Praise for
Me, MySpace, and I

◆

"Dr. Larry Rosen goes beyond the sensational headlines by providing original research on how young people are actually using MySpace. *Me, MySpace, and I* provides parents with a much needed voice in the debate over the role of social networking in the lives of today's totally wired teens."

—Anastasia Goodstein, author of *Totally Wired: What Teens and Tweens Are Really Doing Online*

◆

"Let's face it. We parents need all the help we can get to ensure that we can remain involved in our children's lives—especially their online lives. The better informed we are, the better we can do our jobs in protecting our children and making sure they have the skills and values to make good choices online. Larry Rosen brings his expertise as both a research psychologist and father together in this new book, *Me, MySpace, and I.* He provides great insight and excellent guidance."

—Nancy E. Willard, author of *Cyber-Safe Kids, Cyber-Savvy Teens: Helping Young People Learn to Make Safe and Responsible Choices Online*

◆

Me, MySpace, and I

Parenting the Net Generation

Larry D. Rosen, Ph.D.

palgrave
macmillan

First published in 2007 by
PALGRAVE MACMILLAN™
175 Fifth Avenue, New York, N.Y. 10010 and
Houndmills, Basingstoke, Hampshire, England RG21 6XS
Companies and representatives throughout the world.

PALGRAVE MACMILLAN is the global academic imprint of the
Palgrave Macmillan division of St. Martin's Press, LLC and of Palgrave
Macmillan Ltd. Macmillan® is a registered trademark in the United
States, United Kingdom and other countries. Palgrave is a registered
trademark in the European Union and other countries.

ISBN-13: 978-0-230-60003-4 paperback
ISBN-10: 0-230-60003-4 paperback

Library of Congress Cataloging-in-Publication Data

Rosen, Larry D.
  Me, MySpace, and I : parenting the net generation / by Larry D. Rosen.
     p. cm.
  Includes bibliographical references and index.
  ISBN 0-230-60003-4
  1. MySpace (Firm) 2. Internet and teenagers. 3. Online social
networks. 4. Parenting. 5. Internet—Safety measures. 6. Blogs. I. Title.
  HQ799.2.I5R66 2007
  305.2350285'4678—dc22
                                        2007024917

A catalogue record of the book is available from the British Library.

Design by Scribe Inc.

10 9 8 7 6 5 4 3 2

Printed in the United States of America.

To my four children—Adam, Arielle, Chris, and Kaylee—who are all loving, brilliant, creative, and unique. Their love has been a constant part of my life for the past thirty-two years and every moment I spend with them is special. Every Christmas gingerbread house we build is a constant reminder that we are a remarkable family.

Contents

List of Tables and Figures   ix

Acknowledgments   xi

Chapter 1   Living in a Virtual World   1

Chapter 2   The MySpace Generation   19

Chapter 3   Real People in Virtual Relationships   37

Chapter 4   Me, MySpace, and I   63

Chapter 5   Virtually Exposed   91

Chapter 6   Sex and the Media   117

Chapter 7   Just a Few More Minutes, Mom   151

Chapter 8   MySpace and Your Family   173

Chapter 9   Hate Mail   193

Chapter 10 Proactive Parenting: Teaching Your Children
                to Look Both Ways in Cyberspace   207

Notes   227

Index   253

List of Tables and Figures

Table 2.1   Personal and Work Values of Three Generations: Baby Boomers, Gen Xers, and MySpacers   **21**

Figure 3.1   Example of MySpace Discussion Groups   **50**

Table 4.1   Marcia's Stages of Identity Formation   **74**

Table 4.2   Percentages of Adolescents and Young Adults at Marcia's Identity Formation Stages   **75**

Table 4.3   MySpace Activities   **78**

Table 4.4   Parent Perception and Teen Reality of Information Disclosed on MySpace   **83**

Figure 5.1   Sample MySpace Personality Quiz   **100**

Figure 5.2   Sample MySpace Personality Quiz Psychological Profile   **101**

Table 5.1   List of IM Acronyms and Their Meanings   **103**

Table 5.2   Sample Questions from the Blog Beware Quiz   **110**

Table 6.1   Sexual Relations in Teenagers: Oral Sex Only Compared with Vaginal Sex   **242**

Table 7.1   Parent-Child Internet Addiction Test   **154**

Figure 7.1   Social Cognition Theory Model of Internet Use   **162**

Table 7.2   Sample Behavioral Contract for Internet Behavior   **167**

Table 8.1   Sample Weekly Point System Chart   **187**

Table 8.2   Sample Point System Reward Chart   **187**

Table 9.1   Cyberbullying of Middle School Children   **196**

Acknowledgments

First, I would like to thank the more than one thousand parents and twenty-five hundred MySpace teens whose stories form the foundation of this book, *Me, MySpace, and I*. I would also like to thank the five undergraduate students at California State University, Dominguez Hills who worked with me on the MySpace projects (in alphabetical order): Michelle Albertella, Jyenny Babcock, Cheyenne Cummings, Julie Felt, and Julia Rifa. I am sure that they will all go on to make contributions in the field of psychology.

My family and friends have been with me throughout this project. My parents, Oscar and Sarah Rosen, my sister and brother-in-law, Judy and Michael Heumann, my brother and sister-in-law, Bruce and Liane Rosen, and my cousins Alan, Rhonda, John, and Ellen all have been amazingly supportive. My friend Liz has been there every Monday evening at bowling and has always had encouraging words when it was difficult to write. A special thanks to Joann, who has been the Psychology department stalwart for the past umpteen years. She always has a smile, even when I am asking her to do something in a rush at the last minute. My family and friends encouraged and supported me even when I thought that nobody would publish a book about adolescents living in cyberspace.

A special thanks with love to Vicki, my soul mate, who has stood by me throughout the process of creating this book, even when I was exhausted and grumpy and it cut into our time together as a couple. Thanks for the hugs, love, indie movies, the *Daily Show*, rock concerts, and all those *New York Times* crossword puzzles. I love that the two of us are able to solve them when one of us can't. We are more than the sum of our parts.

I can't have two better colleagues and friends at Dominguez Hills than Mark Carrier, Professor of Psychology, and Nancy Cheever, Professor of Communications. They have helped me in numerous ways on this project, including always being available when I needed them to read and edit a chapter. I am honored that they are my friends.

I have been writing articles for *The National Psychologist* since 1995. My editors, the late Henry Saeman, followed by his son Marty, believed that I had something important to say to psychologists about how technology impacts their lives. Thank you Henry and Marty, since the genesis for this book came from many of the pieces you published. I know Henry is smiling up there right now. Henry always believed in me, even when he had to edit my columns with a heavy hand.

A special thanks goes to three long-time, supportive friends: Bob Indseth (thanks for the tequila and the breakfasts at Denny's and Milton's), Sandy Kaler (thanks for the Indian dinners and all your love and support), and Phyllisann Maguire (thanks for the phone calls, the hugs, and for just listening to me). I have known each for more than half my life and I am a better person because of them.

To Mac: you saved my life so many times. You are one in a million.

To Stacey Glick at Dystel & Goderich Literary Management: thank you so much for believing in me and my book and for continuing to be so positive, even when so many houses couldn't believe that a book on MySpace had any value. Thanks also to my editors at Palgrave Macmillan, Amanda Moon and Luba Ostashevsky, and their assistants, Brigitte Shull and Joanna Mericle. Amanda saw this book through nearly all of the process until she moved on to a new challenge, and Luba saw it through the rest of the way. They were both incredibly helpful and their editing made the book what it is. Thanks to Brigitte and Joanna for having always been available to answer my often confusing, sleep deprived questions.

Thanks also to the most incredible professionals who took the time for my questions-and-answers (Q&A) in each chapter. They include (in alphabetical order): Kerby Alvy, danah boyd, Anne Collier, Matthew

Eastin, Anastasia Goodstein, David Huffaker, Kimberly Mitchell, Stephen Russell, Teri Schroeder, Nancy Willard, and Kimberly Young. A special thanks to Kerby with whom I have worked at the Center for the Improvement of Child Caring for over thirty years. Many of the ideas in this book come from our work together on parenting programs.

A final thanks goes to my children, Adam, Arielle, Chris, and Kaylee. Yes, this book is dedicated to you but I need to say it one more time: I am blessed to have four such fantastic children. I just hope that when I am old and feeble you remember who changed your diapers, let you barf all over his head, read *Goodnight Moon* a zillion times, sang *There's a Hole in the Bucket* more times than I can recall, taught you how to cook, listened when you were sad, and rejoiced when you were happy. I always told people that I had four children to ensure that in my old age at least one would support me financially and be happy to let me live with him or her. I was lying. I had four children because I knew they would grow up to be four amazing adults. Adam and Arielle are already there and Chris and Kaylee are soon to follow.

One final note: I have been teaching at California State University, Dominguez Hills, one of the most multicultural universities in the United States, for over thirty years. The university and its students have always been supportive of my work and me. The students, with their enthusiasm and thirst for learning and knowledge, keep me young and excited. I intend to teach there as long as they will have me. Teaching keeps me young. The students keep me alive and excited to be their professor.

Chapter 1

Living in a Virtual World

♦

"We must see the Internet as a new social environment in which universal adolescent issues such as identity, sexuality, and a sense of self-worth are played out in a virtual world in ways that are both new and old. Adolescents are basically co-constructing their own environments."

—Dr. Patricia Greenfield, Children's Digital Media Center, University of California, Los Angeles, and Dr. Zheng Yan, University at Albany, State University of New York[1]

♦

"We taught our four-year-old how to use our cell phone to call 911 and his grandparents in case of an emergency. That night he asked to sleep with the phone, which he often did with new toys. Ten minutes later we heard him talking to his grandmother and telling her goodnight."

—Mark, parent of Mikey

♦

"I don't call anyone any more—I check their MySpace, IM them, or e-mail them. First thing when I get home, I check my MySpace and am usually on and off until I go to bed. I honestly think that if MySpace weren't around, I wouldn't have a social life."

—Cameron, age 12

♦

Call them what you will—the Net Generation, Millennials, Generation M, the ADHD Generation, Generation Y, the Wired

Generation, or even the "What-I-Want When-I-Want-it Generation"—
they are the first children, tweens, and teens who have grown up in a
technological world where nearly everything is computerized. Their
cribs included an electronic heartbeat bear to calm their sleep and a
video camera for parents to keep an eye on them from the living room
or the office. Their first toys had digital readouts. They learned to use a
mouse as soon as they could sit up on a chair. They were on the Internet and sending e-mail before entering kindergarten. This generation
does not *use* technology, they live it. It is simply part of their world,
which, for many, is a virtual world that exists inside a box, and in their
minds. Many of their friends are scattered around the world. Most of
these global friends they will never meet.

   This is certainly not the first generation to use media that worried
and frightened parents. When the television became a household item,
parents fretted about its effects on their children. On the tube, Elvis
swiveled his pelvis for everyone to see, and the mere appearance of the
Beatles' Paul, John, George, and Ringo sent teen girls into wild scream-
ing fits of excitement—both of which confirmed their parents' suspi-
cions about this new media. The sexual and violent messages conveyed
by comic books in the '50s, drug-laden lyrics in rock music in the '60s
and '70s, heavy metal of the '80s, rap from the '90s, and hip-hop and
violent video games in the first decade of the new millennium spurred
many parents to lobby their congressmen to push for video game, television, and music rating systems to protect their children. Although
children have always done things that their parents either don't understand or approve, what is different now is that the Net Generation is
the first to live their lives completely on a nonstop diet of media. Call
them what you will, tweens and teens are tethered to their media nearly
twenty-four hours a day, seven days a week, which concerns parents
and educators.

   The Net Generation has seen more rapid technological change than
any before. Consumer researchers measure the acceptance of technology—called the penetration rate—by how many years a new form of
technology takes to reach an audience of fifty million people. Radio, for
example, took thirty-eight years; the telephone took only twenty years.
Television, first popularized in the Baby Boomer generation, took only

thirteen years to reach fifty million homes. For the most part, adults drove radio and television sales. In the last decade, though, adolescents have been the ones driving new technology adoption. Cell phones took only twelve years to reach fifty million and cable TV took seven years. The Internet took *only* four years as did instant messaging and iPods. Blogs took only three years and, amazingly, MySpace amassed 125 million members in two and a half years, while YouTube took only one year![2] The accelerated pace is dizzying.

This rapid emergence of technological change did not catch Alvin Toffler by surprise. In his 1974 book, *The Third Wave*, he described an age when each successive wave of technological innovation would emerge faster and faster. Using historical data Toffler noted that as one wave receded and another arose, the point at which they crossed was rife with social unrest including wars, revolutions, and other forms of societal discord. Looking at our world today, it is clear that social unrest is the norm, which is precisely what Toffler would have predicted as waves of new technology continue to rise and fall in a matter of just a few years.[3]

Until recently, adolescents used the Internet to communicate through e-mail, sending instant messages (IM), chat rooms, and gaming sites. Online social interaction was mostly one-on-one or within small groups. The new millennium introduced the idea of online social networking or "virtual communities." The first true virtual community was the Whole Earth 'Lectronic Link (the WELL) started in 1985 by Stewart Brand and Larry Brilliant. Until recently, virtual communities were groups of Internet users who came together around a common bond. Some played *Dungeons and Dragons*, while others discussed weighty political issues. Most were specialized and none were very popular.

Then came MySpace. As we know, MySpace was not the first virtual community to become a "social network." Cyberspace has been hosting groups of people bonded through common interests since the inception of the Internet. In fact, the Internet developed in response to the need for geographically dispersed groups of researchers to communicate with one another. But somehow MySpace was different. Perhaps founders Tom Anderson and Chris DeWolfe were more hip and insightful than previous social networkers. After all, MySpace started in July 2003 as a place for musicians to share their music. The bottom line is that MySpace clicked with the techno-savvy under-thirty crowd and they flocked to the site in record numbers. In July 2005, Rupert Murdock's News Corp bought MySpace for $580 million. With its millions of members, MySpace is the sixth largest "country" in the world and has far more monthly visitors than any other Internet site. To put this in perspective, MySpace gets nearly three times as many hits as Google and one in ten paid Internet advertisements can be found on MySpace. It is the virtual equivalent of the '50s drive-in—the place to be, because everyone seems to hang out there.

MySpace is one of thousands of cyberspace meeting places, but in its brief existence it has experienced more rapid growth *than any other Internet site in history*. Approximately half of MySpacers are under eighteen, and of those, most are under sixteen. Log on and ask to see a listing of MySpacers from your local high school and middle school. You will be amazed.

But nothing this huge comes without its detractors. When Virginia college student Taylor Behl was found murdered by a man she met on MySpace, the response was immediate. A school principal in Vermont blocked MySpace access at school. A diocese school in New Jersey not only banned MySpace on campus, but also forbade students from using it at home. A high school in Iowa, upset about a student's depictions of a teacher on MySpace, suspended the student and restricted all students from using the site. Daily newspapers report on sexual predators roaming MySpace and highlight sexualized photos of young children, profanity, and evidence of drugs, alcohol, and sex found on MySpace.

In fact, NBC's television program, *Dateline: To Catch a Predator*, brought the issue of Internet sexual predation to a national audience. Each week, an adult, posing as a twelve- to thirteen-year-old girl, would talk to adults online, eventually inviting one to visit her at home when, as she told him, she would be alone. When the man arrived, he was greeted by the girl or boy, who would leave to slip into something more comfortable. At that point, Chris Hansen would walk out and inform the predator that he had been caught. An audience of more than ten million viewed each episode, and during the first two shows, they heard the statistic that "*at any given moment there are fifty thousand potential child molesters prowling the Internet.*" This figure was proffered without any validating data and removed after the second show, but even without it, the impact of the show is widespread. Although MySpace is not mentioned directly on *Dateline: To Catch a Predator*, as the preeminent meeting place for tweens and teens, it worries parents that their children may be exposed to online sexual predators. As a response, MySpace now uses a national database of convicted sex offenders to keep predators out of its community.

Parents, who were born and raised before the widespread use of the Internet, are perplexed and worried when they see their children "living" in the potentially dangerous virtual world, happily multitasking for hours on end. As responsible parents, they want answers to a lot of questions, including: "What is MySpace?" "What is my child doing on MySpace?" "Who are the people communicating with her, where do they live, and what types of people are they?" "What are MySpacers talking about and how does that influence my child's values, beliefs, and sense of identity?" "Is spending all that time on MySpace hurting his grades, or making him spend less time with the people in the real world?" "What kind of impact do her online activities have on the quality of our family time?" "Is he safe on MySpace?" "What sexual messages are they sending and receiving?"

As a research psychologist, the phenomenon of MySpace, the behaviors and attitudes of Net Generation children, and the reactions of their parents all fascinate me. It is clear to me, based on more than twenty-five hundred interviews with parents and teens, that adults are concerned about what children are doing in cyberspace in general, and on MySpace in particular. My research explores what tweens and teens are doing on MySpace and shows that although there are potential hazards, adult concerns and fears may be largely unfounded. The evidence shows that MySpace provides a relatively safe forum for children to explore their identity, make lifelong friendships, experiment with their sexuality, and simply practice life. Behind the screen they feel free to try things that are difficult, if not impossible in the face-to-face life at school, home, or the mall. This does not mean that there are no hazards to leading a virtual lifestyle, and we face these issues head-on in this book. But first, it is important to see what exactly children are doing in their technological world.

Even the most technologically savvy parents may need a road map to the Internet, or the Information Superhighway, a phrase popularized by Al Gore in the early 1990s. In 2006, the terms "podcasting," "blogging," "friending," "googling," "wiki," and "phishing" were added to the *Oxford English Dictionary*. Kids use "mapquest" and "google" as verbs to describe what they do online. *"Do you MySpace?"* they ask a new friend. YouTube features more than one hundred million videos, many created by adolescents and young adults; Wikipedia, an online encyclopedia, with information supplied by the public rather than experts, is a popular place for teens to start researching a school paper. Often, four or five IM conversations are open on their computers, and they are listening to music on their iPods, while they are supposed to be doing homework. They sit glued to their X-Box or Wii game console, watch their favorite shows, which they have TiVo'd, talk and text message on their cell phones, and spend a large portion of their waking hours interacting with one form of media or another.

Studies by reputable groups including the Kaiser Family Foundation, Pew Internet & American Life Project, National Center for Missing and Exploited Children, CBS NewsWatch, America Online, Nielsen Media Service, and the Children's Digital Media Project have found that children and teens spend an amazing amount of time using digital media. The best estimate is that media use consumes six hours and twenty-one minutes per day, including television, Internet and computer use (for nonschool-related uses), music, and video games. This means that in a seven-day week, nearly forty-five hours are devoted to the use of at least one form of media. Given that most children and teens multitask (more on this later), this actually equates to eight hours and thirty-three minutes of daily media consumption.[4] Kids are making media a full-time job with overtime.

This certainly doesn't leave much time for interacting with parents, reading, or just doing nothing. Clearly, tweens and teens are completely booked up, with two-thirds of their waking, nonschool hours consumed by media. To quote Dr. Edward Hallowell, an expert on

Attention Deficit Disorder (ADD), our children are suffering from "screen sucking," in which technology literally holds them captive in front of whatever screen they are viewing at the time.[5] Let's take a look at specific media and see what activities are occupying so much of our kids' lives.

- 87% of teens are online, increasing from 60% of twelve-year-olds to 82% of thirteen-year-olds and 94% of sixteen- and seventeen-year-olds.[6]
- Teens are online an average of five days a week, two to three hours a day.[7]
- 67% of teens and 40% of preteens own a cell phone, spending an average of an hour per day talking. Two-thirds of tweens and teens that own or have a cell phone send text messages daily.[8]
- 87% of eight- to seventeen-year-olds play video games, the vast majority of them on a daily basis.[9]
- 75% of online teens use instant messaging,[10] chatting with an average of thirty-five people, for three hours per week.[11]
- 75% of adolescents spend two to three hours per day downloading or listening to music online.[12]
- 80% of twelve- to seventeen-year-olds use MySpace weekly.[13]

Since 1990, researchers have asked teens what technology they absolutely could not live without, or more specifically, "If you were required to give up all of your technology and toys, what is the last you would be willing to let go of?" In 1990 it was a radio or CD player. In 2004 it was the computer and the Internet. In 2006 teens said that they would want to keep their cell phones to the bitter end. One family I interviewed typified how different generations treasure different technologies. Jim, the father of Gavin, age eleven, and Melody, age fifteen, told me: *"They would have to pry my laptop out of my hands and rip out my wireless access to the Internet. And then I would find the closest library and get online there. I literally live online for my job as the vice president of distribution for a paper company. I have to have online access or I can't keep track of my people and we will lose business."* His wife, Franny, had a different perspective. *"With Jim gone on business or glued to the computer and the kids in their rooms doing their thing, I would be lost without my television and TiVo. I have at least ten shows that I watch each week and since I work full time and have to do all the household cooking, I only get to relax and watch TV at night. Please don't let anyone ever take away my flat screen HDTV that I just got for Christmas. I love it!"*

Now listen to the kids. Gavin said, *"I would die if someone took away my Wii that I got for Christmas. It is so much more cool than my X-Box. I only get to use it after I finish my homework during the week but on Saturday and Sunday I get up really early and play on it all day long. Sometimes my friends come over and we do the boxing or golf, but it is fun even if I am by myself. Zelda is so cool with all the hot new graphics."* I had to wait for Melody to finish texting her best friend and IMing her boyfriend to ask her the same question. *"Don't even think of taking away either my phone or my MySpace. I will do anything my mom asks me so that she won't take either of them away. Heck, she even has me cooking dinner once a week—I do great tacos and burritos—and in return I get to have three thousand text messages a month and can mostly be on MySpace any time I have no homework."*

Given that nearly all kids are online, what exactly are they doing? If Gavin and Melody are typical, which according to my research, they are, they are doing everything from buying products to download-ing music, from sharing videos to playing online games. More than three-fourths of tweens and teens also use the Internet to get their news about the world and nearly one-third use it to locate health-related information.[14] Although adults may not trust the Internet as a source of information, kids check Wikipedia—a mostly peer-edited encyclopedia—first in their information searches. Even when they do get news from more traditional sources, they are more than likely to choose the *Daily Show* than network news. Their lives are a steady diet of media, most of which happens on the Internet.

These children are also being allowed to ingest their media diet using technology housed in the privacy of their bedrooms. According to the Kaiser Family Foundation's study of "Generation M"[15]—the "M" stands for media—and Nickelodeon's U.S. Multicultural Kids Study,[16] 69% of six- to eighteen-year-old children have a television set in their bedroom—more than half with cable access and nearly all including a VCR or DVD player. One in three have a computer with Internet access in their bedrooms—my studies of MySpacers show that nearly half have a computer in the bedroom—and those who do use it twice as much as those with a computer in a common area.[17]

Nearly all tweens and teens have some form of music player, including a CD or tape player and a radio. Of course, add in mobile MP3 devices such as an iPod, and you have a complete bedroom entertainment center. If that isn't enough technology, half of all teens own a video game console, and the average home is stocked with at least two. Add to that a television with an average of 104 channels, digital and video cameras, plus a cell phone with text messaging capabilities, and is it any wonder that adolescents come home from school, sequester themselves in their TechnoCocoons[18] and venture out only for snacks and dinner? Jim Taylor, vice-chairman of the Harrison Group which completed a three-year Teen Trends Study between 2004 and 2006, summarized their findings this way: "This generation is unique. Teen life has become a theatrical, self-directed media production."[19]

If these figures seem staggering, indeed they are. Our children are being fed a steady media diet beginning at a very early age. One in five children one year old and younger have a television in their rooms, and the device is on for one hour and twenty minutes a day; this number increases to nearly half of four- to six-year-olds, who watch more than two hours of television a day. Many young children have a VCR or DVD player in their bedroom, plus at least one video game console, and one in three of those with a television in the bedroom fall asleep with it turned on.[20]

Parents aren't helping either. The typical American home has 3.5 televisions,[21] and one in three homes has one turned on all or nearly all of the time. A recent U.S. census found that the number of television sets has surpassed the number of people living in the household. When there are children under the age of six, two-thirds of the homes have the television on more than half the time. Parents are modeling television-watching behavior; children with parents who watch more than two hours of television a day watch a full half hour more daily TV than those children whose parents watch only one hour per day.[22]

Similarly, telephones have always been a youth favorite. With the portability factor, whether it is a cell phone or a cordless phone, teens are talking more from the privacy of their bedrooms than in public areas of their homes. Cell phones are lifelines for teenagers, but this generation is quite different from past ones, because they are rarely "just talking" on the phone. Combine the phone with IM, e-mail, and text messaging and you have what Dr. Christine Wasson calls, "not just objects or communication tools, but portals for keeping in touch."[23]

High school and middle school students that I interviewed told me how, as soon as class is over and students are walking either to lunch or to their next class, everyone, literally everyone, is either talking on a cell phone or texting. I can certainly vouch for that. I was waiting to pick up my daughter after her first day of high school and we had arranged that I would call her on her cell phone to let her know where I was parked. As soon as I spotted students leaving school I called her, only to keep getting a "no service" message. Getting more and more frustrated, I kept trying and trying until I looked up and realized that nearly every student leaving school was on a cell phone. With more than three thousand students at her school they had exhausted the entire available cell frequencies and there was no way I was going to get through. After about twenty tries, I finally got a line and we decided that calling was untenable and it was better to have a standard meeting place.

Cell phones and texting have created an interesting dilemma for schoolteachers and administrators. With nearly every student carrying a cell phone and each having their own special rings—downloaded, of course, from the Internet—constant connection was becoming a problem. Cell phones were ringing like crazy, so most schools made students put them on vibrate. That stopped the constant musical inter-ludes, but did not inhibit text messaging. One thirteen-year-old girl told me that since most of her classes were boring she used the time to text message her friends. *"In Spanish, he has us just doing busy work so I text my friends. Some are in the same class, which is a lot more fun than passing notes, and others are in their classes. We talk about how boring the teachers are, what we are doing for lunch, who's staying after for sports and clubs and pretty much mostly gossip."* When I asked her how she did this without the teacher knowing, she showed me how she could have her phone in her lap or even in her pocket and send a text message. Just like learning touch typing, teens have learned surreptitious texting. She did tell me, however, that many of her teachers are actually happy to let students text during class downtime since it is quieter than having them whisper to each other. However, when one teacher found out that students were text messaging answers across the room during exams, and using their camera phones to take pictures of exam pages and send them to students taking the same exam later in the day, he put his foot down. Now, when the class has a test, students have to put their cell phones in a box by the door.

If teens were using just their cell phones to excess, most parents told me they could understand and deal with it. Rarely, however, can you find adolescents using only their cell phones and no other technology. It is likely that they are hooked into the Internet with three or more IM windows open, a MySpace page, plus several other screens including e-mail and music minimized. Most likely, the television is on in the background and if music is not coming from the computer speakers, it is on a CD player or an iPod. Amanda Lenhart, from the Pew Internet & American Life Project, which studies teen media use, summed up this behavior by saying: "When teens are logged on, they are often multitasking, simultaneously e-mailing and instant messaging, surfing the Web, and if they are fortunate enough to have two phone lines, a cell phone, or a broadband connection, talking on the phone, too."[24]

In a typical response in my research studies, Jennie, a fifteen-year-old high school sophomore, told me, *"I don't see how anybody can just do homework. I would be so bored. I have to at least have my iPod on and most of the time I am IMing someone to ask questions about homework or what they are doing on the weekend. And I know it drives my mom and dad crazy, but I nearly always have the TV on, too. I don't really watch it but if there is something that catches my eye I can back it up with my TiVo and watch it again. It's just really background stuff."* When I asked Jennie if she felt that she could do her homework faster or better without all the distractions, she replied, *"They aren't distracting at all! Silence would be distracting. Besides, I get good grades and always get my homework done so I don't see why I would have to do it in quiet."*

Jennie's mom, Dorothy, agreed. *"We used to worry about Jennie doing her homework and studying with music blasting and the TV and the Internet but how can we complain? She gets great grades, she is a good kid and she never really gets in trouble. I think she would be more trouble if we made her keep the TV off or forced her to do her homework before she got on the Internet. I don't even mind that she takes time out to talk on the phone or text because it never seems to hurt her grades."*

Parents such as Dorothy know that their children multitask all the time and worry about whether their schoolwork suffers. From experience we know that we can certainly drive and listen to music without crashing our cars. But that is because driving and listening to music are both what psychologists call "automatic tasks." I am sure you have often had the experience of driving somewhere and not having much recollection of how you actually did it. In many cases you can't even recall driving, turning, stopping, anything. It is also the case that for most of us, listening to music, and even singing along, is fairly automatic. The fact that we have done them over and over many times means that we do not have to devote much of our brain's processing power to driving or singing along to the music. For these tasks we are good multitaskers.

Now, what happens when one task is automatic and another is not? Take driving and talking on the cell phone for example. According to a yearlong study, sponsored by the National Highway Traffic Safety Administration, cell phones are the number one driver distraction.[25] Why? We can certainly talk to a passenger and not get into an accident. What is it about cell phone conversations that are so distracting? According to the Partnership for Safe Driving,

"Phone conversations have been shown to cause a cognitive distraction in drivers. In other words, the driver's brain is intensely engaged with the conversation, although he may appear to be paying attention to the road. This does not happen with other common distractions, including conversations with passengers. Research has shown that phone conversations cause what is termed 'tunnel vision' in drivers. Although they appear to be looking at objects, their brains are not registering a good portion of what they see. Therefore, a driver is impaired for the entire length of the phone conversation."[26]

Interestingly, we know that there is no difference in attention between using hand-held and speakerphones.[27] Talking on the phone is a cognitive distraction, period. As of January 2007, only three states—New York, Connecticut, and New Jersey, plus the District of Columbia—have banned using hand-held cell phones while driving. California will join that group in July 2008.[28]

In spite of Jennie's assurance that she can concentrate on her work while chatting on MySpace, her homework will most likely suffer. This doesn't mean she won't do as well as she could without distractions, but it is more likely that the more distractions, the longer it will take to complete her work. In fact, information crawling at the bottom of the screen on some television news shows such as CNN can cause you to retain fewer facts about the central message.[29]

Perhaps teenage multitasking partially explains a recent National Sleep Foundation study that found that only 20% of adolescents get the recommended nine hours of sleep on school nights, and sleep decreases as kids get older. This leaves high school students with a "sleep debt," and they only make up a small part of that debt on the weekends, as they are usually out with friends or participating in various activities. More than one-fourth of high school students fall asleep during school regularly, and an equal number fall asleep while they are doing homework.[30] As lack of sleep is directly related to lower grades, increased driving accidents, lack of exercise, and depression, it is important that parents recognize their children's growing sleep debt. Despite this, most of us with teens in our families believe that our adolescent is getting enough sleep at least a few nights during the school week.[31]

In physiological terms, multitasking is controlled by the area just behind your forehead, the "prefrontal cortex," which is responsible for flipping back and forth between multiple tasks. The prefrontal cortex is one of the last regions of the brain to mature and does not reach completion until late adolescence or young adulthood. Interestingly, girls, who have been found to multitask more than boys, have larger prefrontal cortexes, which mature earlier. However, the prefrontal cortex cannot control multitasking indefinitely. It needs rest and recovery time, which is facilitated by sleep.[32]

MySpace provides a perfect multitasking environment. Visualize a child's bedroom with posters of rock stars, loud music, and homework strewn across the bed. Now add a combination yearbook, personal diary, and social club and you have MySpace. If it seems a bit overwhelming, that is probably because you were born before 1980, and did not grow up with videogames, the World Wide Web, e-mail, instant messaging, and cell phones. Certainly you juggled multiple tasks simultaneously, but not nearly to the extent that tweens and teens do today.

A typical MySpace Web page includes a profile with personal information, pictures, music, fancy backgrounds, games, and videos. Most people, however, use the site for communication. They post their thoughts in bulletins, comment on other people's bulletins and journals, instant message, e-mail, blog, and most importantly, collect friends. Anyone wanting to be someone's friend has to ask permission and once he or she is accepted, they become part of a social circle. Each person also gets to select their Top 8 friends whose pictures reside on their Web page.

What is it about MySpace that is so special? According to a Forrester Research national study, 80% of youths twelve to seventeen years old use MySpace weekly.[33] Somehow, in a few short years, MySpace has become an American teen hangout. Not unlike Arnold's Drive-In of *Happy Days* fame where Richie and the Fonz spent their afternoons, MySpace is the ultimate mall where teens can meet and chat. With the exception of any personal pictures posted on a MySpace Web page, MySpace is totally anonymous. Unless a person is already a friend, he or she could be anyone, young or old, male or female, essentially a stranger.

MySpace has garnered intense attention, nearly all negative. Fears of sexual predators, children plotting to bomb schools, threats against teachers, and invitations to drug and sex parties are exposed in the media. Dwarfing these reports by far, however, is a story about a generation that craves life in a virtual world. To investigate their virtual lifestyles, I conducted five research studies of MySpace teens and their parents between 2004 and 2007.[34] One study involved in-person interviews of more than one hundred MySpace tweens and teens, while the other four used anonymous, online interviews to provide an open forum for more than one thousand parents and twenty-five hundred children to express their feelings about MySpace. Each study included questions about how tweens and teens were using MySpace; their experiences with sexual solicitations, cyberbullying, and pornography on MySpace; plus a variety of psychological assessments of their self-esteem, depression, social support, friendships, general psychological well-being, and their perception of parental limit-setting and monitoring. Parents were asked about their perceptions of MySpace, including its risks and hazards; steps they had taken to monitor and limit MySpace usage; and their parenting style. These data have provided the first research-based view of adolescents on MySpace and the issues faced by their parents.

In my research, parents told me how they are concerned and often fearful about what their children are doing on MySpace. They are troubled by media reports of sexual predators and cyberbullies and yet often feel uncomfortable discussing these issues and other concerns with their children. It is also clear from my interviews that many of these same parents are unaware about what their children are actually doing on MySpace and how much time they are spending there. In contrast, their children are, for the most part, comfortable and happy with their virtual lifestyles. In spite of the media coverage, they have told me that they rarely have problems on MySpace and when they do, they handle them with ease and little or no discomfort. It is my opinion, from this extensive research base, that MySpace is a relatively safe forum in which children can develop as persons—explore their identity, make lifelong friendships, experiment with their sexuality, and live life. With a computer screen to shield them, teens feel free to try things that are difficult, if not impossible, in their lives at school, home, or the mall with flesh-and-blood people.

In interviews I have conducted over the years, teens say there are many reasons for having a presence on MySpace. Some are there for friendship, while others just want to have fun. Some want to show off, while others like to pontificate and comment on world events. Dawn, a thirteen-year-old (posing as a fourteen-year-old because the minimum age to be on MySpace is fourteen), told me: *"I am on because everyone I know is on. My cousins, my friends, everyone checks their MySpace page all the time. It's the first thing I do when I get home from school and the last thing I do before I go to bed."* Being on MySpace is almost a given for teens these days. Barrett, a sixteen-year-old from Pennsylvania, told me, *"If you aren't MySpacing then you are a loser. The only kids at my school who don't have a MySpace are geeks and nerds. Anyone with half a social life HAS to be on MySpace cuz that's where it all happens. If you aren't there, then how would you find out about all the parties?"* In contrast, some, like Traci, a fourteen-year-old from the Midwest, wanted to be wanted: *"I have some very sexy poses as my MySpace pics. I know that they are flashy and pretty because I get requests from older men to be their friends all the time. I like it when people think I am a model. It makes me feel important."* Regardless of why they are there, adolescents are serious about what they do on MySpace. In a USC Annenberg Digital Future Project which interviews more than two thousand preteens and teens annually, almost half of Internet users who belong to a social networking site—nearly all on MySpace—feel as strongly about their virtual life as they do about their real-world life.[35]

Dawn, Barrett, and Traci all present issues that worry and concern parents. In fact, in a study by Common Sense Media, 85% of parents of tweens and teens proclaimed that the Internet posed the greatest risk to their children.[36] In the next nine chapters I will explore these issues and probe how living in a virtual world affects adolescents. Using sound psychological theories, extensive research data, and my thirty years of experience working with children and parents, I will provide parents and educators with a structure to help them understand why their children are enjoying their virtual lifestyles and what they can do to ensure that they are safe.

Each chapter addresses an aspect of cyberspace that can affect teens and tweens in either a positive or negative way. I examine how generational differences often make it difficult for parents to understand their multitasking children, who have been raised in a technology-rich environment and have no experience of a world without the Internet. I also discuss how virtual worlds have altered the meaning of a "friend" and how teens use online expression through writing, music, and pictures to help explore their emerging identities. I talk frankly about Internet addiction, sexuality, pornography, and cyberbullying and what parents should do to anticipate potential problems and to react to them if they occur. In addition, at the end of each chapter I pose questions to researchers and scholars who have studied and written about specific issues relevant to the Net Generation—the MySpace Generation. Each interview adds to my psychological and research perspective on raising children who live in a largely virtual world.

I have tried to make my approach fair and even-handed. I attempt to delineate the issues by providing sound research data and solid psychological theory to help you understand what your tweens and teens are doing in cyberspace. Then I support you with a wealth of information and straightforward advice that will help you guide your children through their wired adolescence and into young adulthood. Throughout the book, I incorporate comments from adolescents and parents and provide more context regarding the MySpace phenomenon and ways in which we can ensure that our children's virtual lives are productive and safe. I explore the good, the bad, and the ugly of online life by addressing the issues that parents fear most, and I point out where those fears are valid and where they may be overblown and potentially misguided. The final chapter, using a model of parenting that I have developed specifically for raising today's wired children, provides you with an overall summary of these recommendations, as well as online resources if your children spend much of their day online.

Your children—and you for that matter—live in a virtual world. With virtual networks of MySpace, YouTube, and Facebook, electronic modes of communication such as instant messaging and e-mail, and video games and more media than they can possibly consume, large portions of their time will be spent online. Their friends live online and they need the opportunity to learn and grow socially. If teen life is online, then your teen will want to be online. Just as you teach a five-year-old to look both ways before crossing the street, you must teach your tweens and teens to do the equivalent in cyberspace. I supply the knowledge and tools, you provide the hands-on parenting your child needs, and together you and your child can learn how best to navigate the online world of tomorrow.

Chapter 2

The MySpace Generation

My seventeen-year-old daughter and I arrived home from her school. I quickly made a cup of coffee and by the time I entered her room with coffee in hand, she was talking on her cell phone, had a book open on her lap, the television was on, and she had eight windows open on her computer. One window displayed her MySpace page, another was doing a Google search for a school project, while the other six were instant message screens. I watched for a few minutes while she bounced seamlessly from one conversation to the next, all the while singing along with a song playing on her iPod and glancing every once in a while at a show she recorded with TiVo the night before. I honestly don't know how she lives at this seemingly frenetic pace.

It's hard for me to understand her lifestyle because I am a Baby Boomer and she is a member of the newly emerged MySpace Generation. We coexist in the same world. We use the same technology. But the similarities end where the multitasking begins. As one fourteen-year-old MySpacer so aptly told me,

"I don't understand how anyone can just do one thing at a time. I would be like so majorly bored and probably fall asleep. My mom yells at me all the time to turn off the TV and put away my iPod so I can do my homework. I am doing my homework and I can't imagine not listening to music and talking to my friends at the same time. She just doesn't get it . . . and she never will. We have the same fight every day. It's not like I'm not doing well at school. I'm getting great grades. She says she's proud of me but then she won't let me be and do it my way."

Multitasking is but one way in which MySpacers differ from the two previous generations, Baby Boomers and Generation X. In this chapter I identify some common and also some distinctive features of these three generations. It is important to mention that *not everyone in any generation acts, thinks, and feels the same*. Clearly, your own experiences may be different from those whose thoughts are highlighted in this chapter. Over the past few years, the Kaiser Family Foundation and the Pew Internet & American Life Project have studied thousands of American children, teens, young adults, and their families. Researchers from Carnegie-Mellon University, Massachusetts Institute of Technology's Media Laboratory, and nearly every major university in the United States have chronicled generational commonalities. My own research with MySpacers reveals that they are indeed qualitatively different from earlier generations, because they are the first generation to be born into a technological world where nearly everything is computerized. To the extent that I can make generalizations from these data, I make them in the interest of presenting "typical" members of each generation, which help you understand how your children are so different from you in the ways that they consume technology and other media.

We are in the midst of the three most distinct and qualitatively different generations in history, and it is all due to the rapid emerging prominence of electronic technology. At one end of the historical sequence are the Baby Boomers. Born after World War II between 1946 and 1964, Boomers are the current political leaders, business CEOs, middle managers, and shop owners. The oldest Boomers just turned sixty and many will retire in the next five to ten years.

Although multitasking is a major feature of the MySpace Generation, they were not the first generation to multitask using technology. That honor belongs to Generation X. Members of Generation X, born between 1965 and 1979, are now approaching their late twenties to early forties. They were born before the Internet was a household word. Then came the MySpace Generation. Born after 1979, many MySpacers know no world without hundreds of television channels. The Web is their major source of amusement and information, and they would be lost without a cell phone.

To understand what the MySpace Generation faces in their technological world, it is important to compare their attitudes, values, and behaviors to the two prior generations. In some ways, they are no different than their parents' generation, but in many ways they are quite unique. Those characteristics that best highlight these similarities and differences are presented in Table 2.1, which summarizes personal values—trust, family, political orientation, communication preferences—and work-related values, including career aspirations, work ethic, leadership style, and workplace motivation.

Table 2.1 Personal and Work Values of Three Generations: Baby Boomers, Gen Xers, and MySpacers

Personal Values			
	Baby Boomers	**Gen Xers**	**MySpacers**
Core Values	Optimism, Involvement	Skepticism, Fun, Informality	Realism, Confidence, Extreme Fun, Social
Level of Trust	Confident of Self	Low Trust of Authority	High Trust of Authority
Upbringing	Indulged	Alienated	Protected
Family	Disintegrating	Latchkey Kids	Merged families
Education	Freedom of Expression Is Birthright	Pragmatic, a Way to Get There	Structure of Accountability, an Incredible Expense
Political Orientation	Attack Oppression	Apathetic, Individual	Crave Community
Dealing with Money	Buy Now, Pay Later	Cautious, Conservative, Save, Save, Save	Earn to Spend
Communication	In Person	Direct, Immediate	E-Mail, Voice Mail
Communication Media	Telephones	Cell Phones	Internet, Picture Phones, E-Mail, IM, Text Messaging

Table 2.1 Personal and Work Values of Three Generations (*continued*)

Likes	Responsibility, Work Ethic, Meetings	Freedom, Multitasking, Work-Life Balance	Public Activism, Latest Technology, Parents, Multitasking to the nth Degree
Dislikes	Laziness	Red Tape, Talking It Out, Meetings	Anything Slow, Negativity
Work Values			
	Baby Boomers	**Gen Xers**	**MySpacers**
Career Goals	Build a Strong Career	Build a Career by Trying Many Jobs	Build Many Possible Careers
Work and Family Life	No Balance, Work Is Life	Work Is Work, Life Is What Is Important	Life and Work in Balance
Work Ethic	Workaholics, Work Is Personally Fulfilling, the Process Is Important	Self-Reliance, Want Deadlines but Want to Do It on Their Own Time Plan	Multitasking, Goal Oriented, Social Interaction Is Important, Too
Leadership Style	Collegial, Everyone Has a Voice but the Boss Makes the Rules	Everyone Is the Same, Challenge Others, Ask Why	Team Oriented
Loyalty to Institutions	Cynical	Naïve	Committed
Workplace Interactive Style	Team Player, Loves Meetings	Entrepreneurial	Participative, Social
Workplace Rewards	Title and Corner Office	Free Time Is the Best Reward	Meaningful, Interesting Work
Workplace Evaluation	Once a Year in a Written Evaluation	At the End of Every Project with Lots of Rewards	Whenever I Want It, at the Push of a Button, Often and in Person
Messages that Motivate	You are Valued, You are Needed	Do It Your Way, Forget the Rules	You Will Work with Bright, Creative People

One of my interviews provides a prime example of some of these qualitative differences. I was fortunate to talk with three family members, each representing a different generation. Ron, sixty years old, is the vice president of finance for a national chain of lighting stores. His son Jackson, forty, owns his own computer repair business while his daughter, Janae, nineteen, is a sophomore in college. I spent an hour talking with all three in Ron's home during Janae's spring break and the following exchange typifies the generational differences. I asked them to tell me about their career decisions:

Ron: *"My dad barely graduated high school and worked on a loading dock for nearly forty years. From when I was about five he told me that I needed to get good grades to get into college. There was never a question about whether I wanted to go, I was expected to go. I got my bachelor's degree and then went on to get an MBA. Went to work as an accountant and worked my butt off and paid my dues to get to where I am today. It was a lot of sixty-hour weeks but it was worth it. I'm in charge of the entire western U.S. and have an office on the twentieth floor with a view of all of the city."*

Jackson: *"I got my first job right out of college working for a friend of dad's programming his computers. He wanted me to stay on and maintain the network but frankly I was bored. I tried a couple of other jobs but none of them really turned me on until I went to work for a computer repair company. I liked the work and my boss, who was close to retiring, pretty much put me in charge and let me do my own thing as long as the work got done. When he retired, I bought the business."*

Janae: *"I'm only a sophomore so I don't have a career. I started college as undeclared but I really liked my political science class so I thought I'd take another, more advanced, course and I really liked it so I declared poly sci as my major. But now my dad thinks that I might try a double major in history and poly sci so I'm taking a history class, too. I trust his judgment since he has had a lot of business experience. I'm not sure what I want to do when I graduate but I know it has to be something I can really get into with people I trust and like. I'm thinking maybe about working on a campaign for my local congresswoman cuz some of my friends are going to work for her, too. But I am open to choices and figure that I can always try something and if I don't like it I can find something else more interesting."*

The differences in career choices between Ron, Jackson, and Janae provide a typical example of generational differences. In order to better understand these differences, it is important to look at how each generation faced their own personal growth challenges.

Ron, a Baby Boomer, told me about his upbringing and how he felt that his parents shaped his values and goals. *"There was no doubt in our family that all three children would go to college. There was also no doubt that we were to succeed and create comfortable lives for ourselves. My parents struggled to make ends meet. They didn't want us to have to do the same. We were primed to find a profession that would make us a good living so that we, and our children, would have advantages that my parents did not enjoy."*

Ron's parents are fairly representative of the Silent or Traditionalist Generation. This upbringing created a generation who were both idealistic and competitive. While the Silent Generation had only radio as their source of media when they were teenagers, Baby Boomers grew up with television and saw, firsthand, the world turn itself upside down as the nightly news followed the war in Vietnam, human rights protests, and the Kennedy assassination. With high parental expectations, Boomers went to college in record numbers and developed a solid social conscience and an arrogant, selfish worldview. Often dubbed the "Me" Generation, Baby Boomers questioned authority and spearheaded the human rights movement, women's liberation, and a lifestyle many called "sex, drugs, and rock 'n' roll." They questioned authority on nearly every social issue and believed—truly believed—that they could create a new world.

After college, as young adults, most Boomers jumped right into the business world. Unlike some in earlier generations, who were content to start at the bottom and slowly work their way up the corporate ladder, Boomers wanted it all *now*. They invented the sixty-hour workweek and strove to build an exceptional career. Even when they attained major positions they continued their hectic work schedule, constantly striving for more prestige and recognition. Their title defined them and their lives were vastly affected by their attempts to get to the next rung. They even invented job titles to signify their success. The grocery checker became an "assistant manager," while the manager became an "assistant to the district supervisor." Everyone wanted a title that said, "I am important!"

With such a drive for business success, many Boomers had little time for "fun." Vacations were limited to two weeks a year and so much was crammed into those fourteen days that they needed a vacation to recover from their vacation. Family dinners often saw an absentee father who was either still at work or doing work he had brought home. When extra income was needed to support a lifestyle commensurate with a new job title, moms joined the workforce in droves. Family dinners drifted away and school children returned to a parentless home and a snack in the refrigerator. Like previous generations, Baby Boomers wanted the best for themselves and their children, but they seemingly forgot how to have fun.

Following the Baby Boomer generation, only forty-six million children were born between the years of 1965 and 1979, making Generation X by far the smallest of the three generations. However, what they lack in numbers, Gen Xers have made up for through their creativity, high energy, and frenetic lifestyle. As latchkey children, many Gen Xers grew up with free access to entertainment technologies. Before doing their homework, and while parents were not there to supervise, many children happily occupied themselves with television, video games, and computers. Having been reared on *Sesame Street*, it was only a short leap to VCRs, cable TV, video game consoles, and twenty-four-hour entertainment. Many Gen Xers became attached to their Game Boys and MTV early in their lives.

Gen Xers were the first generation of children to be spoiled and indulged by their parents. Their Baby Boomer parents were the progeny of a generation that had little money and few possessions. Any money the Silent Generation earned was needed to survive. Perhaps out of guilt for not being there during their childhood, or maybe as a way to spend their hard-earned excess money, Baby Boomers indulged their children with material goods. Their children may not have had a parent home after school, but they certainly had enough *toys* to keep them occupied and self-reliant. As twenty-eight-year-old Devian told me,

"When I turned ten my mom and stepdad decided that they no longer needed the nanny to watch me and they let me be home alone after school.

As I remember, I felt proud since I was the first of my friends to get a key and run of the house. My best friend, who hated his stepmom, came home with me and we hung out and ate junk and had a blast. Many days mom would work late and Jack (my stepdad) would be out of town so I made us dinner. I got pretty good at making sloppy joes and tacos which mom said were as good as hers. I don't know if those few years had anything to do with how I am today, but I know that it was the best time of my life. I got to do what I wanted, when I wanted. Six months later, when I got my next report card, my mom lost it. I was a pretty good student before and now I got all Cs and one D in math. I didn't want the nanny again so mom and I made a deal that I would do at least an hour of homework first and then I could play until she got home. My grades went back up so my mom was happy again. For eight years, all through middle school and high school, I felt like the man of the house. When I started college my roommates had no clue about living away from home so I became the dorm dad. I guess I really had to grow up fast and maybe it was too fast but I don't know how fast is too fast."

Many Gen Xers, like Devian, had to grow up quickly without as much parental involvement as in earlier generations. Parental influence, or lack thereof, can be understood by examining early research on infants' attachments to their parents. Psychologists Mary Ainsworth and John Bowlby developed attachment theory, the idea that connections to parents at an early age can explain how many children develop a secure base from which to form close relationships. Ainsworth studied how children reacted when in the presence of their mother and a stranger and, particularly, when the mother left the room and the stranger remained. Ainsworth found that children could be classified as having one of three attachment styles—secure attachment, anxious-ambivalent insecure attachment, or anxious-avoidant insecure attachment. In Ainsworth's studies, a securely attached child was comfortable exploring his or her world when the mother was present, was upset when the mother left the room, and was happy when she returned. According to attachment theory, the child had developed a secure base to turn to in times of stress or need. It is precisely the development of this secure base that helped Gen Xers develop their values about family and relationships.

In Ainsworth's studies, children with either of the two insecure attachment styles—anxious ambivalent and anxious avoidant—were distressed in the presence of the stranger, even with the mother present, or ignored the mother and often treated the stranger the same or better than the mother. When the mother left the room, the anxious-ambivalent child was quite upset, but when she returned the child often ignored her. When the mother tried to interact with her child, her attempts were disregarded. Similarly, when the mother of an anxious-avoidant child left the room and then returned, the child appeared not to care whether or not the mother was there. Considering that many Gen X children spent large chunks of time alone, doing whatever they wanted, it is hardly surprising that they often developed insecure attachment styles with their parents.

Psychologists have adapted child-focused attachment theory to explain the development of adult relationships. Securely attached individuals are seen as being better able to develop trusting relationships, while insecurely attached people are needy and never sure of others' caring (anxious-ambivalent) or are distant and uncomfortable and ill at ease around other people (anxious-avoidant). Based on Ainsworth's theory, psychologists have linked Gen Xers' attachment difficulties to a variety of developmental issues. For example, a recent study by Dr. Tamyra Pierce found that insecurely attached college students had more aggressive thoughts after viewing a newscast about a school shooting than did securely attached students.[1] As Gen Xers enter their third and fourth decades of life, we may be seeing the impact of early attachment style on their online and offline relationships.

With all their technology, Gen Xers quickly learned how to multitask. It is no accident that in 1980 the American Psychiatric Association identified a new disorder called Attention Deficit Hyperactivity Disorder (or ADHD), based on a person's inability to attend to a single task in a constructive way.[2] Because of their multitasking behavior, millions of Gen Xers were (mis)labeled by their parents, schools, and occasionally psychiatrists as having ADHD and were given medication to help them focus on a single task, rather than simultaneously working on many tasks. The response to ADHD was to prescribe drugs (e.g., Ritalin) that helped reduce multitasking. So many children were on

Ritalin during the 1980s that they were often called the ADHD Generation. Years later psychiatrists realized that many of these children did not have ADHD; they were simply excellent multitaskers.

The oldest Gen Xers, now in their late thirties and early forties, have been in the workforce for many years. Their entry into business was quite a shock to their Baby Boomer bosses. While Boomers worked long hours and literally "lived to work," Gen Xers wanted a clear separation between work and play. They were happy to work hard and do their jobs but they wanted to do it on their own terms. As one psychologist told me, "For them life is life, work is work, and never the twain shall meet." Jason, a thirty-two-year-old computer programmer, and a typical Gen Xer, summed it up beautifully when he talked with me. *I told my boss to just give me a project and a due date and leave me alone. He kept asking me to 'report' to him every week and it made me crazy. So, I basically stayed up for seventy-two hours and walked in Monday morning and tossed the completed project on his desk. You should have seen the look on his face. I told him next time he gives me a job he needs to trust me to get the job done and let me do it my way. He couldn't do it and I left two months later.* Jason is not unusual when it comes to interactions between Baby Boomer bosses and Gen X employees. For many Gen Xers, if their bosses don't understand how they prefer to work and don't give them latitude to work their own way, then it is time to find another job. As we shall see, the MySpace Generation has extended this need for career flexibility even further than their Generation X predecessors.

While most Boomers have held one or two jobs their entire lives, Gen Xers such as Jason often move freely from job to job. Unlike Boomers, for Gen Xers a "job" does not represent a "career." It is simply a way to gain experience and then move on to more challenges. Further infuriating their bosses, these new employees expect raises, often within the first six months, or they move on. Gen X workers also expect praise and recognition from their bosses, perhaps in response to busy, sometimes absentee, parents. Their bosses, however, who were trained that these honors are to be doled out frugally to encourage hard work among other employees, are hesitant to do so. Vicarious reinforcement, as this is called in learning theory, simply does not work for Gen

Xers. Lacking proper recognition in their current positions, Gen Xers have felt compelled to seek new jobs, sometimes changing employment yearly. It is hardly surprising that 70% of the dot-com companies were started by Gen Xers who preferred to be their own bosses and set their own rules. Gen Xers want to live life on their own terms.

Tension between bosses and employees often arise around interactive styles. Boomer managers want to meet and talk about goals and the process of getting assignments completed. Gen Xers grow tired of talking. Many Gen Xers hate meetings with a passion and often bring their techno-toys or extra work. It's simply an issue of multitasking. A meeting is a "unitask" and Gen Xers are, for the most part, bored doing one thing at a time. At the first sign of a long-winded speech or intense discussion they phase out and either daydream, fiddle with something, or work on another task. I interviewed Jack, a forty-nine-year-old business executive, and Willie, his twenty-six-year-old son who worked for the same company. Jack told me that, *"I was so upset that Willie annoyed his boss by bringing his laptop to an important meeting."* Willie responded: *"He really wasn't saying anything that he hadn't already written in memos. There was no reason for me to be there and it was taking time away from my work. I hate meetings. They are such a waste of time. If my boss would just let us work we would get projects done in half the time but we have a meeting nearly every day. What a waste!"* When bored at the meeting, Willie chose to multitask to make better use of his time, something that his Baby Boomer father did not agree with or understand.

While Gen Xers such as Willie became expert multitaskers, the MySpace Generation perfected the art and took it to new heights using a variety of technologies. Toting laptops, cell phones, and iPods, they are rarely seen without technology. Walk across any high school or college campus and it is odd to see anyone who is not either talking on his or her cell phone or listening to music, or, in most cases, doing both. They simply can't envision a life without multitasking on their technological gadgets. One recent study showed that within one twentieth of a second, a teenager can determine whether a Web page is worth examining, which is nearly impossible according to current cognitive psychology research.[3] If you don't believe this, watch a fifteen-year-old fly through Web pages. They are almost a blur. I interviewed Lakeisha, a high school freshman, after observing her working on a report in her campus computer center. When I asked her how she knew that she needed to click on a link so quickly, she replied *"I just know. I can tell when something is useful or not and I don't want to waste time on dumb stuff that I can't use."* MySpacers are much more experienced with the Internet than Gen Xers and Baby Boomers, and they use it in entirely different ways. It is not a tool for them; it is a mainstay in their lives. They do not have to think about how to use the Internet, just as many experienced drivers don't have to think about the act of driving.

From birth, MySpacers have been bathed in technology. Their toys were computerized and many started using a computer before they could walk. IMing is a verb, not a technology. Live television is a thing of the past. *"I TiVo everything. Why should I watch something live and have to deal with commercials? I can fast-forward through them and watch a show when I want to watch it, not when it is shown on TV,"* one thirteen-year-old told me. For this generation, MySpace could not have arrived at a better time. It is the perfect "home base" for children who already spend most of their waking hours using technology. MySpace caters to them by providing much of their electronic entertainment under one roof. It is ingenious, and millions of children, teenagers, and young adults are spending two hours a day, seven days a week, on MySpace.[4]

However, judging from front-page stories on nearly every media outlet, parents, teachers, and administrators are not so thrilled. According to my research, nearly half the parents were extremely concerned and fearful about MySpace, but many were unaware of how much time their children were spending there.[5] These parents expressed strong concerns about sexual predators, cyberbullying, and pornography on MySpace. Jeff, the father of a fifteen-year-old MySpacer, told me: *"Although I don't know much about MySpace, I listen to the news and read the papers and quite frankly I don't know what to believe. My son tells me that nothing bad happens on MySpace and I believe him. But I don't know how to reconcile his experiences with all the negative news stories."* Jeff echoed the sentiment of the majority of parents in my research studies. They didn't know what to believe, but they didn't trust that their children were safe on MySpace.

Even though Gen Xers also used technology at an early age, MySpacers are different. They are much more social, more emotionally open, and happier when online. Even offline, dating has become a group activity. This certainly fits with their virtual lifestyles. They meet at the mall and they meet on the computer. To them it is all the same. Their friends are often "virtual," meeting only in cyberspace, and my research revealed that 78% of the MySpacers felt that it was easier for them to be honest with their online friends than with their offline friends. For many parents, the fact that their sons and daughters have online friends is a mystery, and this is one of the features that distinguish the MySpace Generation from many Baby Boomers and Gen Xers. It is natural for MySpacers to reveal their feelings online, for the world to see. Most Baby Boomers and many Gen Xers are uncomfortable with this open honesty and revealing of secrets to the world. This is yet another difference that creates friction between generations. MySpace teens are opening their lives to public scrutiny while their parents are worried about the dangers that this may bring.

MySpacers' online habits have made them more globally aware and more socially conscious. Their world is in environmental and political chaos. They have seen natural disasters destroy entire cities and imperil countries. Global warming, tsunami, levee breaches, and terrorism are part of their everyday vocabularies. On 9/11 they watched the twin towers fall over again and again on the television. Y2K came and went with a whimper, but they have seen more violence in their young lives than any generation should have to witness. YouTube, a favorite of MySpacers, shows video clips of the war in Iraq and violence at home and draws millions. Many of those fighting in Iraq are MySpacers; log on to MySpace and you will see the vast number of servicemen and women posting their thoughts and fears. Video games such as *Grand Theft Auto* encourage young gamers to wreak violence and mayhem. Electronic depictions of violence are ubiquitous in the lives of the Net Generation and the impact of this inundation remains to be seen.

Teachers also treat MySpacers differently. On the positive side, they are praised for their work and their behavior. Teachers use stickers, stars, and pizza parties to reward behavior that was expected of children from previous generations. According to B. F. Skinner's operant conditioning theory of learning, these are excellent strategies for developing good work habits and school success. Based on his decades of research, Skinner asserted that when you positively reinforce behavior, that behavior tends to increase in frequency. Parents and teachers point to better grades as indicators of the success of positive reinforcement. One such statistic showed that in 1968, 18% of high school students had "A" averages. That incredibly jumped to 46% in 2002.[6] Based on these figures, one would assume that high school students are studying more, and that is causing their grades to improve. However, in 1987, 47% of high school students studied six or more hours per week. In 2002 that dropped to only 33%.[7] Learning theorists would acknowledge that perhaps Baby Boomer and Gen X teachers are artificially inflating grades and that, in fact, what they think they are using as positive reinforcers are often simply rewards. A reward, according to learning theorists, is only a positive reinforcer if it changes behavior. It is possible that teachers are awarding higher grades, but MySpacers are actually putting in *less* effort to gain those grades. Once MySpacers enter the workplace, this reward strategy runs counter to how their bosses were evaluated when they went to school. Baby Boomers were, for the most part, reinforced by test scores and semester grades. Gen Xers were reinforced by test scores and grades but also by written comments on projects. Because of all their rewards in school, MySpacers in the workforce expect continuous praise and reinforcement, creating a dilemma for their bosses and perhaps providing an explanation for continuous job changes.

Earlier I provided data from a study published by the Kaiser Family Foundation showing that MySpacers spend more than forty hours per week watching television, playing video games, listening to music, and being online.[8] This enormous media consumption does not allow enough additional time for schoolwork, family obligations, sleep, meals, and outside activities without extensive multitasking. Perhaps due to having too much to do in too little time, adolescents consume caffeine at alarming rates. According to a study by the National Sleep Foundation, three of four teenagers drink one caffeinated beverage—coffee, soda, or power drink—per day and one in three consume two or more, which contributes to their sleep debt.[9] In fact, many MySpacers told me that they feel that caffeine helps them do more work in less time by making them sharper and making it easier to multitask.

Don, a fifteen-year-old, confided that unbeknownst to his parents, he has a Starbucks every morning because *"there is just too much to do in school and coffee helps me focus on my work. I can listen to the teacher and do my homework at the same time. Between fourth and fifth periods I need to get a soda from the machine so that I can stay alert and do my work in class."* Jordan, his seventeen-year-old brother, revealed: *"I get a Red Bull on the way home so I can do my homework really quickly and then jump onto MySpace. If I don't drink a Red Bull or something like it I work too slowly to have enough time to go online before I have to go to bed."* Although Don and Jordan feel that their caffeine helps them multitask, researchers are divided. Overall, the consensus appears to be that while drinking caffeinated drinks does enhance cognitive performance, even on two tasks at the same time, it also induces fatigue and sleeping difficulties in adolescents. More importantly, a recent study in the journal *Pharmacology* found that as fatigue increases, the benefits of multitasking decrease.[10] This suggests that although teens may feel that they are performing better and faster after ingesting caffeine, the bottom line is that in the long run they are paying for this by poorer performance and an increased sleep debt related to caffeine stimulation. While the MySpace Generation may thrive on their ability to multitask using technology, their increased use of caffeine to do so diminishes that ability.

Despite having so few hours for anything other than eating, sleeping, and school, MySpacers are encouraged by their Baby Boomer parents—who realize that they themselves work too many hours and have too little recreation—to supplement schoolwork with outside activities. According to one Kaiser Family Foundation study, eight- to eighteen-year-olds spent almost one and a half hours per day in some physical activity and another hour pursuing a hobby or participating in a club.[11] Soccer practices after school, coupled with dance lessons, acting in local plays, and other extracurricular activities on the weekend, occupy an already limited amount of "down time" for the MySpacer. A teenager's life is often scripted down to the minute and adding in additional activities necessitates more multitasking, often supplemented by caffeinated drinks, to remain awake and alert. Maria, a fourteen-year-old, told me that she's thinking of quitting either soccer or basketball because she is so exhausted every night that her grades are dropping. When I asked her mother about this she said, *"I just want her to have all the opportunities that I missed. She is a star on the soccer team and her coach said if she keeps it up she could play varsity and eventually get a scholarship to college. I know she needs to keep her grades up but she'll have more opportunities to get into college playing soccer than she will getting high grades."* When I looked at Maria for her response she just shrugged.

Overall, the MySpace Generation is defined by their immersion in technology. Many MySpacers are effectively plugged in and turned on during every waking minute. They are nearly always wired, constantly multitasking, and leading rapid-paced lives in a pixelated world that blurs the distinction between real and virtual. MySpacers are intensely curious, self-reliant, assertive, and experiential. They crave novelty and welcome diversity. They are clearly different from previous generations, but is their captivation by virtual worlds such as MySpace positive or negative? Overall, based on my extensive research, the impact of the MySpace lifestyle on child and adolescent development has been positive. It has provided a safe forum for expressing feelings and appears to enhance relationships and psychological well-being. Clearly, there may be some potential pitfalls in spending so many hours in cyberspace, and I will explore these problems and the benefits of a virtual lifestyle, and provide parents with a framework that they can use to enhance the positive developmental impact of MySpace and minimize the threats to their tweens and teens. Although these children live in a world that those of us from previous generations may not understand completely, and face issues that many of us cannot fathom, this is a crucial period in defining their lives. With the benefit of my research and interviews, and an understanding of psychological and social development, you will have the information and tools to guide your children through their virtual worlds and make those experiences valuable, positive, and enhancing.

I interviewed Anastasia Goodstein, Publisher of Ypulse, an online blog with reviews and commentaries about Generation Y, and the author of *Totally Wired: What Teens and Tweens Are Really Doing Online*. Here are her thoughts on generational similarities and differences:

Q: What do you think are the most important differences between Generation Y and those that have gone before, particularly Gen X and Baby Boomers?

Goodstein: The biggest difference is that Generation Y or Millennials have grown up using the Internet and other digital technology, so that it has become an integral part of what it means to be a teenager. They use it to stay connected to their friends, to express themselves, and experiment with identity. They are consuming more media and more marketing than any of the past generations, making them savvier about what is being pitched to them. They also constantly multitask with media and technology, especially when they're doing their homework. There has been a lot of debate over whether media multitasking actually helps or hurts academic performance.

They are also considered the most parented generation in history. They are constantly busy and tend to be stressed out about schoolwork, getting into college, and getting jobs as adults. Some would call this "helicopter parenting" in that parents remain heavily involved in their children's lives even when they become young adults. This is different from the latchkey kids who made up Generation X and the Boomers, whose parents were experimenting with a more relaxed style of parenting. As a result Millennials are seen as having closer relationships with their parents and having a sense of entitlement when they enter the workforce.

Q: How do you see Gen Y interacting in a business world with Gen X and Baby Boomer bosses?

Goodstein: I see them as being very adept at using technology and wanting the flexibility to work remotely, from their laptops or PDAs. They come in expecting a lot of responsibility right away and don't really have the concept of paying dues as previous generations have. And if they don't get it, they may go somewhere where they do or start their own company. They value a balance between work and life and don't want a job that takes over their lives. Most of all, they want to be heard. And even if they go about it in a way that feels entitled or abrasive, they are the future and often have incredible ideas that shouldn't be ignored.

Q: How do you feel Gen Yers are different Internet consumers than previous generations?

Goodstein: Going back to your first question, I think it's less about using technology to transact—find a plane ticket, look up a movie time, send an e-mail—and more about using technology to interact—chat with friends, post comments, rate a person or product, share videos, and photos.

Q: What aspects of MySpace have made it so attractive to Gen Yers?

Goodstein: The DIY [do it yourself] nature of the site and being able to completely customize their page, add video, lyrics, songs, and different layouts is huge. MySpace pioneered the concept of your Top 8 and having everyone connected through Tom. I also think it's about critical mass at this point, everyone's on it—including most bands, movies, and TV shows all offering additional content. But there's a lot of competition now so MySpace will have to keep innovating and coming up with more things to do or else teens will spend more time somewhere else.

Q: Do you see any downsides to MySpace or general Internet use that are particular to Gen Yers?

Goodstein: I think the downsides are not inherent to any particular Web site or technology. It's human nature and desire that creates the downsides—predators have always been out there, they now have a way to get in touch with kids more or less anonymously. Teens have always bullied each other; they can now do it virtually. Human drama becomes virtual human drama. I think the public nature of these sites and the viral nature of the Internet just magnify these issues.

Chapter 3

Real People in Virtual Relationships

◆

"Americans are more socially isolated than they were twenty years ago. Nearly a quarter of people surveyed said they had 'zero' close friends. More than 50% named two or fewer confidants, most often immediate family members. Both of these figures represent a surprising drop since 1985."

—Dr. Miller McPherson, Duke University and the University of Arizona, Dr. Lynn Smith-Lovin, Duke University, and Dr. Matthew Brashears, University of Arizona[1]

◆

By age four children already know the meaning of the word "friend." To a young child, a friend is a playmate, someone he or she can sit next to on the floor playing with trucks or dolls. At first, friends engage in parallel play; they play next to each other, but not together. School-age children gradually learn how to share toys and play together. This concept evolves and changes until adolescence, when friends are defined as those people who share common interests, spend time together, and provide emotional support. The process of forming friendships defines the teenage years. Friends become confidants who share a burgeoning need for intimacy, companionship, and self-validation.

During this developmental stage, larger groups of friends are also critical. The transition from elementary school to middle school and then to high school is defined by the development of what psychologists call "crowds" and "cliques." As children move from level to level, several small elementary schools feed into one larger middle school and then often several middle schools join together into one large high school. Old friends move too, but in larger schools there are more classes and more opportunities to make new friends. During this time teenagers form small subgroups (cliques) and larger ones (crowds). Many adolescents belong to more than one clique, often defined by shared classes or outside activities.

Psychologists have studied two types of crowds over the years in order to discover how children and adolescents develop friendships. On the one hand, "merged crowds" are formed from combinations of preexisting cliques or one-to-one friendships, while on the other hand, "reputation-based crowds" are larger, less structured units defined by common interests, beliefs, or styles. Jocks, nerds, Goths, and brains are a few examples. In some multicultural schools, crowds may be defined by culture and ethnic background. Although the concept stays the same, crowds differ from school to school and most certainly across generations. Crowds impact the teen's entire school experience by defining her or his social status and identity. When teens were asked what it takes to get into a "good crowd" at their school, the number one criterion for both boys and girls was personality, followed by clothes and reputation for girls and reputation and athletic ability for boys.[2]

On the Internet, and particularly on MySpace, online friendships are the name of the game. MySpace is all about friends. A MySpace page prominently announces both the adolescent's number of friends and their Top 8 best friends. Teens may have anywhere from zero to thousands of friends. Discounting those with impossibly large numbers of friends, based on the over twenty-five hundred interviews that I conducted, the average MySpacer had 168 friends with more than half sporting upwards of one hundred. One statistic from my research, which interestingly enough is corroborated by another national sample of teens,[3] is that teens listed an average of thirty-seven people as "close friends" and admitted that their friends list included quite a few whom they had never met in person. In fact, one-third of MySpacers have met only one in four of their online friends.[4]

On MySpace, someone must request to be on your friends list. When teens are deciding whom they want to accept, their decision process most probably echoes what I was told by John, *"If I know them in person, then I add them,"* or Melissah, *"Only school friends or relatives."* Other typical answers included:

- *"If I know them or if they look rather cute."*
- *"It depends on the person's profile, their hobbies. If the person is interesting, cool or cute, I will add them."*
- *"I pretty much add anyone who asks."*

Accumulating friends is a major goal for many MySpacers. Several teens told me that they had more than one thousand friends, and one enterprising young lady had 24,506. Perhaps the most telling interviewee, a fifteen-year-old girl, told me she had recently pared her friends list "down" to six hundred from more than one thousand. When I asked her how many of those were close friends, she replied, without batting an eye, *"All of them, of course."* Is it possible for the typical teenager to have hundreds of friends? How can she possibly keep up with that many people? When I did the math and told her that even if she spent one minute a week talking to her six hundred close friends, it would total ten hours, she informed me, in a tone that only an adolescent can carry off, that she spent way more than one minute a week with each of them. "How long are you on MySpace?" I asked. *"About three hours a day,"* she replied. "Well, again doing the math, that means you have twenty-one hours a week to talk to six hundred people. So, each one gets about two minutes a week." She looked at me like I was an alien and said, *"You are assuming that I am only talking to one at a time. Some are in groups I belong to so I can talk to them at once and I never have fewer than five IMs at a time."*

Psychologists have determined that friendship, whether individual or group-based, provides four types of support. First and foremost is social companionship. Friends participate in activities that lend social support and, in turn, enhance the friendship. Second, friendship provides informational support, which helps someone understand something that may not have made sense. For example, friends often offer information about sexuality through their blogs, Web sites, or one-on-one conversations. Third, friends offer self-esteem support, imparting a sense of value and worth, and validating feelings. Finally, friendship gives instrumental support in the form of tangible items or services that help improve quality of life.

What exactly is a friend to a teen or tween, and are these online friends "true friends" or just acquaintances? A friend, according to most psychologists, must possess several important characteristics. First, they must share interests, values, attitudes, and beliefs. On MySpace, with the main focus being communication, it is easy to determine if someone is like you in these critical ways. For example, simply reading someone's profile tells you about their personal characteristics, including their tastes in music, their attitude toward world events, their social interests, and much more. Some write blogs, while others receive comments from other friends. Some belong to discussion groups sharing views on a variety of topics. The information on the profile provides a wealth of information about similarities and differences between MySpacers.

Second, friends must be emotional confidants who are willing to listen to someone's problems without being judgmental. Online social networking sites, such as MySpace and Facebook, foster this emotional connection through a combination of anonymity and self-disclosure. According to Dr. Patti Valkenburg and her colleagues Drs. Alexander Schouten and Jochen Peter, being online means that you are communicating anonymously, even if you know the person on the other end of your discussion offline. This anonymity fosters self-disclosure that, in turn, promotes reciprocal liking and emotional bonding needed for confiding in another person. Valkenburg and her colleagues describe two theories about who might benefit from developing online friends. The rich-get-richer theory suggests that extroverted teens, those who are outgoing in their offline world, develop emotional bonds with online friends. In contrast, social compensation theory claims that socially anxious adolescents find it easier to make friends online, because they can be more open and honest via the Internet.[5] My research data, and that of others, support both theories. For example, as support for social compensation theory, I found that shy teens felt less shy and more honest online, which then led to the accumulation of more MySpace friends and enhanced self-esteem. Teens in my studies who were shy offline actually had more MySpace friends than those who were outgoing at school and with their friends.[6]

The third criterion for true friendship is providing support and understanding in times of need. Once an emotional connection is made online, and teens disclose personal problems and struggles on their MySpace pages, friends comment freely, most often with empathy, advice, and guidance. In my study of over twenty-five hundred MySpacers, three-fourths posted comments on their friends' pages, and more than four out of five reported that reading those comments was one of their top uses of MySpace. Mark, a sixteen-year-old, told me, *"The first thing I do is check comments from my friends. The other morning before school my parents had a major fight and I wrote about having a tough time dealing with their arguing and worrying about if they were going to split up. By the time I got home from school there were at least ten comments, some from people I hardly know, about how they dealt with their parents' divorces. I felt really supported and it made me realize that if they got through it, I could, too."*

MySpace's Top 8 feature encourages adolescents to identify their best friends—at least their best friends at the moment—by prominently displaying the pictures of these eight friends on the main MySpace page. Although 70% of the MySpacers told me that they pretty much leave their Top 8 alone, 30% swapped people in and out. Fourteen-year-old high school freshman Sandie told me that she changes her Top 8 daily, *"depending on who I talked to that day and who I am trying to get to know."* John, a school friend of Sandie's, told me, *"I have to kind of rotate people so nobody gets their feelings hurt. Of course, my girlfriend is number 1, and I have to put my brother on there or he'll kill me, but the rest change all the time. Sometimes I will meet someone and put their picture on my Top 8 so that they will want to talk to me on IM."* Poignantly, sixteen-year-old Danae told me, *"I hate Top 8. I feel so obligated sometimes. For example, my friend put me on his Top 8, so of course, I had to put him on my Top 8. The bad thing is that there are only eight spots you can fill. So if a friend puts me on their Top 8 and I don't do the same, I feel kinda bad and it sucks. So instead, I put my favorite bands on my Top 8."*

MySpace now has expanded the Top 8 and offered the option of making it a Top 12, Top 16, or even a Top 20. Danae told me that to her, *"The Top 16 or 20 is stupid. You still have to leave some people off and then they are hurt. It's my least favorite part of MySpace."* A high school senior said, *"Well, I had a Top 8 with my best friends and boyfriend, but now have a Top 12 so I could add some other close friends. I think I might even do a Top 20, but I think that is a bit crazy. I'm thinking about going back to just eight and figuring out who I really want there."*

Another way of accumulating friends is through a Buddy List. In the late '90s, America Online Instant Messenger (AIM) popularized a system of real-time messaging. With this technology, as soon as one person typed and sent a message, another person on the Internet could read it and respond in real time. *"I have 329 people on my Buddy List,"* says Nan, a fourteen-year-old MySpacer. *"There are school friends, band friends, D&D friends, and a whole bunch more groups. When I go on AIM I always have at least 50–100 people to talk with. It feels like I am at a big party and I know everyone there."* AIM's millions of users are mostly under eighteen and active MySpacers. Research by the Pew Internet & American Life Project found that more than half of all Buddy Lists included more than fifty screen names and 28% had more than one hundred. In essence, a Buddy List defines an adolescent's extended network of friends.[7]

Instant messaging is an important part of teen life. According to the Pew study, three-fourths of all teens online use it to communicate with their friends; half use it daily. When a buddy logs on to AIM, a message is sent to everyone who has that person's screen name on his or her Buddy List. A note pops up on the screen informing the group that he is available to chat, a tone sounds, his name lights up on the Buddy List, and a symbol indicates his status as online, idle, or away. It's a simple system that provides infinite opportunities for one-on-one conversations. Although much of what is discussed on IM is fairly pedantic, such as making plans, discussing homework, and gossiping, IM does promote the development and maintenance of friendships by having omnipresent buddies to provide emotional support when needed.

One would think that with so much flashing on screen, typing and communicating would be difficult, but Amee, a fairly typical sixteen-year-old, told me, *"I live on IM. Does it make me crazy? No way! It's great! It makes me feel like I have a whole world of good friends out there that care about me and want to talk with me. Any time of the day or night I can count on someone to IM. Just last night I talked to Evan from about midnight to three a.m. He was bummed about Clare, his girlfriend—who is one of my best friends—so I helped talk to him. He didn't know it but for most of the time I was also IMing Clare and telling her what he was saying."*

For the same reason that teens love IM, they have embraced text messaging on their cell phones. According to a recent study, 40% of fifteen- to seventeen-year-old boys and 57% of fifteen- to seventeen-year-old girls text message on a regular basis.[8] Although text messages are limited in length, they are used by teens when support is needed. Fay, a sixteen-year-old, told me, *"The other night I was freaked out because there were police cars near my house and I couldn't drive home. I didn't know what was going on and so I called Jessie, my best friend. Her mom wouldn't let her talk on the phone because she was supposed to be studying for a chemistry test, but she was able to keep texting me until the police let me through. She was great. She kept sending me messages that everything was going to be OK and to just relax and sit in my car and listen to music. She really calmed me down."* Again, this points out what a powerful influence electronic modes of communication can be on friendships in the MySpace Generation of children raised on technology. Through text messaging, Jessie was able to provide Fay with emotional support that she needed to get through her crisis.

The Process of Friendship

Traditional friendship development most often begins with spatial proximity. When we meet someone in person, we are usually very cautious about revealing too much about ourselves. At the beginning of a face-to-face relationship we spend time telling the other where we go to school or what we do for a living, and how we like to spend our leisure time. Only after we have established a measure of trust do we then start to reveal more about ourselves, including our deepest inner feelings.

In contrast, online friendship usually begins with a flurry of e-mail messages or IMs back and forth with early self-disclosure by both parties. Where offline friendships may take weeks or months to develop, many online friendships can literally spring from nothing to best friends in a matter of days. Jeenie, a fifteen-year-old, described it this way when talking about how she met Frankie, her best friend: *"We met through a friend who thought we might like each other. She e-mailed me and we decided to IM. We talked for hours. I think we sent like a million IMs from about ten at night until two in the morning. The time flew by and we talked about everything—boys, parents, school, everything. I even told her some things I never told anyone. That week we probably spent twenty hours on IM, and I know that she and I are friends for life. She lives pretty far away but we already are talking about me flying out during spring break to see her."*

Self-disclosure is critical for both formation and maintenance of friendships. So, what makes it so much easier and so much faster online? When we meet someone in person we are immediately struck by outward characteristics—hair color, clothes, height, eyes, and more. Psychologists refer to these as "gating characteristics." One classic comic strip shows a dog typing on a computer, with the caption: "On the Internet, nobody knows you're a dog." In essence, without any cues, other than verbal ones, there is no basis for prejudice.

Dr. Adam Joinson coined the term "disinhibition" and defined it as "any behaviour that is characterised by an apparent reduction in concerns for self-presentation and the judgment of others."[9] In essence, disinhibition is what you do or say online that you would not do or say offline or in person. In one research study, for example, Joinson had pairs of people discuss topics either face-to-face or online and found that online discussions led to more than four times the amount of self-disclosure. In another study Joinson found that if a person felt that the chances of rejection by the other person were high, and was given a choice of communication mode, they preferred to hold the conversation online rather than face-to-face.[10]

Parents have told me that they worry about their teenagers communicating online with "friends" and possibly forming friendships with teens, whom neither the parents nor the teenagers have ever met. From dozens of research studies, and evidence from MySpacers like Jeenie, we now know that indeed they do form strong bonds online. Dr. Joe Walther, a pioneer in the study of electronic communication, uses the term *hyperpersonal* for these written conversations, in which the two parties feel anonymous, distant, and safe. According to Walther, the participants infer the information that may be lacking online to develop an impression of another person by "filling in the blanks."[11] Making assumptions about someone you have never met can easily lead to a trap Sigmund Freud called projection, a defense mechanism through which a person attributes thoughts, motivations, desires, and/ or feelings to another person, based on his or her own needs and wishes, rather than on direct information about or from that person. So, if John is talking online to Mary, he may think that she is very kindhearted and empathic without any evidence to support this conclusion, because he wants (and needs) her to be kindhearted and empathic.

On MySpace, online conversations can quickly lead to friendships. Feeling disinhibited leads to hyperpersonal, self-disclosing interchanges that then can generate a feeling of an emotional connection. This connection fosters trust, or a belief that the other party will act kindly, ethically, and supportively toward you. Psychological research has shown that both mutual interest and repeated interactions enhance trust, which, in turn, is a key to fostering friendship.[12]

Regardless of the mode of communication, trust consists of at least four elements. First, we trust someone who possesses information, abilities, or skills in a specific area that is the basis for our interaction. Recently, I completed a study that examined whether people trusted peers or experts dispensing advice in a variety of online situations. When asked about online book reviews, for example, most people trusted peer evaluations such as those found on Amazon.com. In contrast, when seeking information concerning health issues, over three-fourths of the 414 subjects in this study trusted expert opinions over those of their peers.[13] Clearly, when it comes to our health, we trust those who are trained medical professionals.

A second element of trust is benevolence, or the expectation that others will want to do good so that we will then feel comfortable reciprocating their trust. Without the assurance that another has good intentions, we may be hesitant to extend ourselves, which makes it difficult to develop a trusting relationship.

Third, trust implies that we expect others to act in accordance with socially accepted standards of honesty and ethics. In developing real-world friendships we use a combination of behaviors (Does this person act in a way that demonstrates trust?) and additional nonverbal visual cues, including facial expressions, word inflection, and body language, to help us determine whether someone is trustworthy. Online we need to use different criteria to determine trustworthiness. On the Internet one helpful barometer of trust is responsiveness. If, for example, a person were to ask someone a question online, he would trust the person more if he received a rapid response. On some intuitive level, we believe that when a person answers a question immediately they are more trustworthy.

A fourth element of trust is a person's willingness to disclose personal information. We have a sense that if someone is willing to tell us his or her deepest, darkest secrets, then we can trust him or her with ours. With the online world promoting disinhibited, hyperpersonal communications, deciding whether to trust someone can be difficult. After talking to more than twenty-five hundred MySpacers, it is clear that the vast majority enter their virtual world with a predisposition to trust others.

One MySpace teen expressed this sentiment: *"I think that when I meet someone new, since I have no reason to believe they are lying, I would rather believe that they are someone I can trust. In five years of being on the [Inter]net, I have only had this illusion shattered twice and both times I should have seen it coming. But in ninety-nine out of one hundred times I am meeting or talking to someone I don't know they seem to deserve my trust. I guess I just believe that deep down inside people are real and sincere and not out to mess with me."* Clearly, trust in the online world can be an issue when it comes to people, such as sexual predators and cyberbullies, who may enter MySpace with dangerous motives. These potentially misplaced trust issues are discussed in later chapters.

Since the '60s, psychologists have studied the impact of friendship on mental health and found that teens who have more friends are more confident, more altruistic, less aggressive, more involved and better adjusted in school, and earn better grades. Additional work has shown that those teens who have more supportive friends—people with whom they can talk about personal problems—are less depressed and exhibit higher self-esteem than teens with fewer supportive friends, who are more psychologically distressed and more apt to have suicidal thoughts.[14] How does this translate from real-life friends to online friends? My research on MySpace demonstrated that teens with more MySpace friends experienced less depression, were more self-confident, and found it easier to be more honest online, but they were also more likely to be addicted to the Internet.[15] Online honesty can, however, lead to situations in which trust is placed in people who have ulterior motives. Another study of fifteen hundred adolescent Internet users discovered that girls who were emotionally troubled, or who had high levels of conflict with their parents, were more likely to use online friendships to make themselves feel better. Boys who had more emotional problems or had little parental interaction were also likely to do the same.[16] Taken together, it is important to ensure that MySpacers develop healthy online relationships.

To assess the power of online friendship, the Pew Internet & American Life Project studied social ties formed in cyberspace. Their national survey found that Internet users have larger social networks than nonusers. Estimating "core ties"—very close friendships characterized by frequent contact and strong emotional intimacy—and "significant ties"—important friendships, but with less frequent contact and not as strong an emotional connection—the Pew study found that Internet users had about the same number of core ties as nonusers, but had many more significant ties. One-third of Internet users in the Pew study insisted that being online increased their social network, with an equal number claiming that the Internet increased both core and significant ties.[17] Although this national study did not examine social networking among MySpace users, it is likely that the impact of being online would be even more substantial if we included the number of friends that are being made on MySpace. Having more friends enhances opportunities to develop both core and significant ties.

To explain why and how we create emotional ties from social interactions, Stanford psychologist Dr. Albert Bandura proposed social cognition theory. Bandura coined the term "self-efficacy" to represent the self-evaluation that influences decisions about what we do, our confidence in performing tasks, and how we feel about ourselves. According to social cognition theory, when we have positive outcomes from social interactions, we feel satisfied, proud, and confident. Negative outcomes leave us feeling dissatisfied and disappointed in ourselves, both in the moment, and in the long term. These positive and negative interactions provide us with feelings that we integrate and use to form our feelings of self-worth.

As stipulated in social cognition theory, adolescents are continually revising their sense of self, based on positive and negative online interactions. Online communication can make this self-evaluative process easier than face-to-face communication, by providing teens the option of discontinuing negative communications that may reduce self-efficacy. For example, if someone makes a negative comment on a teen's MySpace page, he or she can simply ignore it, delete it, or even block the person from making further comments. E-mail, IM, text messaging, and chat work the same way. With online communication the teen has the option simply to ignore negative feedback, knowing full well that just around the corner (or at the bottom of the screen) is someone IMing them with positive strokes and wanting to be their friend. A teen with hundreds or thousands of online friends will always have someone to provide positive feedback and, hence, increase his or her self-evaluation. MySpace affords many opportunities to foster self-efficacy through individual interactions over which the teen can exert control. It can be a delicate balance, however, as one seventeen-year-old girl related,

> *"A friend of mine had met a guy online that she thought I might like. She gave him my IM name and we started talking. At first I was flattered. It felt good to flirt with someone and he said lots of nice things about me like how cute my photos were on MySpace and how smart I seemed. But then he started IMing me all the time and getting pushy about wanting to go out on a date. I got a creepy feeling about him and tried to ignore him but then he started to say really mean things and bad-mouthed me to my friend and she kinda got mad at me. It really became a mess and I guess I could have just blocked him but I felt bad so I decided to get a new IM name."*

MySpace, and other social networking sites, provide a variety of vehicles to establish a sense of community. Chat rooms, discussion groups, and bulletin boards are all available through MySpace. Unlike crowds and cliques, these communities do not depend on space and time. While school friends are mostly restricted to the seven- to eight-hour school day (and perhaps after-school and weekend activities), the online world is wide open. Interacting with groups of people online, as opposed to in-person, is a qualitatively different activity from both individual online friendships and real-world groups. One college freshman told me that he is actively involved in an online Web site that is built around playing a specific game:

> "I have been into this for years now and many of my closest friends are part of this board. We game together but we also talk outside of the game about other stuff. It's a small group, maybe seventy-five of us, who have been doing this probably ten hours a week or more for at least four years. Strangely, I have not met any of them but I feel like I know them. If I have a problem, something that's not even part of the game, I know I can find someone online to talk to. We are working on a plan to all meet next summer somewhere 'live' but we tried last summer and it fell through. It's gonna happen this time, I know it. But even if we never meet, I feel like I have a group of lifetime friends who I feel closer to than nearly anyone else in the world."

Being part of a group requires the teenager to learn how to cooperate, take different perspectives, gain social support, and develop a sense of intimacy. Groups are both more and less than one-to-one friendships, and they fulfill quite different needs. They allow a sense of identity and a frame of reference for future individual behavior in a group environment, such as college or the workplace. MySpace in particular and the Internet in general have always fostered group interaction. From its earliest inception in the early '80s, the Internet hosted specific topic-based discussion groups on Usenet, where users left messages on a remote computer system for others to access and then add their own comments. Imagine a gigantic bulletin board with thumbtacked messages and you have the general idea of a Usenet newsgroup. On any given day, anyone could log on, read the posted messages, and either pen a response or post a new message. At the same time another type of discussion group, a Listserv, performed a similar function, except that messages were not only posted, but were e-mailed to all registered subscribers.

Regardless of the format, online discussion groups have always produced group cohesion. Lifetime friendships were forged through these groups, producing a true global community. Today, Usenet and List-servs have been replaced by a combination system in which members can choose either to read posts online or to have them e-mailed. For example, Yahoo! hosts thousands of discussions on any topic imaginable. When a friend of mine had a sudden appearance of hives, she joined a Yahoo! group and talked to others who had experienced similar problems. Through this group she was able to gain information about possible causes and treatments. Granted, the discussants were mostly lay people and not medical professionals, but their caring was apparent. Several people e-mailed her outside of the group to make further suggestions and she still talks with one of them relatively often and considers her a friend, although the two have never met.

MySpace provides similar types of groups and forums on every imaginable topic. Figure 3.1 displays an assortment of MySpace group categories followed by the number of groups in parentheses—thousands of groups are available. It is particularly noteworthy that there are more than 270,000 fan clubs, plus an additional 347,000 groups discussing music. Given that friends share hobbies, values, attitudes, and beliefs, these groups are definitely a source of community and friendship centered on mutual interests.

Many MySpacers I have interviewed talked about participating in groups. For example, John, a seventeen-year-old high school senior,

Figure 3.1 Example of MySpace Discussion Groups

Groups by Category

Activities (97297 groups)	**Health, Wellness, Fitness** (26986 groups)
Automotive (54512 groups)	**Hobbies & Crafts** (36433 groups)
Business & Entrepreneurs (20446 groups)	**Literature & Arts** (33827 groups)
Cities & Neighborhoods (45078 groups)	**Money & Investing** (12395 groups)
Companies / Co-workers (42140 groups)	**Music** (347023 groups)
Computers & Internet (19910 groups)	**Nightlife & Clubs** (65335 groups)
Countries & Regional (16759 groups)	**Non-Profit & Philanthropic** (20734 groups)
Cultures & Community (89838 groups)	**Other** (2123208 groups)
Entertainment (414962 groups)	**Pets & Animals** (40584 groups)
Family & Home (49157 groups)	**Places & Travel** (21145 groups)
Fan Clubs (270880 groups)	**Professional Organizations** (50011 groups)
Fashion & Style (76492 groups)	**Recreation & Sports** (145552 groups)
Film & Television (58978 groups)	**Religion & Beliefs** (116268 groups)
Food, Drink & Wine (47166 groups)	**Romance & Relationships** (87313 groups)
Games (66677 groups)	**Schools & Alumni** (195319 groups)
Gay, Lesbian & Bi (44084 groups)	**Science & History** (10643 groups)
Government & Politics (33570 groups)	**Sorority/Fraternities** (36111 groups)

regularly posted comments on a music discussion group called "Green Day," which at this writing has an astounding 6,332 members, all discussing the rock group with this name. John told me, *"I check in with 'Green Day' at least once a day, if not more, just to see who has left comments and if anything is going on. I also belong to about a dozen other groups, some of which I don't really use all that often. The only one I really like is this one because the people on there are really up on what's happening with the group."* For John, who happens to be rather shy, the group forum allows him to freely express his feelings. I asked him whether such a free forum creates problems. *"Sure, there are some a-holes who just want to argue about anything and everything but mostly we ignore them. For the most part, I think I feel at home there. I don't have a lot of friends at school, never have, but I feel like on MySpace I have zillions. It's made me feel like I am not such a freak."*

John and countless others involved in discussion groups experience what psychologists call homophily, which is the tendency of individuals to associate and bond with others with similar interests and ideas. The more we share in common with someone, the more we are able to discuss, and the more likely it is that we will get emotional and social support for our opinions. Without a Green Day group, John might not be brave enough to talk about his favorite band to anyone at school. But online he has thousands of "friends" who share his love. Research has shown that sharing interests leads to an increased sense of belonging and self-validation. Being part of the group has made John feel welcome, trusted, and valuable, something that he may not feel at school.

Online communities are also playing a major role in helping people deal with catastrophic events in life. When a disgruntled student opened fire and murdered more than thirty people on the Virginia Tech campus in April 2007, students immediately turned to MySpace and Facebook for further information. Pages sprang up where students and other young adults could leave their thoughts and feelings about the tragedy. Interestingly, Virginia Tech officials chose to warn the student body by sending a campus-wide e-mail; however, most students didn't get that e-mail, because for them, social networking is their main source of communication, not e-mail. They check their MySpace page constantly, but only read e-mail a couple of times a day.

By promoting and reinforcing communication skills, online communities are helping teenagers learn how to create enduring friendships. However, it is important to ask whether these online relationships interfere with creating and maintaining real-world relationships. In my research with parents and teens, I have found consistently that only a small percentage of parents worry that time spent online interferes with offline relationships. Most responded like June, who talked about her fourteen-year-old son Ben:

> *"I was worried that Ben was spending too much time on MySpace so my husband and I sat down with him and talked about whom he was talking to online. It turned out that most of his online friends were from his school and he told us that he found that if he was able to IM kids from his classes it was easier to talk to them at school. He showed us how he could look up which kids from his high school had MySpace pages and then told us about how he needed to know how to do a homework problem, so he found one of his classmates, IM'd him, and got the homework and then they talked about school and he discovered that they really had a lot in common."*

Like Ben, many teens in my studies reported that by talking online they felt more confident talking offline. In a study of 816 Dutch adolescents, Dr. Patti Valkenburg made similar findings. She reported, "Our study clearly showed that the Internet is positively related to the closeness of existing friendships for both lonely and socially anxious groups."[18] This is not, however, the case with all MySpacers.

Some MySpacers use the Internet to escape from their problems in the real world. It is important for parents to stay aware of this possibilty and, like June, keep an open line of communication with their children. If your teenager would rather stay home all weekend and talk online than go out with friends, that may signal a potential problem that needs to be addressed. It is important to have frank conversations with your teenager about friendship. One strategy is to ask your teen to list his five best friends and then talk about who they are and whether they are online or offline friends. Don't seize this as an opportunity to criticize or belittle online relationships, but rather view it as an opening to discuss the value of friendship. Don't deny the value of online friends, because this may well be alienating and divisive. Instead, ask about each online friend as you would about a school friend. Remember that your teen most likely sees no difference between online and offline friends and in fact may feel more kinship with his online friends. It is important to reinforce the value of both kinds of friendship while, at the same time, providing opportunities for your teenager to spend time with offline friends.

Although early adolescent friendships are most often same-sex relationships, teens begin to develop strong opposite-sex friendships, many of which lead to romance. Soon crowds, cliques, and friendships become secondary to boyfriend-girlfriend relationships. By the seventh grade, 34% of teens are romantically involved. This increases to 59% in tenth and eleventh grades, and to 72% in twelfth grade.[19] Based on my interviews with MySpacers, some of these relationships start online.[20]

Online dating at sites such as match.com or eHarmony is a billion-dollar industry catering mostly to adults. MySpace and similar social networking sites, although billed as friendship networks, also function as vehicles for dating. The formation of an online romance is most certainly affected by the rapid process of "getting to know you" online. Combined with the lack of gating cues, easy self-disclosure, and Freud's defense mechanism of projection, it is possible to imagine how teens might fall in love without ever having met. One college student told me that he had an online girlfriend for five years whom he had never met. She lived in the Midwest and he went to school on the East Coast, but they planned to meet during summer break after his freshman year.

Between 2003 and 2005, I completed a series of five studies of online daters.[21] One in three online daters found a serious relationship through a combination of sending e-mail messages, talking on IM, eventually moving to the telephone, and finally meeting in person. In addition, the amount of emotionality and self-disclosure in an initial e-mail message from a man to a woman or a woman to a man strongly influenced the receiver's impression of the sender. Highly emotional messages and those with moderate-to-high self-disclosure were seen as more positive and the sender as more attractive. Although no research has been done on teen online dating, these results may indicate why adolescents might be attracted to online romance. Disinhibition and the hyperpersonal nature of online interaction make MySpace, which is rife with self-disclosure and highly emotional communications, a perfect place to form deep romantic connections with people without any physical contact. I suggest that parents make a special effort, in their talk about online and offline friends, to note any potential romantic entanglements and address them in a neutral, nonjudgmental manner.

With so many friendships and potential romantic relationships available online, mention MySpace to a parent and the first response usually concerns fears of adolescents interacting with strangers. My research indicates that this is clearly a concern of most parents. In my most recent study of 482 parents of MySpace teens, 59% were concerned about their teenager having close friends on MySpace and meeting them in person. From my interviews it is clear that most MySpacers spend at least some time talking to strangers, people who they have never met in the real world. Of the 482 teens in this latest study, 12% did, in fact, meet an online friend in person. Similarly, a national survey found that 55% of online adolescents conversed with people they did not know and 7% of these teens and preteens actually met their online friend face-to-face; of those, 23% did so alone.[22] Another 2006 study of 1,160 online teens, sponsored by Cox Communications and the National Center for Missing & Exploited Children, validated these data, finding that 14% had met someone face-to-face whom they had known only through the Internet. Strikingly, 30% of the adolescents in the Cox study had *considered* meeting someone they knew only online.[23]

The idea that teens are communicating with and meeting strangers online fuels the media and presents a potential nightmare for parents. However, I don't believe that parents need to do anything special or out of the ordinary to meet this challenge. If your son or daughter told you that they were going to meet a new friend at the mall or go to a movie, you would most likely ask questions about that friend. Who is he? Where did you meet? What is he like? What do his parents do for a living? Parents need to be more vigilant with online friends as their children are meeting them and getting to know them in the virtual world. Based on my most recent study, however, nearly one in three parents have never seen their teen's MySpace page, and 75% review it less than once a month. More telling, however, only one in four parents asks their teen about online friends, and 41% are not even sure whether their adolescent has online friends. The solution is proactive parenting.

There are two basic ways of parenting—proactively and reactively. Reactive parenting, often the choice for the busy parent, involves responding to every situation as it happens. When a problem arises, the reactive parent is forced to think on the spot and make quick decisions. Because the act of children pushing boundaries set by their parents often gives rise to such situations, it is common for reactive parenting to be punitive. The teenager who stays out too late is grounded for a week. The twelve-year-old who keeps playing video games after being told to come to dinner may lose video game privileges. Proactive parenting involves anticipating problems and establishing limits and providing guidance *before a problem arises*. It is, of course, easier simply to react to problems by imposing consequences. It is much more difficult to foresee potential harmful situations and react proactively. In the case of online friendships, proactive parenting is a must. Parents cannot simply wait until their teen has made an online friendship and met that person offline. Parents must act proactively when it comes to their adolescent's online social interactions. Here are seven suggestions for parents to engage in proactive parenting:

1. Have your teenager show you his or her MySpace page. Look at their list of friends and ask about any you do not know. Pay particular attention to the Top 8 as those are your teen's best friends and usually the ones they communicate with most often. Find out how they met and glean any information you can about their age, geographic location, and personal information. The easiest way to do this is to click a friend's photo and visit their MySpace page. Be advised, however, that the information there may or may not be true. If you are concerned, ask your teenager to tell you what he or she thinks about the validity of that information.

2. Try to maintain a neutral attitude about online friends. Most will match what they say on their profile. If you are concerned that a friend may be misrepresenting himself or herself, ask your teen for more information. Remember, that these friends serve a purpose in your adolescent's life, because interactions with friends are critical in navigating adolescence.

3. Pay particular attention to comments on your teen's MySpace page. You can learn a lot about their friends from the comments they leave and clicking on the picture or icon associated with a comment will take you directly to that person's MySpace page.

4. Look at your teen's IM Buddy List, and once again ask about any names you do not know.

5. Talk with your child about the meaning of friendship and how important it is to have friends, particularly people they know in the real world. Don't put down their online friends, but suggest that they have a balance between online and offline friends.

6. If you are worried about your teen's interactions with a particular person, ask to see any e-mail correspondence or IM conversations between them. This is a last resort, and you should be forewarned that e-mail messages can be deleted and IM conversations disappear once they are terminated. In this situation you may need to proactively insist that your teen save all e-mail messages and IM conversations and provide consequences if they delete any of them. You may need to monitor this by insisting that you be able to look at what is on their computer screen at any time, including reading any ongoing conversations. Again, be alert to your teen quickly closing any windows. My suggestion is that you set up a rule in advance that, if you attempt to look at your teen's computer and you see any windows being closed, there will be reasonable consequences. For example, you can establish that the first time this happens Internet access will be restricted for the remainder of the day. With each additional infraction you can add on reasonable penalties. If your penalties are too harsh, you will only alienate your teenager and force her to be even more surreptitious.

7. Consider placing the computer your teenager uses in an area other than his or her bedroom. Half the teens in my studies access the Internet from their bedrooms and those who do so are 50% more likely to make new online friends and are more likely to divulge their full name and the name of their school.[24]

Given the amount of time teens spend on the Internet, and the limited time they have for face-to-face activities, MySpace serves three functions. First, it allows the teen to keep in touch with current friends, both from school and other parts of life. Second, it gives adolescents an opportunity to make friends among people that they might never have met if not for the Internet. Finally, through various communication tools, MySpace provides a twenty-four-hour network where a friend is always there, ready to talk. These are all incredibly valuable functions in the teen's struggle to find a sense of identity and self through adolescence. However, parents need to practice proactive parenting to help monitor these friendships. In chapter 4 we explore how proactive parenting helps provide a safe environment to answer the all-important teen question, "Who AM I?"

I interviewed danah boyd, a University of Southern California Fellow at the Annenberg Center for Communications, and a pioneer in studying teen and young adult behavior on social network sites such as MySpace and Friendster.[25] Here is what she had to say about online friendships:

Q: Teens are making many friends online whom they will never meet offline, in the physical world. What do you see as the positives and negatives of these virtual friendships?

boyd: First, it is important to ask ourselves which teens are making which friends online and how significant are those friendships? Just becoming involved in online gaming and meeting someone online every day to play a game most likely does not mean you are "friends." One father told me that his son had been talking to another boy for about a year on WoW (World of Warcraft). When the dad asked his son, "Do you want to meet him? We could arrange a trip to his town and get together," his son answered, "Why would I want to do that?" Teens go online for many reasons, but adults are typically more interested in meeting strangers for offline encounters than teens. Teens are looking for support and validation, but they are primarily interested in enriching their offline connections—talking to a stranger online doesn't help build a teen's reputation at school. That said, for marginalized teens such as queer youth, finding a community of like minds often only happens online.

It is important to remember that status is a core feature of teen life. Making more friends is often not as important as making the "right" friends. There are strangers that can provide offline credibility. One adolescent told me that he made friends with a well-known band that had a MySpace page and that one of the band members made some comment on his profile. This made him look good in front of his peers.

One of the most negative aspects of online friendships—although I think this is truer for adults than kids—is that you invest a lot of energy into connecting with someone and often that does not build into a relationship. Often it just fizzles out but sometimes it simply can't turn into an offline friendship. This is best exemplified by the attention given to celebrities. For example, suppose a teen is obsessed with Angelina Jolie and learns everything about her life—which, by the way, is so easy given the fact that our mediated society allows anyone to gain access to extensive information about celebrities. Now, suppose the teen has a meltdown and needs to reach out to someone for help. Reaching out to Angelina is impossible. A fan is a nonperson to her. Another example concerns bloggers who build up their identity online, writing about their thoughts and feelings. Those who read a given blog may think the blogger is a close friend, because after all, the information is so intimate, so real. But is this friendship? The blogger doesn't know anything about the reader. What does it mean that you can know so much about someone when they know nothing about you? Such unbalanced connections are not friendship, even if they are marked as "friends" online.

How teens conceptualize online friendship is quite different than adults' understanding. Part of this has to do with language, part of this has to do with generational differences. Teens are very aware of the differences between an online "friend" and a deep personal connection, even if they use the same term. Teens have "throwaway friendships" where they meet someone, have a great time, and then never see the person again. People get together online, talk, disclose, and then simply stop talking or disappear. Such connections occur offline—at the mall, at the beach, and so forth—and they also happen online in networked publics. Stranger danger obfuscates the benefits of meeting new people for brief encounters. Meeting people of diverse backgrounds in public settings helps socialize young people into society and such encounters breed tolerance. We understand this when people have defined roles— bus drivers, shopkeepers, janitors—but what about the person just walking down the street who smiles and says, "Have a nice day"? Can teens (and adults) foolishly trust an untrustworthy person? Of course. Can they get involved in risky situations? Of course. But treating social encounters as a binary choice and encouraging young people to trust no one also has extremely dire consequences.

The bottom line is that public life is important. Sociality is constructed through people's encounters with others. The Internet is helping a networked public life emerge and much of what is taking place there mirrors and magnifies what takes place offline.

Q: Why do you feel that some MySpacers "collect" hundreds of friends?

boyd: Young children love to collect things like baseball cards. Collecting is a part of competition. Some younger teens replicate this tendency on MySpace. Yet, having lots of MySpace friends is not universally acceptable to teens. While some people see collecting as cool, others label such collectors as "MySpace whores." The average MySpace teen has hundreds of friends for a variety of reasons. First, it is very difficult to say no to a friendship request if you know the person or even if you only sort of know him or her. Most schools have hundreds of teens and thus it is not uncommon to see teens that have hundreds of MySpace friends, all from their school. The politics of saying yes or no to friend requests are complicated. Should you say yes to someone from school that you don't know but is in a class with you? What about someone you see around town? Once you start accepting requests from anyone you recognize, why not accept requests from people who look interesting? Where's the appropriate boundary? Just because teens have hundreds of "friends" does not mean that they're close with all of them. In academic papers, I capitalize the word Friend when talking about these online acquaintances because the word means something different. On MySpace, Friends are used to construct an imagined audience—the people that you want to pay attention to your profile and comments. Through this imagined audience, teens have a sense of the social context and, thus, what is appropriate and expected behavior.

Q: Online teens are more apt to disclose their personal secrets to others. How do you feel this enhances or detracts from the process of developing relationships?

boyd: Teens disclose "personal secrets" to their peers all the time; what is different online is that more people can see these secrets. People regularly reveal personal information to others to build social ties. The process is simple: you share with someone and then they validate and reciprocate. This helps build bonds. Teens tend to do this more than adults simply because they are in the process of building their friend group. Of course, the desire to get validation through exposure can be problematic, particularly when individuals are seeking any attention they can get.

While face-to-face encounters allow you to immediately see someone's response, digital encounters make it difficult to gauge people's reactions. You don't have to see the sneer or scowl when someone reacts negatively to something you said. It is an imagined audience, not a real audience. There are no external cues to stop you from disclosing. As you write yourself into being online, you craft a nearly complete persona before you get any reaction . . . this is quite different than when you say something and adjust immediately based on the reaction you receive.

Kids are taught at a young age the difference between what you do in public and what you do in private. Conditioning starts as young as a two-year-old is told that "we don't pick our noses in public." Kids don't question why until they are older. Growing up is a continual process of building and testing and pushing at the edges to see how far you can go, to see what is acceptable. To learn what is acceptable in different situations requires experiencing different social situations.

Adults take access to private spaces as a given. They see their home as their own domain. It is a place where they can sing with music alone and know that nobody will see or judge them. Young people do not have the same experiences with privacy. While their bedroom may feel somewhat private, teens for decades have bemoaned their parent's response of "well, it's my house!" whenever their efforts to control their bedrooms conflict with their parents'. For teens, privacy is when they have control over the space or audience. While home is not a private space for all teens, teens also don't have access to the types of publics that adults take for granted. Their mobility is heavily controlled through structural, social, and political limitations.

For many teens, networked publics like MySpace are the only large-scale publics to which they have access without being under constant surveillance (although this is rapidly changing).[25] Publics are critical for teens to "grow up," test the social boundaries, and develop a sense of self that is situated in the broader world. Given the lack of access to other publics, it is not surprising that teens are turning to online spaces to have some form of public life. These spaces are also where they turn to have "private" encounters with a smaller group of friends.

Chapter 4

Me, MySpace, and I

◆

"MySpace provides a fertile ground for identity development and cultural integration. As youth transition from childhood, they seek out public environments to makes sense of culture, social status, and how they fit into the world."

—danah boyd, University of Southern California Fellow at the Annenberg Center for Communications[1]

◆

"People sometimes need to hide a bit or stay put a while before moving forward. But as long as they're using the Net in the spirit of self-reflection, they're making the most of life on the screen."

—Dr. Sherry Turkle, Massachusetts Institute of Technology[2]

◆

In the '50s and '60s Professor Erik Erikson formulated his model of how we struggle from birth to define our identity. To Erikson, this struggle is precipitated by a continual onslaught of crises. During infancy, we grapple with who to trust, and then how to assert our growing need for independence. In childhood, our crises surround our abilities and self-esteem. Once we hit adolescence, however, Erikson says we move into a psychosocial crisis between our personal identity and role confusion. Teenagers continually wonder what they are doing with their lives, who their real friends are, and how the world sees them. It's an awkward time fraught with much angst.

A teenager's job is to discover his place in the world. When he is young, he spends the majority of time with his parents, and his identity comes from them. When he is around seven years old, he spends about as much time with his peers as he does with his parents, and by eleven or twelve, the preteen spends roughly 40% of his waking hours with his friends. At fifteen or sixteen, he hardly sees his parents, spending three hours with his peers for every one spent with his family. So during Erikson's psychosocial adolescent crisis, the teen must turn to his friends to develop his values and beliefs. Gabriel, age fifteen, exemplifies this process well:

> *"From the moment I get home until I go to sleep I'm hooked up. If I'm not IMing my friends, I'm in some group talking about the latest bands. This is the one place where I can say what I feel and nobody comes down on me. Sure, sometimes I'll say something and get flamed but I don't know what I would do if I couldn't talk to my dudes. They have helped me out when I was really down about school and stuff and saved my life a time or two. And I do the same for them. One guy I was talking to the other day was tripping about his girlfriend and some other guy who was hitting on her and I talked him down. Took over two hours but it was cool."*

The Internet, in general, and MySpace, in particular, provide a unique forum for adolescent identity development. A MySpace profile expresses an "individual's digital representation."[3] MySpacers supply multiple photographs of themselves and their friends; self-descriptions of likes and dislikes; evidence of their tastes in fashion, music, and other media; results of personality quizzes; blogs expressing their views, ideals, and values; and a host of other clues to their adolescent identity. They use the power of MySpace's social network to form communities of like-minded people and develop a larger sense of group identity.

In earlier generations, identity development was done primarily face-to-face. Teens hung out after school and on the weekends on their neighborhood streets, or met at malls, parks, or other safe public locations. Many of those previously safe public gathering places are no longer safe or available. With their focus on technology, MySpace and other social networks provide a lifestyle that affords adolescents virtual social worlds. This existence, however, is foreign to many adults. As expressed by Dr. Henry Jenkins, codirector of the Comparative Media Studies Program at Massachusetts Institute of Technology, "Most parents understand their children's experiences in the context of their memories of their own early years. For the Baby Boom Generation, those defining experiences involved playing in backyards and vacant lots within suburban neighborhoods and socializing with their friends at the local teen hangout. Contemporary children and youth enjoy far less physical mobility, have less time outside of adult control, and have fewer physical places to hang out with their friends. Much of this activity is being brought online . . . where young people feel more comfortable sharing aspects of their lives."[4] MySpace has become the teen hangout of the new millennium.

Two communication modalities—IM and chat—provide venues for adolescents to develop their sense of self. In a one-on-one instant message setting, adolescents are able to divulge feelings in a safe, private environment with any of hundreds of buddies, many of whom are school friends, but others are online friends. Although this communication is simply an exchange of words without any additional cues about the other person's feelings or motives, as noted earlier, research shows that teens who have more peer-to-peer interactions are more confident, more altruistic, less depressed, and have higher self-esteem. Sabrina, a thirteen-year-old MySpacer, explained why, for her, IM is a perfect place to share those deep, dark secrets, literally 24/7:

> *"I have 127 people on my buddy list but they're not all really 'friends.' Some are kids I met in camp over the summer, others are from school, some from dance class and the rest are just like people I know from somewhere. When I need someone to talk to I know that there's always someone around. Even one time when I couldn't sleep cuz I was so bummed about breaking up with my boyfriend I found Jessie on MySpace at 3:00 a.m. She is such a great friend. She talked with me for hours until I finally crashed."*

Boys are also talking about their feelings. Even though more girls than boys are members of MySpace—my research shows that six out of ten MySpace adolescents are girls[5]—boys are well-represented when it comes to talking about their feelings. Unlike a school or other face-to-face setting, where boys usually talk to other boys, a national survey showed that 71% of boys preferred to talk online with girls. The most common reason given was "emotional support." Jordan, a sixteen year-old high school student, told me,

> *"My buddy list is about half my guy friends and half girls I know. If I'm just BSing, I can usually find one of the guys I know to hang with. But when I really want to talk, on my buddy list I have a separate group of five girls who I know are always around and who will listen and not make fun of me. It's nice to know they're there, you know, and only one of them is from my school, but she's cool. The others are from all over. One I met playing RuneQuest [an online game] and another I know from my old school. There's always someone on, you know, any time."*

When preteens make the jump from elementary school to middle school, they enter a world that is quite different from their earlier educational experiences. In addition to having up to seven different teachers, they often find themselves in a school that is usually three to four times larger and more diverse than their elementary school. Inseparable eleven-year-olds now spend less time together as they discover new friends. One-to-one friendships now take a back seat to crowds and cliques. Over time, as both boys and girls become interested in the opposite sex, two same-sex cliques will merge together to form a loosely based crowd of both boys and girls. As adolescence draws to a close, these groupings start to disintegrate as couples emerge and time spent with the rest of the group begins to wane.

These groupings come at a critical juncture in adolescent identity formation. The teen is at that awkward stage dealing with puberty and body awareness, hormone-induced mood swings, burgeoning sexual awareness, parental expectations, and rapidly fluctuating self-esteem. It is precisely during this period of life that teens turn to their friends for help in navigating their topsy-turvy world—and all of their friends are on MySpace. No wonder they rush home and boot up the computer. They don't have the roller rink or burger joint of the '50s and '60s, or the mall, basketball court, or street corner of the '80s and '90s.

After school they either have to go straight home, often to an empty house, or they are schlepped from soccer practice to piano lessons to whatever outside activity their parents think they need to become more well rounded. They crave autonomy and their friends and yet we are afraid that the world is too scary to let them just hang out at the mall. So their lives become a continuous loop of school, activities, home, and sleep.

If they can't physically hang out with their friends they find other ways to get together. Many are too young to drive and are alone until their parents get home from work. And traditional methods of keeping in touch, such as the telephone, restrict the communication to just one person. How then can the whole clique spend time together if they are all home alone? MySpace offers a solution to this strong adolescent need for bonding with friends. Nobody put it more succinctly than thirteen-year-old LaShonda:

> *"I take the bus home, dump my backpack, grab a snack, and get on my computer. I know that Jamie and Alishia will already be on MySpace cuz they live close to school, but Kendra's still at track practice and Wanda's got after-school piano lessons. By four o'clock we're all together, talking a mile a minute on IM to each other. Usually Alishia and I are on the phone since she's my bestest friend but her mom's pissed at her for going over her cell minutes so mostly now we have to IM."*

As I mentioned while comparing the MySpace Generation to Baby Boomers and Gen Xers (in chapter 2), teenagers such as LaShonda and her friends have perfected the art of multitasking. Recent national research by Arbitron and MindShare[6] found that teens multitask *at least 75% of the time*. MySpace is all about multitasking and communication. When you look at what they are doing when multitasking it is nearly always based on communication—IM, chat rooms, e-mail. They are talking with their peers. That is exactly what teenagers do. Being online just makes it easier to talk to all their friends at the same time. Decades of psychological research have shown that those adolescents who interact more with their peers show improved interpersonal skills and more poise and competence in social situations, making their MySpace interactions all the more critical in their identity quests.

Erik Erikson's theory of identity search through crisis resolution attempts to explain how we change our relationships with all parts of our world. When the child reaches adolescence, he enters a "psycho-social moratorium," a time when Erikson noted that adolescents get to try on different identities. He likened it to going up to the attic and playing dress up with mommy and daddy's old clothes. A virtual world provides the perfect venue for trying on new clothes. Put a comment on your bulletin that is controversial and see how others react. Vicari-ously watch others getting reactions to their actions. Ask that cute girl in your fourth period class out on a date. She may turn you down but being rejected online is a whole lot easier than in person. Fifteen-year-old Emilio described it this way:

> *"There was this girl in my Math class that I had been watching every day in class. I thought she was way outta my league but I couldn't get her out of my mind. I could barely listen to the teacher. Jorge told me that she told Sylvia that I could ask her out but I thought that Jorge and Sylvia were just teasing me. I decided what the heck and got her IM name and IM'd her. We talked for like hours and I finally got up the nerve to ask her out and she said yes. Wow! I coulda never done that in person. Man, I was like sweating in front of my computer like I was actually there in her face."*

Dr. Sherry Turkle, a professor at Massachusetts Institute of Tech-nology, likened the computer to a Rorschach Test. Based on what you see when a psychologist shows you various ink blots, and decades of research on what those answers might mean, the psychologist can get a picture of how you are thinking and feeling. In her book, *Life on the Screen: Identity in the Age of the Internet*,[7] Turkle explains that com-puter users employ the machine much like a Rorschach Test as a way to display their feelings, literally using the computer as a mirror to their inner selves. This fits well with data from my research showing that adolescents feel more confident and more creative online than in real life (or RL, as Turkle calls it).

In support of Erikson, Turkle referred to the adolescent morato-rium as: "a time of intense interaction with people and ideas. It is a time of passionate friendships and experimentation. It is a time during which one's actions are, in a certain sense, not counted as they will be later on in life. They are not given as much weight, not given the force of full judgment. In this context, experimentation can become the norm rather than a brave departure."[8] This moratorium is what allowed Emilio to ask for a date online and provides many teens with the courage to take actions online they might feel awkward and embarrassed doing offline.

Behind the Screen

Turkle introduced the concept of being "behind the screen" as a metaphor to explain why the computer seems to be freeing for many people. As the adolescent struggles with his identity, Turkle feels that having a computer screen between him and the world makes it easier to "try on new clothes." This is nothing new to psychologists, who in 1959 described the "stranger-on-a-train" phenomenon,[9] in which people riding on a train with someone they will never see again are comfortable disclosing deep secrets. Extending the notion of the stranger on a train to computer behavior, research shows that people will disclose more personal information if they are doing so through a computer rather than face-to-face.[10] My research on online dating demonstrates this phenomenon perfectly. People meeting online with the intent of eventually having a date were much more willing to self-disclose, even in the first or second e-mail.[11] If they are told they will never meet the person at the other end, they disclose even more.

This feeling of anonymity is so strong that psychologists have dubbed it the "disinhibition effect" to explain not only why we feel comfortable revealing ourselves to strangers, but also feel freer to speak our minds with people we know, as long as we are doing it electronically. Dr. John Suler has identified two types of disinhibition—benign and toxic.[12] Benign disinhibition is simply the act of telling someone something online, either about your own feelings or in response to something they have written. In this case, your response is either neutral or positive. When Sabrina's friend walked her through her breakup in the middle of the night, most likely benign disinhibition was at work. Across MySpacers I have interviewed, 78% felt they could be more honest online, and 49% stated that it was easier to make friends online. Together, these findings show that adolescents feel less inhibited and able to be more straightforward and honest in a virtual world.

Toxic disinhibition, the act of visiting the "dark underworld of the Internet—places of pornography, crime, and violence—territory they would never explore in the real world,"[13] is quite prevalent on MySpace. One MySpacer told me, *"A kid at school told me on IM last night that I was a lowlife scum and when I saw him at school the next day he acted like nothing happened. That seems to happen a lot here [on MySpace]. It's as though people don't give a damn if they hurt your feelings as long as they're not looking at you in the face. I don't get it how someone can be so mean on IM and oh so nice in person. It's sorta like he's two different people like that Dr. Jekyll and Mr. Hyde dude."*

Whether it is benign or toxic, self-disclosure is more uninhibited behind the screen. MySpacers have said repeatedly that they like being able to "play act." Badwhar, valedictorian of his class, told me that he had a second MySpace account where he pretended he was a seventeen-year-old girl. When I asked him why, he just shrugged and said *"I don't know. It's just kinda fun to see how people treat you differently when you're a girl. Somehow it seems like a metaphor for the intolerance I feel when people act funny toward me when they think I might be some sort of Arab terrorist because of the way I look. I really get a kick out of seeing how girls treat girls and how boys treat girls. I can say the same thing as a boy to someone and get a totally different reaction than if I say it as a girl. It's mind boggling."* Teens have told me that they have entered chat rooms and said things like "I am worried about my friend" separately under an identity as a boy and as a girl. As a girl people would ask more questions and offer suggestions, while as a boy, the comments would often go without response.

While Badwhar plays at what psychologists call "gender-bending,"[14] other teens try on being older while some heterosexual teens observe reactions when they broach their interest in homosexuality. Some MySpace young people have told me that they like to pretend to be dumb just to see what other people do and say. One guy got a date with a girl by pretending to be a "C" student and when she met him and found out he was a "brain" she canceled the date.

A recent national study of one thousand teens and their parents by the Pew Internet & American Life Project found that more than half the teens provided false information on their social network profiles.[15] While some teens lie about their age to bypass online age restrictions, others, such as Badwhar, do so to see what it is like to be someone different. In psychological terms, they are each experimenting with how they present their "self."

In 1959 Professor Erving Goffman published a seminal book entitled, *The Presentation of Self in Everyday Life*.[16] Goffman likened our interactions to being an actor in a play—what he termed "dramatic realization." Our performer must play to the audience and present the image that he wants others to see. Goffman said that we continually monitor how people perceive us and adapt our presentation of ourselves to the people and the particular situation. In essence, we put on a persona through which we want others to view us in the most positive light. Goffman asserts that by putting up a false front—what he terms the front stage—we conceal any negative aspects of our personality backstage, so that we can shape and control how others see us. I saw an actress being interviewed recently on a talk show and portraying herself as altruistic and kind, someone who wouldn't hurt a fly. As soon as the cameras went off, she went into a rage about wanting the interview to focus on her new movie, not on her personal life. Unfortunately for her, someone in the audience caught her on videotape and the next day her rant was posted on YouTube. Her front stage behavior was exposed as quite different from her backstage reality.

Extending Goffman's work, Dr. Carl Rogers, founder of humanistic personality theory, said that we collect all of our experiences, both conscious and unconscious, and combine them to form our unique "true" self. Rogers also sees the self as a result of interacting with the real world, but he extends Goffman's ideas to insist that we are not actors in a play, but rather humans seeking our own concept of who we are by matching responses of others to our fluid concept of how we see ourselves. According to Rogers, we are not one actor playing a constant role, but rather an improviser, continually modifying our projected self based on our experiences with people in the real world.

Based on the work of Goffman and Rogers, psychologists have identified three separate aspects or parts of the "self"—true self, ideal self, and ought self. The true self is your presentation of who you or someone else feels you are as a human being. The ideal self is how you would like to be seen by other people, while the ought self is how you think other people expect you to act. This ought self is akin to Goffman's version of the self that continually plays a role on the stage of life.

Psychologists who study how we present ourselves both online and offline have discovered that we use virtual worlds to explore our various selves. For example, researchers have found that people who were lonely or socially anxious in face-to-face encounters were more able to express their true selves online and, in fact, were able to develop online relationships that could then be moved and maintained offline.[17] In my interviews, boys often told me about how they use MySpace to practice talking to girls to gain confidence to speak with them in person at school. Surprisingly, girls have told me that they too talk about sensitive topics on IM that they would not have the nerve to say face-to-face and that doing so then makes it easier to talk about the subject in front of a friend. One sixteen-year-old said,

> "I was really angry with my best friend, Angel, because she told me that she cheated on a test and acted like it was no big deal. I IM'd a friend from a different school later that night and we talked about it and she gave me some ideas about how to let Angel know that I didn't approve of her cheating, without ruining our friendship. The next day I was really nervous, so nervous that I had written down what I wanted to say and at lunch I talked to Angel and I was so surprised that she listened. She even told me that she liked the way I talked, that I was not acting judgmental, but just concerned."

In another interesting study about the benefits of communicating online, subjects entered a psychology laboratory and were first asked to list ten traits that they believed they expressed to others in "live" social gatherings (their "ought self" traits), as well as ten that they felt uncomfortable sharing. For example, at a party, a man might feel that he "ought" to act like he is a good listener when he is talking to a woman he has just met, but in reality he is uncomfortable letting on that he has difficulty talking about emotional subjects with women. Next, subjects either talked face-to-face with another person or conversed with someone in an online chat. Following their talk, whether it was online or offline, subjects were instructed to quickly list traits they felt they possessed. Those who talked face-to-face were more likely to list their ought self traits, while those who talked online were more apt to list those uncomfortable traits, which meant they were better able to express their actual or true self online. Interestingly, when these same people who talked first via an online chat met their online partner, they tended to like each other more than those who talked face-to-face.[18]

Dr. Katelyn McKenna and her colleagues at New York University investigated people in an online discussion group and found that those who expressed their true selves in the group were more likely to make long-lasting friendships. In fact, they found that the vast majority of online relationships were still intact two years later and were as successful, or more so, than relationships begun face-to-face.[19] The authors concluded, "Rather than turning to the Internet as a way of hiding from real life and from forming real relationships, individuals use it as a means not only of maintaining ties with existing family and friends but also as a means of forming close and meaningful new relationships in a relatively nonthreatening environment." They went on to add, "The Internet may also be helpful for those who have difficulty forging relationships in face-to-face situations because of shyness, social anxiety, or a lack of social skills."[20]

I have found similar results in my interviews with adolescents, particularly from those who are shy or suffer from low self-esteem. In my most recent study, teens who reported being shy in the real world found it easier to make friends online and easier to be honest on MySpace and, consequently, felt more positive about themselves both online and offline.[21] According to the research, this benefit has little to do with either how much time the teen spends on MySpace or how many friends he or she accumulates. Living in a virtual world is a boon for kids who might be unable to say what they feel in RL. Many of them say that they feel more free and uninhibited online and that this spills over into their school life.

The Process of Identity Formation

Perhaps the best view of how adolescents develop their true sense of self is in the work done by Dr. James Marcia. In Marcia's identity status model, he extended Erikson's work to include the idea that not only do adolescents go through crises to explore their identities, but they also make decisions that he calls "commitments." Marcia proposed four stages of identity formation, as seen in Table 4.1. Each stage deals with identity in terms of aspirations, skills, ideology, sex roles, and religion.

Marcia's model has been used extensively to track adolescent identity development. Table 4.2 indicates what percentage of adolescents and young adults fall into each category based on research using extensive interviews.[22]

The data in Table 4.2 make some very strong impressions about the process of identity formation. First, middle school children, roughly eleven- to thirteen-years-old, are, as might be expected, either in the identity diffusion or foreclosure phase. When I asked Arthur, a tween MySpacer from Wichita, Kansas, to describe his experiences on MySpace and what he planned to do with his life, he told me, *"I mostly just hang on MySpace. I don't really want to meet anyone or talk to anyone other than my friends. Sometimes people ask me to become their friend but I always say no. I have no idea what I want to do. I like math and science but I don't really think I can hack being a scientist. I guess I have lots of*

Table 4.1 Marcia's Stages of Identity Formation

Identity Diffusion	• No identity crisis yet • No commitments • Often confused and overwhelmed
Foreclosure	• May or may not have experienced a crisis • Made commitments based on outside forces (e.g., parents, society) but not through their own process • Often make quick choices without consideration
Moratorium	• Major crises • No commitments, but working on them • Lots of rebellion, dissatisfaction
Identity Achievement	• Experienced, struggled with, and resolved crises • Made commitment decisions on their own • Still worry about achieving goals, but do well under stress or anxiety

Table 4.2 Percentages of Adolescents and Young Adults at Marcia's Identity
Formation Stages

Age Level	Identity Achievement	Moratorium	Foreclosure	Identity Diffusion
Pre–High School	5%	12%	37%	46%
High School Freshmen and Sophomores	9%	15%	37%	39%
High School Juniors and Seniors	21%	14%	36%	29%
College Freshmen and Sophomores	23%	28%	26%	23%
College Juniors and Seniors	40%	16%	31%	14%

time until I need to figure it all out although it makes me a little crazy to think I have to decide all this stuff in the next couple of years."

Second, early high schoolers are struggling with their identity formation, like Emilio, the fifteen-year-old who shared his experience of asking a girl out on MySpace and here talks about his feelings about his future:

"Hey dude, how should I know? No, seriously, my parents are telling me that they think I would make a good high school teacher, maybe math or history, but I don't know. High school teachers are mostly idiots. Except my math teacher. He's cool and funny and all. He also talked to me about maybe being a math teacher, too. I guess I'll just take the math classes and see what happens. If I do well, maybe I can try to be a teacher."

Emilio is clearly in foreclosure, following along with his parents' career ideas. Notice how he didn't seem to put too much thought into his course of action. Foreclosed adolescents usually just make choices along the lines of what others expect them to do, although they tend to do it without much conviction. That's the lack of commitment to one's own values driving Emilio's path at this point in his life. He is still young and easily swayed by authority figures like his teacher and his parents.

Next, consider Marvin, a senior in high school, who said, *"I have a scholarship to play ball at Texas and I'll probably major in communications. My junior and senior years were crazy with a whole bunch of schools trying to get me to come there. My mom and dad pissed me off most of the time. They only cared about me going to a school that might lead to a baseball career. For a month or two, while I was trying to decide, we hardly talked. I think I mostly ate dinner in about thirty seconds and ran back upstairs. They're OK with me going to Texas, but I don't know how I feel. I guess if it doesn't work out I can always transfer."* Marvin's identity formation is somewhere between moratorium and identity achievement. He certainly is in what Erikson and Marcia call a crisis and at some level he has made a commitment although it appears to be a soft commitment with an escape clause. Marvin is similar to most adolescents who are still struggling with their identity throughout high school and beyond. More than half of Marvin's fellow graduating class find themselves in a similar struggle. They are not alone. According to Dr. April Vogensen's study,[23] the majority of eighteen- to twenty-two-year-old college students is either identity diffused or in the moratorium stage where they have not yet resolved their Eriksonian crisis and made a commitment to their future. Marvin's situation is hardly surprising given the generational values discussed earlier. MySpacers, such as Marvin and Vogensen's college students, are searching for interesting, meaningful lives, and they are doing so by keeping their options open and building many possible careers. These values are precisely the ones that would place them in the moratorium stage, working their way to identity achievement.

MySpace usage seems to support the theories of Erikson, Goffman, Rogers, and Marcia's identity search. A MySpace page contains a combination of photographs, music, art, video, blogs, comments from other MySpacers, pictures of the Top 8 friends, a count of all friends, and more. In essence, the page reflects the MySpacer's interests and personality. It can be bland or creative, static or ever-changing. It is a place for an adolescent to question his or her identity.

As the adolescent or preteen logs on to his MySpace page after school (the most popular time to be on MySpace, according to my research, is between 5:00 P.M. and midnight), he anxiously checks to see who has commented on his personal blog. Perhaps last night he wrote something about drugs and a party he might go to this weekend, where there is sure to be marijuana and beer, just to test the waters and see how people responded. Sure enough, he has five comments, three from school friends and two from "online friends." Since research shows that he likely has upwards of one hundred friends, some of whom he has never met, he can anticipate a variety of reactions. His school friends, who are not part of the stoner clique (that is, not into getting high on drugs), make some decidedly negative comments while at least one online friend tells him about how cool it is to smoke weed. It is all a process that is typical of what teens attempt to do in their real-world lives. Except our adolescent has "tried drugs" (or at least the prospect of drugs) in an online environment and has gotten feedback from a variety of sources. All of this helps him gain a better sense of self by weighing opinions from a variety of online and offline friends.

The MySpace Web page is Sherry Turkle's Rorschach Test in action. My research revealed that 39% of the MySpacers spent one hour per week working on their Web pages, while 22% spent two to three hours. One-fourth of the MySpacers worked on their pages more than three hours per week by adding to and changing their pages.[24] MySpace pages are most certainly a reflection of adolescent attempts to continually test what others think of them by how they represent themselves. They don't just alter their MySpace page because it is something to do. They do it to reflect their ever-changing, constantly evolving values. It is an outward expression of their emotional identity development. Table 4.3 shows the percentage of MySpacers who engage in these activities. Note that they range from presenting identity information like photographs and music to communicating with others, which is an important way for the teen to present and receive personal feedback.

The MySpace Web page provides a perfect opportunity for the adolescent to look to others to assess the appropriateness of attitudes, behaviors, and values. With the vast majority writing, reading, and commenting to their network of friends, they are certain to gain feedback no

Table 4.3 MySpace Activities

MySpace Activities	Percentage of MySpacers
Post new photographs and video on MySpace page	88%
Modify MySpace profile	85%
Read comments on their MySpace page	83%
Post comments on friends' MySpace pages	73%
Use IM or e-mail	70%
Read comments on friends' MySpace pages	64%
Add and change music on MySpace page	61%
Talk with people who share common interests	54%
Post bulletins on their own MySpace page	52%
Write a blog or journal	46%
Make new friends	40%
Work with friends on homework and study for exams	40%

matter what they write. For some it can be akin to "testing the waters," while for others it is simply cathartic to dump their feelings. As danah boyd says, it is their "public display of identity."[25]

Another interesting use of MySpace involves adolescents creating shadow Web pages, as we saw earlier with the example of a gender-bending page created by Badwhar. One fifteen-year-old told me that he made a whole separate Web page under an assumed name that was totally separate from all of his friends. When I asked why, he told me that he felt that it might be a place where he could say some things that he wouldn't feel comfortable saying in front of his MySpace friends. When I asked him what things he wanted to say at this alternate site, he just shrugged and said *"you know, embarrassing stuff. Stuff that I wouldn't want to have the kids at school know about."* I didn't press him, but I would guess that his other Web page presented an "alter ego" experiment. My latest research found that 11% of teens had a MySpace page where they presented themselves as a different person, and, as noted earlier, a Pew Internet & American Life Project national study found that more than half of teens post false information in their online profiles with 8% admitting that "most or all of the information on the profile is fake."[26] Having a shadow site may serve an important function in helping to reconcile adolescent identity crises. Consider, for example, the teen who is struggling with her sexuality, political views, or any other topic that might cause distress or embarrassment among her friends if posted on her MySpace page. The shadow page allows free expression, echoing Sherry Turkle's comments about adolescent moratorium and the possibility of experimentation without embarrassment or consequences.

Proactive Parenting in Support of Adolescent Identity Formation

By the time a child reaches mid-to-late adolescence, his parents have provided the majority of their guidance and influence. With most interactions now occurring between peers, the parents' role takes a back seat. However, there are ways that a parent can facilitate a child's exploration and search for identity. Here are eight suggestions for dealing with children and preteens as they struggle with their identity diffusion and foreclosure stages.

Be Aware of Their Virtual World

No matter what you read, MySpace is not just another fad. Certainly Web sites may come and go, but according to all my interviews, adolescent MySpacers are not going anywhere but MySpace. The number of members continues to rise. Older users, particularly college students, are finding that MySpace is not for them anymore and they are moving to other virtual communities like Facebook, LiveJournal, or Friendster, but for tweens and teens, MySpace is home. What is clear is that the percentage of MySpacers under eighteen is increasing. According to the latest national polls, 80% of teens have profiles that they visit weekly.[27]

Teen life is online. In 2000 73% of teens were online. That increased to 87% in 2004 and 93% in 2006. More importantly, the percentage of teens who use the Internet daily increased from 42%, to 51%, to

61% across those same years.[28] Although MySpace is often the focus of teen activity, it is not the only part of their virtual world. YouTube and Wikipedia, now major teen sources of entertainment and information, did not even exist three years ago. Nobody can predict the next teen virtual hangout, but there are ways to keep up with the trends. My recommendation is to periodically visit www.ypulse.com. At Ypulse, Anastasia Goodstein, author of *Totally Wired: What Teens and Tweens Are Really Doing Online*,[29] provides invaluable daily news and commentary on trends in the life of tweens, teens and young adults. She posts her thoughts daily about news and does an excellent job of staying on top of the adolescent lifestyle, both online and offline.

Keep an Open Communication Line

Parents have told me that they were unsure about what their children were doing online, but didn't know how to approach the subject with their teens. Even if you don't understand sites like MySpace, it is still important to let your children know that you are available to talk about any issues that arise. MySpace is a forum for identity development for many adolescents and the issues that arise most likely have nothing to do with being on the Internet. Your children are going to face these issues on or off MySpace. Make sure that they know that you are available if they need to talk about their experiences. Take heart, this is easier if you adopt a proactive parenting style that promotes discussion on a regular basis. I recommend that you plan informal family meetings on a weekly basis to check in with your children about issues that may have arisen on the Internet. It is best to set a standard time for these meetings—after dinner works if you all eat together—and make them short. These should not be times for parents to complain about how much time their kids are spending online. These meetings should provide opportunities for parents to raise concerns proactively about issues related to online activities.

Parents have also indicated to me that they feel that their child's MySpace use is interfering with their other activities, both at home and with their face-to-face friends. In some areas, such as schoolwork, and offline relationships, most parents and children agree that MySpace has little negative impact. However, parents and teens disagree on how MySpace impacts family time, doing chores, and outdoor activities. Parents feel that the time their teens spend on MySpace directly reduces the time they have together as a family, while teens do not agree. In addition, parents are worried that chores are not being done and outdoor activities are being neglected as their children spend hours in the virtual world, which can be located anywhere there is Internet connectivity. Their children disagree.[30] This disparity in perception suggests that these are issues that should be discussed in regular family meetings before they become serious family problems. If any of these issues are already negatively affecting your family, it is important to make sure to discuss them in those weekly meetings.

Create Your Own MySpace Page

Anyone can create a MySpace account. Simply go to www.myspace .com, enter your e-mail address, create a password, and you now have a Web page. There is no need for you to do anything with your page. Simply use your access to visit some MySpace pages and get an idea of what adolescents are doing online. Once you sign up, you will be assigned your first friend, Tom Anderson, the cocreator of MySpace. If you click on his picture you will be taken to his Web page. I recommend that you scroll down to where people leave comments on his page and click on any of their pictures. That will take you to their personal pages. Spend an hour visiting a sample of MySpace pages to get a feel for what is out there.

Do not use your own account to spy on your children. According to Pew Internet & American Life Project studies in 2000, 2004, and 2006, "Teens are now more aware that their parents are 'checking up' on them after they go online."[31] Besides, according to my research, there is no reason to spy on your MySpacers, because more than 70% of them said that they would feel comfortable having their parents look at their MySpace page. In an interview, the father of a thirteen-year-old boy commented, *"One night after my son went to bed I noticed that the computer—which is in the living room—was still connected to MySpace. I looked at his MySpace page and didn't like some of the things that his friends had written. When I talked to him about this the next day he got so angry with me and stomped off to his room. We talked later and I tried to explain that I wasn't snooping but he asked me how I would feel if he went into my bedroom and read private letters that I had written to his mom when we were dating. This really hit home and we made a deal that I wouldn't look at his MySpace unless he was there to show it to me."*

Spying on your children will just make them more likely to mistrust you and be unwilling to talk with you. One recent phenomenon, mentioned earlier, is for children to create shadow sites where they let their parents view their safe MySpace page while maintaining another where they really reside. If you try to look at what they are doing on MySpace, you will doubtless find that your teenagers are amazingly adept at switching and closing screens as they hear a parent coming to check on them.

Share Your Child's MySpace Page

You absolutely need to ask your child to show you his or her MySpace page. According to my research, 34% of parents said they had never done so, nor had they talked with their children about their MySpace use. Another third of the parents checked their teen's MySpace page every few months *at the most*. Basically, only one-third of the parents actually monitored their child's MySpace page on a regular basis. In addition, 40% of the parents had never seen the photographs that their children posted on MySpace.

It is critical to ask your children to let you see how they represent themselves in their virtual world. You need to read comments on the page and check who is listed in their Top 8. If you do not know some of the people there, ask your child who they are and why they are on the Top 8, and have your child click on their pictures and visit their Web pages. It is important that you do this together so that you give your child a fair chance to explain how he or she is using MySpace. If you read comments on your teen's MySpace page that seem harsh or potentially harmful, remember that teens face similar comments at school and with their friends. On MySpace, however, those comments are in written form and available for others to read at any time. If someone is being nasty or overly critical, they can be easily blocked from your teen's MySpace page. This makes it even more critical that you and your teen view and discuss their MySpace page together at reasonable intervals.

Table 4.4 Parent Perception and Teen Reality of Information Disclosed on MySpace

Information Disclosed	Parent Perception		Teen Reality
	Yes	Not Sure	Yes
Full Name	29%	29%	45%
Address	4%	28%	9%
School Name	44%	31%	69%
Telephone Number	8%	31%	23%
E-Mail Address	34%	34%	51%
IM Name	35%	37%	55%
Information about Social Activities and Their Location	20%	41%	41%

It is also important to see what information your child is giving out and talk about the ramifications of making private information public. In my research, I asked the children if they gave out certain information on MySpace and asked the parents if they were aware if their children were giving out personal information. The results, summarized in Table 4.4, clearly show that at least one-third of parents are simply not sure if their child is giving out any of the information; and when they are sure, they drastically underestimate how much of that information is divulged. Posting information such as school name—which is one of the first pieces of information you are asked about on your MySpace profile and which students use to find schoolmates' MySpace pages—and the location of social activities can be sufficient, along with a MySpace photo, to identify and locate someone such as Chandra, a seventeen-year-old high school senior and editor of her school newspaper who said: *"I was at our end-of-the-year newspaper party when this dude comes up to me and says 'hey, you're CC Writer from MySpace'. It was incredibly creepy that he knew who I was and found me at the party. He didn't even go to my school but since someone posted directions to the party, he just showed up."* An innocent posting about a party on MySpace,

coupled with other personal information, can make it easy for someone online to locate a MySpacer offline. When you visit your teen's
MySpace page with them, check for postings of these types of information, not only on her page, but also on those of her friends. If you
are typical of the parents in my research studies and others,[32] you may
find that your son or daughter and their network of friends are revealing much more than you think. Although your son or daughter may
not think twice about giving out personal information, you need to be
proactive and discuss this before any potential problems arise.

It is also important to remain aware of how much time your child is
spending on MySpace. From my research almost all parents are aware
of how many hours a day their children are on the computer; however, nearly four in ten don't know that much of that time is spent on
MySpace.[33] Although parents do pay attention to when their children
are on the computer, and many do set time limits, they need to make
sure that they are alert to how much of that computer time is spent
visiting virtual communities such as MySpace. Since MySpace plays
a major role in identity development, we need to be mindful of our
children's daily visits.

Encourage Safe Exploration

In my research, most parents expressed several major concerns about
their teens' safety in MySpace, including their teens posting sexually
explicit content or photos, viewing sexually explicit content or photos,
being approached by sexual predators, making friends on MySpace,
and posting personal information. They were also concerned about the
potential of teens having a lack of physical activity, becoming addicted
to the Internet and MySpace, and becoming socially isolated.[34] These
are very valid concerns and need to be addressed with your child or
adolescent. Some of these issues are realities on MySpace, which this
book addresses (see chapter 6). There *are* sexually explicit photos in
spite of MySpace's efforts to remove any evidence of nudity or partial
nudity. Indeed, people do make friends on MySpace and then meet
them in person. All of these issues should be discussed with your child
in advance so that both of you are clear on acceptable parameters for
MySpace use.

Encourage Peer Support

Research shows that having peer support helps increase interpersonal skills, develops a sense of self-esteem, and enhances psychological functioning. Given that most of your child's friends are online and that the vast majority of his or her interactions are with school friends or other peers who are known offline, it is important to encourage your child to use any avenue to consolidate his or her sense of self. MySpace provides a multitude of opportunities for your teenager to share feelings online that may be difficult to discuss offline, and the structure of MySpace makes it simple to gain the feedback necessary to help the teen work toward identity achievement. Spend time with your teen reading comments and help your teen differentiate between MySpace friends whose advice may be valuable and those who may create more identity confusion. Identity development requires interactions both online and offline. Spending time talking with your teen about online interactions is a good entrée to discussing how offline friends are playing a role in their identity development.

Keep an Open Door Policy

Children have built TechnoCocoons in their bedrooms complete with all their technological entertainment. My research and that of others has found that many of these children access the Internet from their bedrooms.[35] A Kaiser Family Foundation national study found that if a computer was in a common area, it was used by the child or teenager an average of forty-seven minutes a day. *If it was in the bedroom, it was used an average of ninety minutes a day.*[36] This does not mean that you cannot house a computer in your child's bedroom. Often, it is the most convenient place. However, a bedroom computer should come with an "open door policy." This means that you and your child should have an understanding that the door remains open and that you may enter at any time and view what is on the computer screen. This includes the agreement that you can read any instant message screens (IM conversations are saved until that IM screen is closed). You should feel free to scroll back and read what your child is saying to others. Also, learn how to use the computer's "history" and "cache" functions so you can view what your child has been doing and where he or she has been visiting.[37]

This should not be done in a punitive way, nor should it be done surreptitiously, but it is important to have this constant supervision to help promote healthy use of the Internet and MySpace. Since most teenagers reported that they were comfortable having their parents view their MySpace page, an open-door policy affords this opportunity.

Set Clear Limits and Boundaries

Research has shown that the majority of parents set limits on their children's use of the Internet. However, half of those teens say that their parents do not actually monitor those limits.[38] Proactive parenting means setting clear limits and boundaries on behavior and *adhering to those boundaries*. Obviously, we often believe that we are setting limits, but we are not sticking to them. This is another issue that should be discussed in family meetings. Children need limits and they also need to know that those limits are real and not simply empty talk. Make sure that those limits are reasonable and be willing to negotiate with your teenager. Spending time online is important so keep that in mind when setting limits.

Remember that a large portion of your adolescent's social life is online and MySpace is most assuredly a major part of their virtual, electronic world. It is not a fad, but rather, it is an enormously popular, important virtual universe where children and teenagers congregate and work on their answers to the question *who am I?* The suggestions I have provided above will help make that process more productive while keeping parents happy and children safe.

I interviewed danah boyd, a University of Southern California Fellow at the Annenberg Center for Communications, and a pioneer in studying teen and young adult behavior on social networking sites such as MySpace and Friendster. Here is what she had to say about online identity formation:

Q: How do virtual worlds such as online social networking sites help teens develop their sense of identity?

boyd: The way you develop your identity is to put things out there, get feedback, and adjust accordingly. You develop an internal model of yourself and balance this with reactions from other people; this is what Erving Goffman calls "impression management." Doing this online allows you to be more reflective earlier about whom you are. On MySpace, for example, you have to write yourself into being; in other words, you have to craft an impression of yourself that stands on its own. Is it the end-all and be-all in developing your sense of self? Of course not. But online expressions are a meaningful byproduct of identity formation. For today's teens, it's just another step in the path of figuring out who you are. And figuring out who you are requires being social.

Q: In what ways do anonymity and the ability to self-disclose "behind the screen" influence how teens develop their sense of self?

boyd: I think that it was Alan Kay that said, "technology is anything that wasn't around when you were born." When it comes to Web technology, I would modify his statement to say that "technology is anything that wasn't around when you were coming of age." The Internet is not a newfangled technology to teens—as far as they are concerned, it was always there. Social network sites came about as they were coming of age—they assume participation to be a natural progression. They don't think about being "behind the screen"—it's just another medium through which they share what they're doing with their peers. Being online is just another way to access friends. Adults don't think of talking on the telephone as being "behind the phone." It is just a way to call friends. The same goes for the Internet when it comes to teens.

Remember the old *New Yorker* cartoon, "On the Internet, no one knows that you're a dog"? I was amazed at how many 1990s scholars thought that the Internet would make race, gender, age, attractiveness, etc., disappear. It didn't happen. Teens hang out with people that they know; their online identities are tightly connected to their offline ones and you don't get any "street cred" if you're anonymous. For the most part, teens are trying to be pseudonymous to hide from two different audiences: those who hold power over them (parents, teachers, law enforcement, college admissions officers, etc.) and those who want to prey on them (primarily marketers). It is important to note that some teens attempt to be anonymous so that they can bully other teens, but most bullies are quite honest about their identity. The other main use of anonymity by teens is when there will be a huge social cost for being open about who they are. I'm thinking about the queer teens who are trying to figure out their sexuality while living in a repressive social environment, or the teens who are abused by their own parents who are trying to find help online.

Q: What do you see as the role of parents in helping teens express themselves online?

boyd: For the most part, I ask parents to relax. The Internet is not the devil, but it does mirror and magnify a lot of what's happening offline. This means that most behavior that we see online we also see offline. At the same time, because parents aren't privy to what happens in the school locker rooms, the Internet makes the trials and tribulations of "teenagedom" far more visible to adults than ever before. I'm in awe of watching healthy families take the Internet as an opportunity to talk about teen life, public and private expressions, and the pressures of socialization. Unfortunately, these healthy encounters are few and far between. Too many parents see problematic expressions online and blame the Internet, block their teens' access, and assume that the problem will go away. It never does. The sad reality is that the Internet does not build trust between parent and child, but it can destroy any burgeoning trust that existed if parents fail to understand their children's Internet activities from the perspective of their child. I've watched numerous parent-child relations disintegrate over MySpace; these fights tend to make children more vulnerable because the child's response is more often than not to rebel.

Teens live in an environment that is fundamentally different from the one they experienced growing up. When it comes to the Internet, the way that teens must negotiate context and sociality is unlike anything that their parents ever experienced (unless they were celebrities). We know how we're supposed to interact in a restaurant because we learned this from our parents; teens are setting the rules for what's normal in networked publics—this is not something that a prior generation can teach them. Teens are in an environment where all of the contextual information is different and constantly changing. They are forced to interact with adults and their peers simultaneously and they are bound to make terrible mistakes according to parents' standards and experiences as they attempt to be validated by other kids online. As a parent, it is important to explore, not judge. It is critical to not project your old ideas about friendship and identity onto MySpace interactions. It is important to have candid conversations with your children about the architecture itself, so you can see what it is they do online and learn from them. Rather than telling them that they can't do this or that, start by understanding and respond by offering "what if" scenarios involving college admissions, employment, misperception, etc. Don't force them to make choices between your value system and theirs. Listen and try to understand the culture of your online child on his or her own terms because saying, "back in my day" simply will not work, because in no way is their world anywhere near what yours was back in your day. You have a choice. You can project your values and rules onto kids or you can attempt to learn from them. They are not just here to teach you how to program your VCR; let them teach you about their world with its different structure and different norms.

Chapter 5

Virtually Exposed

♦

"Think of anything you post as a tattoo on your forehead.
Who do you want to be looking at that tattoo tomorrow,
six months from now, six years from now?"

—Cliff Van Zandt, former FBI profiler[1]

♦

A blog is a cross between an online newsletter, a daily journal, and a diary. Unlike the pink flowered book that is kept under lock and key and hidden in a drawer, a blog is online and available for anyone to read. Various studies have attempted to estimate the number of blogs in cyberspace—referred to as the "blogosphere"—but this is a daunting task. Technorati, an online blog-tracking company, has estimated that as of early 2006 more than twenty-seven million blogs were on the Internet and this number was doubling every six months. According to Dr. Susan Herring and her colleagues at Indiana University, nearly all bloggers are under thirty years of age and one-third are adolescents.[2] My research shows that 40% of MySpacers write and maintain a blog, mostly on MySpace, although some do so through other sites such as LiveJournal.[3] Most blogging research has found that more than half of all teen blogs are written by girls although the gap between boy and girl bloggers appears to be diminishing.[4]

On MySpace, communication is the primary activity. This includes blogging (writing one or reading and commenting on other blogs), presenting a profile, and IMing. Teens write their version of blogs in the form of bulletins or commentary and invite their "friends" to make comments. Although the site allows its members to limit who has access to their blog postings, most MySpacers allow anyone to read and comment on them. Many teens post several blog messages a day and a single blog entry can generate quite a few comments. So, by the end of a week, the MySpacer may have dozens of comments. What do they talk about? Some entries are merely recitations of daily life—what they did today, who they saw, where they went. Others include political commentary. Many are as personal as a locked diary. As Janice, a sixteen-year-old high school student, told me: *"I used to see a shrink but now I just write out how I feel and see what my friends have to say. It's pretty freeing. And it saves my mom a ton of money. I think that I get better stuff from my friends anyway."* Janice allowed me to read some of her blog entries and the comments from her friends, which was quite enlightening. A portion of that conversation is reprinted below. Before you read it, think back to when you kept a diary, or, if you never did, recall any writing you might have done about your personal feelings.

Thursday July 20, 2006

I am so bummed today . . . well, not just today. I've been this way for almost a month. School is so much these days. Lots of tests and I'm not doing so well. My mom will be so p-od if I got a D on my math test. Even if I do, I think I'll still have a C still but I'll be close to a D. The other classes are not much better. I feel like there's not much left. What if I fail my classes? I'll have to go to summer school and that's a real downer. No wonder I'm feeling so blue.

6:12 p.m.—3 Comments—Add Comment

JONNYBoy	Wow I never saw you so down. Why do you think your mom will be so pissed? Has she done that before? When you think about what she might do, what do you imagine? Posted by JONNYBoy on Thursday, July 20, 2006 at 6:33 p.m.

WHIRLeeBird	Stop your whining. You just need to buckle down and study. Get off MySpace and get back to work! Posted by WHIRLeeBird on Thursday, July 20, 2006 at 6:37 p.m.
CarMeN2006	Janny, I think you are acting a bit too soon about this. You still have 3 tests and you haven't gotten your grades yet. Perhaps it won't be as bad as you think. I remember other times when you thought you failed that you actually passed. Remember? Keep studying and you might do better than you think. Posted by CarMeN2006 on Thursday, July 20, 2006 at 6:39 p.m.

Unlike a personal, private diary, Janice put herself and her problems out in the open, for all to see. Granted, the comment from WHIRLee-Bird was not particularly helpful (or even kind), but the other comments were empathetic and gave Janice good counsel. Some comments even mimic specific psychological approaches.

CarMeN2006's comments were particularly interesting. Once again, her style mimicked that of a psychologist by providing advice on how Janice's thought patterns were irrational or distorted. In seeking out help through blogging, Janice is not alone. As shown in a recent AOL study, nearly half of the surveyed bloggers consider it a form of therapy, one-third write about self-help or self-esteem topics, and two-thirds feel free to write about "anything and everything."[5] The AOL study concludes, "That's six times as many people who prefer to seek help and counseling from a professional." Strikingly, one out of three bloggers say that when they need psychological help, they either write in their own blog or read the blogs of other people who are dealing with similar issues.

A blog is extremely attractive to an adolescent, a young adult, or any-one who has thoughts they wish to share. On MySpace it is particularly appealing for several reasons. For one, no programming is necessary. Users type their blog into an already formatted template. Responding to a blog is also quite straightforward, as each entry has a comment section where "friends" or others post their thoughts. Discussions can be "threaded" so that a comment is clearly identified as being secondary and not necessarily a response to the main message. For example, in Janice's blog above, if WHIRLeeBird had made a comment in response to CarMeN2006's message, it would have been indented under CarMeN2006's and then if Janice had put another post in response to WHIRLeeBird, it would have been indented under his. This can develop into quite a few back and forth comments, which can form an online discussion.

Blogs are also attractive because they are time-stamped, so that the writer can tell when a friend's comment arrived. They can be updated frequently and an unlimited amount of material can be written at no cost. To facilitate back-and-forth conversations, postings are done instantaneously so thoughts and responses can be posted as they occur, simulating a live conversation. If someone makes a comment that the MySpacer wants to follow up on in "real time," IM is readily available. MySpace makes it all quite easy by indicating which friends are currently online and available to IM. Blog postings are maintained forever so it is easy, and often helpful, for the teen to go back in time and read earlier posts to see how feelings have changed.

As you saw with Janice, the act of writing down problems and getting advice and feedback can be very therapeutic. But it also comes at a price, according to Nancy Willard, Director of the Center for Safe and Responsible Internet Use: "Teens will argue that their posts on social networking sites are part of their private lives. Public posts are not private."[6] Anyone can read a blog. Although many parents who are Boomers or Gen Xers feel that it is problematic to write about private feelings in a public forum, according to the teens that I interviewed this lack of privacy does not concern them. Hank, a nineteen-year-old, told me: *"I see blogging as sorta like reality TV. When you watch* Survivor *or* Next *people are honest and say what they feel. Sometimes it hurts other people like when some dude Nexts a girl after just seeing her walk off the bus, but I like being able to go on MySpace and just write down what I am feeling at the moment. I think I can be more honest than if I was talking to a friend on the phone or even face-to-face."*

Shyness and Honesty
"Behind the Screen"

As mentioned in earlier chapters, two aspects of online life are important in looking at how and why online teens feel more comfortable sharing their feelings: teens feel that they can be more honest online, and shy kids find it much easier to share thoughts online behind the safety of the screen. For example, Eric, the twenty-year-old son of a friend, told me a story about how he played online RPGs (role-playing games) with Joe, an online acquaintance who was delightful, witty, and a good gamer. When Eric tried to arrange to have Joe join an ongoing game at Eric's house, Joe declined numerous offers. Another gaming friend told Eric that he had played a "live" RPG with Joe a year ago and found him to be so nervous that he was unable to play the game very well.

Being behind the screen can play a major role in blogging. Even if the blogger and commenter know each other, the research mentioned in chapter 4 shows that the discussion is more open, honest, and sometimes brutal when it is online rather than face-to-face. As psychologists have found, there is something about being "behind the screen" that allows a person to express feelings that would otherwise stay hidden.[7] As Tina, a seventeen-year-old high school junior, told me, *"I don't know why, but I can say stuff to my friends easier on their blogs than at school. It's funny that I can tell a friend something one night on MySpace and the next day at school we just don't talk about it. Sometimes it comes back through someone else at school but nobody seems to get pissed off when it's online. I guess I feel that same way when a friend hurts my feelings on MySpace. It's not that I don't care, it just seems less hurtful when it's done in my blog."*

Many teens I interviewed echoed Tina's feeling that they can accept negative comments more easily when they can't see the person. This is also true of engaging in opposite sex conversations. Teens seem comfortable making or breaking dates online and several reported that they had broken up with a boyfriend or girlfriend via IM.

David Huffaker and Dr. Sandra Calvert of the Children's Digital Media Center at Georgetown University have studied teenage blogs.

Although they conclude that "interestingly, the blogs created by young males and females are more alike than different," they do note that nearly half the blogs they studied held comments about relationships, equally split between boys and girls. One in six discussed homosexuality, mostly by teenage boys. Female bloggers tended to self-disclose more, were more polite, and attempted to reduce any tension created by the comments. Males, on the other hand, used more impersonal language, were more fact-oriented, and were much less concerned with being polite. Although males seemed to be surer of themselves and their opinions, expected differences in language patterns representing aggression and cooperation did not appear.[8]

Blogging and Teen Identity

Earlier, in chapter 4, I explored the adolescent's search for identity on MySpace. There I focused on how teens use chat and IM to explore their identities with their friends. Clearly, a blog is an excellent means of pursuing the search for the "self." It allows the teen to present an array of "possible selves" and get feedback from friends. Teens can learn about how others perceive them, practice various identities, and see which ones get reinforced by positive responses. In addition, the fact that blogs can be stored on MySpace for posterity allows a continual backward glance at the chronological perusal of the teen's process of coming of age. Comments stay forever, which means that the teen has a complete record of everything. Lidia, a nineteen-year-old who is on both MySpace and FaceBook, told me,

> "I use FaceBook to talk to my college cohorts, but MySpace is special. I have been on since my senior year of high school and I love to go back and see how my feelings have changed in just a short time. It's like I have a diary but I not only get what I write but what my friends write back. The other day I was feeling bummed about some stuff with a guy and another girl in my dorm and I went back and found what Jeremy, my boyfriend in high school, wrote to me when we were having troubles. It really helped to read that and then to read what my best friend Ashley said right after Jeremy's post. It really helped me put things in perspective and realize that it was

like déjà vu—like I had gone through something similar before and I just forgot about it."

Lidia was able to go back and reflect on her own blog and use her thoughts and Ashley's comments to help deal with her current problems. This is one of the most important aspects of keeping a personal blog, and MySpace makes it easier for adolescents to navigate the four stages of identity formation in their quests to eventual identity achievement.

In addition to blogging, instant messaging is a popular way for teens to communicate. Recent national research by the Pew Internet & American Life Project found that 75% of online teens and 66% of online young adults have used IM. For communication purposes, the Pew project found that 46% of teens preferred IM over E-mail (33%) for online communication, and they used IM regularly, with the majority using it for thirty to sixty minutes daily. One-third of the teens IM'd more than an hour a day. If you have ever watched over your teen's shoulder, you know that it is rare to see only one open IM screen. The majority IM with multiple friends simultaneously, with only 4% saying they never IM more than one person at a time.[9]

IM'rs have a buddy list that includes the screen names of their "friends." Often organized into categories, buddy lists are frequently huge, with one study indicating that three in four include more than twenty buddies, and 40% of IMing teens have *more than one hundred buddies*.[10] Having a buddy list is a badge of honor for most teens and tweens. Just like having hundreds of MySpace friends, teens feel more popular with more buddies. "Buddy" and "friend" are interesting word choices. They both connote someone belonging to an inner circle. Imagine how it must feel to have hundreds of people who are close enough to call a friend or a buddy. With this huge extended network, there is always someone online to IM.

So, what are they talking about? Actually, the answer is pretty innocuous. The Pew Internet & American Life Project study found that 82% use IM to make plans,[11] while other researchers report that 68% say they are just using IM to pass the time and talk about things that happened during their day.[12] And mostly they are talking with those school friends who were already involved in precisely the same activities they are discussing. So why don't they just use the phone to talk about all of this important stuff? Most teens have told me that they love IM because they can talk to more than one person at a time—remember, multitasking is their forte—and when they look at the list of who is available it makes them feel like they are a member of a larger community. Paradoxically, a Carnegie Mellon study[13] showed that teens judged their IM friends as less psychologically close than their phone friends. But, when it came to seeking advice, they did so equally often on the phone or via IM. While earlier generations would only talk about personal issues face-to-face or on the telephone, the MySpace Generation still uses their cell phones for intimate talks, but supplement those conversations with instant messaging and comments on their blog and on their MySpace profile.

Similarly, danah boyd likens MySpace profiles to conversational anchors, providing a basis for communication.[14] It is yet another way that adolescents may leave themselves virtually exposed. MySpace profiles can be plain and simple, using a standard template with no frills, or they can be fancy, full of color, photos, music, art, and a passel of information. No matter what they contain, you can't doubt their importance as 86% of MySpacers in my study spent some time each week working on their profile page; 46% told me that they spent more than two hours per week, and half of those teens spent more than four hours per week tweaking their MySpace page.[15]

Essentially, the profile is a virtual reflection of the MySpacer's personality. Photographs provide images of the teen, her friends, and often her activities. One main photo is displayed any time that person is depicted as a friend or makes a comment on someone's blog. Change the photo and it changes everywhere it appears on MySpace. The MySpacer's chosen nickname can also provide initial clues to the person's personality. Choosing a nickname like WispyLady might tell one thing while a moniker such as HotANDSeXy paints an entirely different picture. Pictures tell more of the story. A photo of the person with her best friends at the park paints a different picture from one showing her chugging beer at a party.

Profiles also display clues about our MySpacer, such as age, sex, and location (referred to online as a/s/l), school, marital status, sexual orientation, body type, ethnicity, education, occupation, income, zodiac sign, whether the person smokes or drinks, and pretty much any other information the MySpacer wants to offer. Additional profile information highlights the teen's interests and may include: her favorite movies, television shows, and music groups (with links to all); discussion groups to which she contributes; a link to her blog and attached comments; a count of the number of her friends; pictures of her Top 8; and comments left by friends. Clearly the MySpace profile is a flexible system and a work-in-progress for most teens. As I mentioned earlier, teens reveal quite a lot of personal information on their profiles, and parents need to be aware of the safe and risky options available for their teenagers to express their unique personalities.

One interesting addition to MySpace profiles is the personality quiz. Teens, particularly those under sixteen, appear to love taking these quizzes and posting their answers. A popular one, "Tell Me About Yourself," includes an amazing array of questions, as seen in Figure 5.1. It starts out quite innocently with questions about physical features and then progresses into much more intimate questions. There are hundreds of such quizzes—mostly generated by MySpacers—floating around MySpace pages, some yielding psychological profiles like that seen in Figure 5.2. All of them have a link encouraging others to take the same test.

The profile can tell you a lot about the teen, if it is truthful. I have yet to see data on this but in a study of online daters I found that nearly every profile had an inaccurate portrayal.[16] I have no doubt that the same is true for MySpace. However, regardless of the veracity of these quizzes, the impact is the same: they allow the MySpacer to add more information to the profile, which, in turn, paints a more complete picture of how the MySpacer wants to be seen publicly. Depending on how the information is utilized, the adolescent can gain valuable insights into his or her personality and perhaps, through the expressive, written nature of the profile, become more aware of issues that may be important during adolescent development. As a parent, it is important for you and your teen to visit their MySpace profile often as kids are adding material and modifying their profiles on a daily basis.

Figure 5.1 Sample MySpace Personality Quiz

TELL ME ABOUT YOURSELF - The Survey	
Name:	XXXXXXXXX
Age:	15
Birthday:	July 15
Birthplace:	OC baby!
Current Location:	sunny san diego
Eye Color:	green-blue-hazel... something along those lines i guess
Hair Color:	brown
Height:	5'1 and 3/4" (in my mind im 6')
Right Handed or Left Handed:	right
Your Heritage:	uhhh...no fricken clue
The Shoes You Wore Today:	flip-flops... like a true californian =)
Your Weakness:	boys boys boys
Your Fears:	bees, spiders, um... theres lots more
Your Perfect Pizza:	cheese
Goal You Would Like To Achieve This Year:	finish school in one piece
Your Most Overused Phrase On an instant messenger:	lol
Thoughts First Waking Up:	need...more...sleep
Your Best Physical Feature:	...eyes?
Your Bedtime:	when i get tired i guess
Your Most Missed Memory:	last summer :-)
Pepsi or Coke:	root beer!
MacDonalds or Burger King:	ewww
Single or Group Dates:	both
Lipton Ice Tea or Nestea:	soda
Chocolate or Vanilla:	vanilla
Cappuccino or Coffee:	ha! try a double chocolate chip frappucino (you kno it jessie! =D)
Do you Smoke:	nope
Do you Swear:	hell yeah
Do you Sing:	do i sing? ya. do i sing well? no way
Do you Shower Daily:	for sure
Have you Been in Love:	nope, not yet
Do you want to go to College:	yes
Do you want to get Married:	eventually
Do you belive in yourself:	hmmm...
Do you get Motion Sickness:	i used to
Do you think you are Attractive:	on a good day
Are you a Health Freak:	sometimes
Do you get along with your Parents:	sometimes
Do you like Thunderstorms:	i love em
Do you play an Instrument:	nope
In the past month have you Drank Alcohol:	no
In the past month have you Smoked:	no way
In the past month have you been on Drugs:	no
In the past month have you gone on a Date:	yep :-)

Figure 5.2 Sample MySpace Personality Quiz Psychological Profile

Advanced Global Personality Test Results					
Extraversion	||||||||||||	60%	Romantic	||||||||||||	70%
Stability	||||||||||	46%	Avoidant	||||||||	36%
Orderliness	||||||||||||	60%	Anti-authority	||||||||||	56%
Accommodation	|||||||||||||||	63%	Wealth	||||||||	50%
Interdependence	||||||||||	56%	Dependency	||||||||||||	63%
Intellectual	||||||||||||||	70%	Change averse	||||||||	50%
Mystical	||||||||	36%	Cautiousness	||||||||||||	70%
Artistic	||	10%	Individuality	||||||||	43%
Religious	||	10%	Sexuality	||||||||	50%
Hedonism	||	10%	Peter pan complex	|||||||||	43%
Materialism	||||||||	36%	Physical security	||||||||||||||	76%
Narcissism	||||||||||||||	70%	Physical Fitness	||||||||||||	70%
Adventurousness	|||||||||||||	63%	Histrionic	|||||||	36%
Work ethic	||||||||||	50%	Paranoia	||||||||||	56%
Self absorbed	||||||||||	50%	Vanity	||||	23%
Conflict seeking	|||||	30%	Hypersensitivity	||||||||||||	63%
Need to dominate	||||||||	36%	Female cliché	||||||||||||	70%

Strategies for Profile Self-Presentation

According to Dr. Joseph Dominick, who studied the contents of 319 personal home pages—which are the same as MySpace profiles—there are five strategies of Web self-presentation based on work by the late social psychologist Edward Ellsworth Jones:[17]

1. Competence—This profile page author needs to be seen as skilled and qualified so he or she lists accomplishments, qualifications, and the like.
2. Intimidation—This profile page is designed to demonstrate power and uses strong language, threats, and anger.
3. Ingratiation—This person wants to be liked by others, so he or she says positive things about other people and, often, mildly negative or modest things about himself or herself.
4. Exemplification—This home page portrays the author as morally superior or possessing high standards. Often this profile page will include strong commitments to causes, a display of self-sacrifice, and examples of self-discipline.

5. Supplication—This profile page is designed to show the author as helpless so that others will want to come to his or her aid. Usually, the author presents a profile that is self-deprecating and includes pleas for help.

Dominick found that the majority of Web pages or profiles used ingratiation, followed by competency, as ways of self-presentation. This suggests that MySpacers either need to be seen as eager to be appreciated and liked by online and offline friends or need to be viewed as smart and successful. These self-presentation strategies are clearly messages showing the world how the MySpacer wants to be seen. Through comments from friends, this self-presentation will either be reinforced or modified in a continual search for identity.

Profiles, blogs, comments, and instant messages are all written, one-dimensional forms of communication that, for the most part, are devoid of the ability to transmit emotions and feelings. Since physical gestures are impossible when people are online, MySpacer teens have developed their own language, often called "netspeak," incorporating abbreviations, slang, emoticons, leetspeak, and additional online jargon. Known as "paralanguage" because of its mostly nonverbal nature, netspeak has effectively created a culture of its own. Blogging, commenting, and IMing are ways of maintaining and enhancing that culture through language.

Abbreviations like BRB, LOL, or CYA are quite common and, in fact, you may have used them in your own online communications with family, friends, or coworkers. POS and P911, for example, are more generation-specific in that they are ways teens tell their IM friends that a parent is close by and may be reading the IM conversation. POS means "parent over shoulder" and P911 says "don't say anything that might make my parents mad." Table 5.1 displays a few acronyms that are commonly used by the MySpace Generation. Other acronym lists can be found on the Internet.[18]

Emoticons, or smilies, are another way teens present emotions or feelings, with which you may already be familiar. They are so popular that IM users, for example, only need to click on an icon to put a smiley face, a sad face, or any of dozens of emoticons to express feelings in

Table 5.1 List of IM Acronyms and Their Meanings

Acronym	Meaning
ASL or a/s/l	Age, Sex, Location
BF/GF	Boyfriend/Girlfriend
BRB	Be Right Back
GTG	Got to Go
IDK	I Don't Know
LOL	Laughing Out Loud
ROTFLOL	Rolling on the Floor and Laughing Out Loud
LMAO	Laughing My Ass Off
W/E	Whatever
WTF	What the (you can fill in this word)
TTYL	Talk to You Later
JK	Just Kidding
IMHO	In My Humble Opinion
CYA	See Ya

their instant messages. The smiley face may even be animated, which transmits an even stronger feeling of happiness.[19] For a complete list of smilies visit http://www.smileyworld.com/emoticons.

Another strategy adopted by teens to transmit information beyond the printed words is to enclose a word or phrase indicating a physical action with stars, brackets, or some other nonalphabetic character. For example, typing *hug* tells the message receiver that had the sender been there live, he would have gotten a hug. Typing in capital letters typically denotes that the author is shouting and angry.

Video gamers and other teens and young adults have created their own language called leetspeak. Originally designed to prevent Internet filters from recognizing certain words that might be offensive, leetspeak is now part of mainstream adolescent culture. In this language, letters may be replaced by numbers or characters that resemble the letters, and words may be altered or shortened. For example, 1337 spells leet, which is short for elite. The numeral "1" looks like a lowercase "L," the "3" represents a reverse "E," and the "7" stands for "T." Leetspeak becomes 13375p34K. Interestingly, it has gone from a special gamer's language to mainstream advertising (Sears used HE4T to name one of their clothes dryers) and television (CBS's popular show *Numb3rs* uses the "3" to stand for an "E"). It's all very bewildering to many parents, especially because the replacement letters and numbers are fluid and interchangeable rather than fixed, but teens who use it can read it fluently. One word that seems to have arisen in leetspeak is pwn3d (pwned), which means to not only defeat an opponent, but to rub it in his face.

Marc Prensky, founder and CEO of Games2train and author of *Don't Bother Me Mom—I'm Learning: How Computer and Video Games are Preparing Your Kids for Twenty-First Century Success and How You Can Help*, has described adolescents as "digital natives," meaning that they are native speakers of the digital language of computers, video games, and the Internet. According to Prensky,

> "Those of us who were not born into the digital world but have, at some later point in our lives, become fascinated by and adopted many or most aspects of the new technology are, and always will be, compared to them, Digital Immigrants. As Digital Immigrants learn—like all immigrants, some better than others—to adapt to their environment, they always retain, to some degree, their 'accent', that is, their foot in the past. The 'digital immigrant accent' can be seen in such things as turning to the Internet for information second rather than first, or in reading the manual for a program rather than assuming that the program itself will teach us to use it. Today's older folk were 'socialized' differently from their kids, and are not in the process of learning a new language."[20]

Just watching your teen communicate via IM or a blog should show you the prevalence of netspeak. In one study, David Huffaker, coauthor of *Gender, Identity, and Language Use in Teenage Blogs*, found that 63% of the bloggers he studied used emoticons, with females using them more often than males.[21] In another interesting study, researchers found that in a moderated chat room (where one person oversees and controls the conversation), moderators who used emoticons were seen as more dynamic, friendly, and valuable than those who did not.[22]

Does all of this netspeak help our children be better writers or better students? David Huffaker most certainly believes that blogging is important as he says "blogs can be an important addition to educational technology because they promote literacy through storytelling, allow collaborative learning and provide anytime-anywhere access."[23] Education has long taken advantage of storytelling to enhance learning. Beginning at a young age parents and children read bedtime stories. Upon returning from kindergarten, and then later elementary school, the child recounts events of the day. Stories lead to writing and blogs promote storytelling, creativity, and imagination.

Many parents have told me that they are concerned that their children, with all the acronyms, abbreviations, and netspeak, will be unable to write correct sentences in the English language and will lose their ability to spell as they rely on spell checking programs. Research indicates that this is not true. Using writing samples from thousands of English language examinations for sixteen-year-olds, Alf Massey of Cambridge University discovered that, despite parental concerns, teenagers today are using more complex sentence structures, a wider vocabulary, and are, surprisingly, more accurate at appropriate use of capital letters, punctuation, and spelling compared with those in previous years.[24] A study of eleven-year-olds found that those who sent more text messages were better at spelling and writing than those who composed fewer text messages.[25] According to psychologists and linguists, regardless of the use of abbreviations and shortcuts, today's teens are producing more writing than earlier generations, which is helping them develop their English language skills.[26]

Given MySpacers' interest and experience in writing online, schools are beginning to realize the power of blogs in fostering both scientific and creative writing. Since many students maintain online blogs, it is an easy transition to school-based online discussions. Using the Internet for school blogs also ensures that students will have access and even find it fun and interesting to do their schoolwork. Journalism classes have used online blogs to present and group-edit student articles. Science classes have used similar tools to help students critically examine experimental projects. One class assigned a group project in which the data were collected at home and analyzed and discussed in a blog format. The results show that students write more actively when using an online writing vehicle, rather than paper-and-pencil. Countless other studies have shown that blogs can improve critical thinking, literacy, and the ability to take material and prepare logical arguments. Further, blogs encourage collaborative writing and debate, which are no different than posts and comments on MySpace.

In spite of the enhanced writing skills of the MySpace Generation, putting their lives online can leave them virtually exposed. One major problem is that you don't know who is reading your musings today nor do you know who might read them tomorrow, or next month. A blog is permanent. As the quote from Cliff Van Zandt asserted at the beginning of this chapter, blog material is eternal. By their nature as personal diaries written "behind the screen," blogs often lead to public self-disclosure of private information. Anything written online can be copied, saved, and potentially distributed to others as Congressman Mark Foley discovered when his sexually explicit IM conversations and e-mail messages with young congressional pages were made public and he was forced to resign.[27] As the MySpace Generation continues to communicate electronically, using the printed word, it remains to be seen whether there are any long-term ramifications of putting your life online.

Privacy is clearly a major issue with teens writing personal thoughts online. As an experiment, I went onto MySpace, clicked on Tom Anderson's picture and randomly clicked on photos of some of his one hundred million friends. On each page, I clicked on a link at the top that said "Subscribe to this Blog." Immediately, I was able to read each MySpacer's blog even though I had not met that person, nor did they know who I was. Some of the blogs were quite descriptive, with tales of drunken parties, rants against teachers, and clear personal information.

Online comments have already created problems for some people. As reported by ESPN, Mark Cuban, owner of the Dallas Mavericks basketball team, wrote comments in his blog criticizing the referees in a playoff game. Consequently, he was fined by the NBA.[28] An article on blogging in *Wired Magazine* began with the question: "What do a flight attendant in Texas, a temporary employee in Washington and a Web designer in Utah have in common? They were all fired for posting content on their blogs that their companies disapproved of."[29] A *USA Today* article recounted several instances in which something a student had written online came back to haunt them, including an applicant to college who was denied admission because of blogged comments disparaging the campus, and high school students who have been suspended for comments made on MySpace.[30] The lesson for your teenager is that what he writes online is available to anyone.

As we have seen, online blogs, IMs, and e-mails are equivalent to using a permanent marker. Consider the following scenario. A college graduate, who has not written a word on MySpace for several years, applies for a job at a major aerospace company. He has an excellent interview and looks like a perfect candidate. But then the director of human resources visits MySpace and finds his profile with pictures from his partying days and material he wrote when he was in high school about beer bashes, drugs, whatever. The company hires someone else.

This may seem far-fetched, but, in fact, it has already occurred. There are federal regulations about what future employers can ask in an interview, but there are no laws forbidding them to visit MySpace, Google, or Archive.org (which records much of the material on the Internet using its Wayback Machine) to search for further information about candidates. Googling someone is now a common verb. Anything that you have written on the Internet is probably saved somewhere on some computer. You don't have to be an Internet sleuth to find this material either. It's there and it's easy to locate. The Internet truly is the great storage garage of the new millennium.

As I mentioned earlier, teens freely divulge personal information on MySpace and many parents are unaware of the extent of this disclosure. Setting aside the current media paranoia about sexual predators, disclosure of so much personal information can lead to future problems. I included a sample MySpace quiz in this chapter, with answers by one fifteen-year-old girl. Glance back at this quiz and you will see many opportunities for innocent, seemingly harmless teenage self-disclosure.

Self-disclosure does not just include your own MySpace page. As Kevin Farnham, author of *MySpace Safety: 51 Tips for Teens and Parents*, reminds us: "This is, of course, the primary purpose of the World Wide Web: to conveniently spread information globally. The reality is: any information you make available on any blog or Web site on the Internet immediately ceases to be fully under your control. Data you enter into MySpace lasts forever. You should assume that it may be archived and available somewhere on the Internet for a very long time into the future."[31]

What you say online can also cause emotional distress although many teens minimize the problem. Eric, a college freshman MySpacer said: *"There is really no risk in saying anything you want on someone's blog. If the person has a problem with it, just disappear. Change your screen name, open a new MySpace page. It's easy. People do that all the time."* I have found in my interviews that a large number of "friends" are online friends only. When asked what percentage of MySpace friends teens had met in person, 47% had met less than half their online friends and 33% said they had met less than one-quarter. If you have never seen someone live, in the flesh, and are talking to him or her online only, there is little to keep that person from acting out against you. That can hurt.

Eric went on to say that even if someone doesn't hurt you directly, they can do it by other means. *"One time I was having a pretty intense IM conversation with Sarah, going back and forth, and getting heavier and all of a sudden there was nothing. No response. Nothing. I waited and still nothing. After about fifteen minutes I gave up, not knowing what I said that drove her away. We had been talking like this for days and she just up and disappeared. I felt awful."* Luckily, Eric is an emotionally healthy kid and he realized that it wasn't his fault, but would a younger child know this? We will talk more about this in chapter 9.

What Can You Do?

NetSmartz Workshop is an interactive, educational safety resource from the National Center for Missing & Exploited Children and Boys & Girls Clubs of America for children ages five to seventeen, parents, guardians, educators, and law enforcement officials. As part of its Web site, NetSmartz has an online instrument titled "Blog Beware Quiz." The issues it raises are valuable and can be the source of a parent-child discussion. In Table 5.2 I have selected a few questions that I feel are important. It should be clear which answers might raise red flags, but I have highlighted those issues to which NetSmartz recommends parents pay particular attention. If your child answered any of the gray highlighted answers, use those questions for a discussion starter. Even if he or she did not give any of those answers, the questions themselves may be good discussion points.

Here are some general suggestions for helping your adolescent understand the ramifications of putting thoughts online.

1. Discuss the potential pitfalls of putting information on MySpace that will last forever. Use this opportunity to talk about what your tween or teen might plan for his or her future and explain that what is discussed today on MySpace may hinder chances in the future.

2. Talk to your teen about the inherent dangers in posting personal information on MySpace. Use the "Blog Beware Quiz" items as a stepping-stone to talk to your teen about what might happen with material that is posted online, not only on MySpace but anywhere. Recommend that he or she set his or her MySpace profile to private, which means that someone has to request to be allowed to see more than the main photo, gender, age, and location (which can be stated as broadly as "California"). Teens appear to be doing a fairly good job of guarding the privacy of their profile. According to a recent nationwide study by the Pew Internet & American Life Project, 59% of teens who have an online profile restrict access to their friends. Interestingly, teens with parents who know they have an online profile are more likely to set their profile to private access than teens whose parents are not aware that they have an online profile.[32] Be careful not to play up the "sexual predator" angle. My research showed that while 67% of the parents were concerned about sexual predators on MySpace, only 32% of the children agreed. I also found that while 71% of parents believed there were quite a few sexual predators on

Table 5.2 Sample Questions from the Blog Beware Quiz

Blog Beware Quiz
Which is the safer screen name to have for your social networking site? A. Katie_ny13   C. YankEEfan7444 B. Cute14girl   D. Grade10hottie
Which is appropriate to post on your profile or blog? A. The name of the school I attend B. The location of the party I went to on Friday night C. Names of movies and celebrities that I like
Which item is OK to post on your profile or blog? A. Your religious affiliation   D. Favorite movie B. Your favorite food   E. Your hometown C. Your ethnic background
Which is the safer entry for your blog or personal profile? A. Full name, name of school, hobbies B. Nickname and state C. First name only, school mascot, photo of yourself
If you were to post a picture on your social networking site, which is the better choice? A. A picture of just yourself B. A picture of yourself with friends or family C. A picture of your sports team D. A picture of your car E. A picture of your local hangout F. A picture of your favorite celebrity, sports team, or singer, author
Which is the safer password? A. Your pet's name: Fluffy B. Your birthday: 5131991 C. The street you live on: 1224 Tibbling Lane D. A code: i8p1Zza2day (I ate pizza today)
Of the choices below, what would be an appropriate entry for a blog? A. "I am feeling depressed and sad; no one likes me" B. "I scored 16 points at my basketball game last night! GO TIGERS! ON TO STATE!" C. "I had a great weekend filled with fun. I went to the movies with my best friend and then we went for ice cream." D. "Today at school Connor Bodally made fun of me. Just because his dad owns the Drive-Ins in Beach Town, he thinks he is the coolest kid around. I hate him" E. "I walked to work after school like usual. I really hate that we have to wear these stupid purple uniforms (see pic) . . . I mean we're just serving hamburgers right?"

MySpace, 18% of the teens said that sexual predators were rare and another 36% said there were some predators, but not many. The media has championed this issue into a "moral panic" and when asked about the media portrayal of sexual predators, 69% of parents felt that it was either "pretty close to the truth" or an underestimate, while only 46% of teens expressed the same feelings. Clearly the media is influencing parents' perceptions of what is happening online. My advice is not to buy into the panic over sexual predators, but to include it in your discussion about posting personal information.

3. Talk to your teens about how what they say on MySpace might seriously hurt someone's feelings, whether intentionally or unintentionally. Have a frank discussion of how online friendships develop quickly and what impact that might have on the level of personal feelings your teen discloses. Include in your conversation an examination of how simply disappearing can hurt someone who feels they are talking to a "friend." It is clear that most teens have either done this, had it happen to them, or know someone close who has been "dumped" online. It may seem harmless, but not when it happens to your teen. A friend of mine has a daughter who is a high school senior. She had been talking to Randall online for five years. They had been as intimate as you can get online, and had shared secrets that most boyfriends and girlfriends don't share. They lived near each other and discovered that they had similar interests and values. They made plans to meet and suddenly Randall had other plans and they could never quite coordinate a meeting. Over the next few months Randall spent less and less time on IM and finally disappeared. When my friend's daughter asked one of her other online friends what had happened to him, she told her that Randall had a new IM screen name and was not really using his old one. She also told her, quite bluntly, that Randall really didn't want to talk with her anymore. My friend's daughter was devastated as she truly thought this was her one true love—her soul mate—and she had invested a lot in the relationship. Sadly, she had not dated at all in high school as she felt as though they were going steady. It hurt for quite some time. It is important for you—as a parent, but

also as a member of a different generation—to be aware that having an online boyfriend or girlfriend might seem foreign to you but to the MySpace Generation it is just another indication of how important the Internet is to their social life. Keep in mind, when you are talking about online relationships with your son or daughter, that MySpace is, for many, a place to fulfill their social needs and this includes friends and potential love relationships.

These suggestions involve "talking" to your teen. In one of my research studies, I asked both parents and their adolescents how much time they spent talking and how many meals they shared during a typical week. One-third of both teens and parents estimated that they talked one hour or less a day and another third said they talked between one and two hours a day. The average number of shared meals was somewhere between five and seven per week. Granted, with parents working full time, and kids being involved in many after-school activities and having mounds of homework, it is difficult to find time to share a meal or talk. However, somehow these teens found a way to spend two hours a day on MySpace alone, and this doesn't count other Internet or computer activities. My study also showed that 36% of the parents had no idea how much time their children spent on MySpace, but those who did accurately estimated the same two hours per day.

My suggestion for sharing meals with your tween or teen is twofold. First, mealtime is an excellent opportunity to talk and, second, there *is* time to share a meal, even if the time is short. Here are some tips for making those moments more productive:

1. Schedule a regular time for the meal, preferably dinner, at home. This can be eating dinner the same time every day, or, if schedules change daily, planning the night before when you are going to eat and letting everyone know the schedule. If you can make longer-range plans, post a calendar on the refrigerator with shared meals highlighted. A fascinating study found that kids who eat family dinners often get mainly As and Bs in school compared to those who eat together infrequently.[33] Other studies have shown that teens who take part in regular family meals are two and a half times

less likely to smoke, three times less likely to use drugs, and one and a half times less likely to drink alcohol. They are also less apt to get depressed, develop eating disorders, or consider suicide.[34] Teens who share family meals report being able to talk to their parents about serious problems. Have the meal planned in advance. Make sure that everything you need is ready. Prepare as much of the dinner in advance as you can. If you are harried while cooking then the dinner will not be as productive. If you don't have time to cook, bring in food to preserve that special, valuable time.

2. Don't allow any outside distractions. Turn off the television. Believe it or not, most families eat with the television on.[35] This is a distraction that gives everyone in the family an opportunity to focus their attention elsewhere.

3. Ask questions and then listen. Don't interrupt. An excellent way to show your teen that you are listening is to ask follow-up questions. Don't ask judgmental questions. Keep them "informational." And, watch your facial expressions. Nonverbal communication is a powerful way to transmit information. If you grimace when your son or daughter tells you about their MySpace experiences, you will discourage them from sharing.

4. Compliment your child often. Behavioral psychologists call this "catch them being good." Give at least three compliments at each meal. It doesn't have to be something important that they did. Just tell them that you liked it. Make sure that you compliment them on specific things they did that you like. Just saying that they are being good is too general and does not reinforce specific behaviors. The key to "positive reinforcement" is to focus on a specific behavior. You will know it is working if the specific behavior stays good or gets even better. Trust me, when one behavior increases, it also helps others to increase.

5. Don't just ask questions of your teen. Share information about your day, as well. Try to engage them in appreciating what you do. Focus on the positive. Don't complain about your day. That turns them off.

6. Ask your kids for advice about household matters. This may sound strange, but teens have lots of excellent ideas and truly like

to be asked their opinions. If you are buying something new, ask them what they think. You can even have them do some online research for you. When my television exploded due to oxidized wiring, I asked my two teenagers to go online and find what televisions were recommended. Teens are on the cusp of being adults—now is a good time to make them feel that way.

7. Give your kids responsibilities for parts of dinner and don't just make this setting the table and cleaning up. Make them responsible, periodically, for planning and preparing parts of a meal. Encourage them to find recipes on the Internet and create an appetizer or dessert. These are "extras" and have more prominence because they are first or last. Personally, I have found that having kids make dessert is great because it keeps them at the table longer. Make sure that no matter how it tastes you find something about their creation to compliment. Make a big deal out of it and they will feel good and want to do it again.

Above all, talk to your children. Find opportunities to sit down quietly and chat. Remember, it is more important to catch them being good than to point out where they have done something wrong. Positive reinforcement is more powerful in changing behavior than punishment.

I interviewed David Huffaker, coauthor of *Gender, Identity, and Language Use in Teenage Blogs*. Here is what he told me:

Q: Teens on MySpace spend hours writing blogs, comments on other blogs, and bulletins. Why are they so willing to put their thoughts on paper when often it is difficult to get them to write school papers?

Huffaker: There are probably a dozen reasons why teens use blogs, including both popularity among peers and a positive outlet for creativity and expression. From a developmental perspective, blogs let teens construct and share the stories of their lives, and provide a "voice" possibly stifled in other venues, while connecting with friends and other bloggers, fostering community and sociability.

The reasons blogs are different than school papers have to do with both content and style. In terms of content, blogs allows teen to choose their own subject matter rather than completing an assignment (in other words, the writing is emergent rather than allocated). In terms of style, blog writing is more informal than school writing, not only with the language itself (stories and narratives rather than essays and reports), but also the types of content that can be created (text, photos, videos, music) and formatted (colors, spacing, fonts, design).

Q: What do you think they get out of blogging? Is it just a fad or have they really discovered a tool that is helpful to their adolescent development?

Huffaker: Since Internet technology continues to advance, it is difficult, if not impossible, to predict the longevity of blog use by adolescents. For example, Web cams are also popular and video blogs (or vlogs) could be a next step. It's hard to tell. It is interesting that social networking sites such as MySpace and Facebook, which are inundated with adolescents, have blogs implemented in their applications, demonstrating that online communities must utilize blog applications to thrive.

That said, I have always believed that blogs are useful for adolescent development in several ways. First, they allow teens to explore a personal narrative and thus experiment and construct an online (and offline) identity. As adolescents approach adulthood, it is imperative that they begin to construct a cohesive narrative, or life story. Second, blogs foster community through the reading, commenting, and linking with other bloggers. Perhaps the most important aspect of adolescent development is the cultivation of friendships and peer relationships. Third, it promotes literacy development through the written and multimedia posts that bloggers devise. Of course, improving verbal and digital literacy is vital to success in the real world.

Q: How do you feel that writing on the Internet affects writing in school? Do you think that the language of the Internet (acronyms, shortened words, emoticons) negatively affects the way they write in school?

Huffaker: This is a popular criticism of the Internet, that teens are learning bad language habits such as misspelling words, and using informal or disjunctive language. Surely, Internet language is about shortcuts—communicating as quickly and efficiently as possible. However, this does not necessarily carry over into formal writing, such as the kind of writing found in school settings, and I have not seen any empirical studies to suggest that Internet writing has any effect on school writing. By contrast, I would argue that the fact that kids are writing so much on the Internet is advantageous because it allows them to practice communicating, as well as provide opportunities to be creative with language.

Q: Many people have cautioned teens that anything they write online can be used against them down the road. Why do you think that teens ignore this caution and write about anything and everything?

Huffaker: I can only speculate here, but it is possible that teens do not see beyond the immediacy of their local social networks, or worry too much about the consequences of today's post. It is also possible that given the sheer size of information and content available on the Internet, the plethora of URL addresses, avenues and corners, and the relative anonymity that being online provides, teens feel tucked away and concealed in the sea of bits, creating a sense of protection or fearlessness. In other words, who's gonna find me on the World Wide Web?

Q: Should parents talk to their kids about blogging? If so, what advice would you give the parents before they talk to their children?

Huffaker: I think it's better for parents to openly talk with their kids about the consequences of blogging, such as privacy issues (i.e., words or pictures can get one into trouble), sexual predation (i.e., stranger danger), or cyberbullying (i.e., harassment by schoolmates), rather than read their kids' blogs behind their back (which creates trust issues), or enforce draconian Internet constraints (which pushes kids to surf the Internet outside parental jurisdiction).

My only advice is that parents spend some time reviewing Web sites like YouTube, MySpace, or LiveJournal before they talk to their children, so that they understand the terrain. If parents sound terribly uninformed when talking with their teens, their frankness or warnings will likely be ignored.

Chapter 6

Sex and the Media

◆

"Geez, I'm in my bra and panties. Nobody can see anything. I don't see why everyone's so upset."

—JuneBug 14, Des Moines, Iowa

◆

"The Internet is transforming the experience of growing up in America. It is also transforming the job of being a parent in America. The Internet brings the world—the good, the bad, and the ugly—to the American family's doorstep. It brings the ruins of ancient Athens to that doorstep, but it also brings the red light district of Bangkok."

—Third Way Culture Project, Washington, D.C.[1]

◆

"Although it has long been normative behavior for adolescents to seek out images that are sexually explicit (e.g., viewing one's first *National Geographic* and *Playboy Magazine* were once rites of passage for many boys), adolescents are bombarded with sexual content in everyday media sources that are to some extent difficult to escape. Images meant to tantalize are embedded in most advertising in television, billboards, and print media and programming such as music videos, soap operas, and movies contains highly sexualized images and content."

—Dick Thornburgh and Herbert Lin, National Research Council, Washington, D.C.[2]

◆

Multitasking is a way of life for children, tweens, and teens. The MySpace Generation consumes and is consumed by media. By the age of eighteen, children have watched hundreds of thousands of hours of television, mostly in the privacy of their bedrooms. They have also listened to countless hours of music, seen hundreds of movies, read magazines, and surfed the Internet from the time they could push keyboard buttons and move the mouse.

What exactly are they watching, hearing, and reading? According to a two-year study published in *Pediatrics*, these children and adolescents are consuming a "sexual media diet" or SMD.[3] A seven-year Kaiser Family Foundation study highlighted the extent of part of this SMD. Between 1998 and 2005 the number of sex scenes on television doubled. A staggering 70% of the twenty most-watched teenage shows portray some sexual content, with 45% displaying sexual behavior. In a typical one-hour prime-time show, six scenes will portray sexual content. For those top twenty–watched teenage programs this increases to seven scenes an hour. Over the seven-year study, the percentage of sexual content on television has increased to new highs across all types of shows.[4] A study by the Campaign for a Commercial-Free Childhood found similar results, with 83% of the top twenty–rated shows containing sexual content, including 20% depicting sexual intercourse.[5]

Television is only part of the sexual media diet. What about movies, music, magazines, newspapers, and the Internet, which make up the remainder of the SMD? Add in the sexual content from those sources and children and adolescents are consuming massive amounts of nudity, sexual relations, innuendos, petting, and discussions about having sex. What is the impact of thousands and thousands of hours of a sexual media diet? If we were talking about consuming too much food, we would certainly expect negative health consequences. Later in this chapter I take a look at specific impacts of each medium, but in brief, research overwhelmingly shows that an overall diet rich in sexual content is strongly *negatively* related to sexual attitudes and behaviors. Teens who were highest in SMD were more than twice as likely to be sexually active than those who consumed the lowest sexual media diet and were also more likely to have permissive attitudes toward sexual experimentation.[6] A RAND Corporation study found similar results:

twelve- to seventeen-year-olds who watched a lot of sexualized media were twice as likely to engage in sexual intercourse. In fact, according to Dr. Rebecca Collins, the RAND scientist who conducted this study, those twelve-year-old heavy TV watchers behaved sexually like fourteen- to fifteen-year-old light TV watchers. Collins's study also found that it was not watching sexual activity per se that was the problem. Strikingly, watching sex being discussed on television affected teens as much as viewing sexual behavior. According to Collins, "talk on television had virtually the same effect on teen behavior as depictions of sexual activity. This finding runs counter to the widespread belief that portrayals of action have a more powerful impact than talk."[7]

The RAND study demonstrated the negative impact of television sex, but are teen TV viewers getting any positive messages about sex? The Kaiser Family Foundation study found that only 10% of the top twenty teen shows presented messages about safe sex, and few of these messages were a primary part of the show. In addition, the study found that references to the risks and responsibilities associated with sex have decreased dramatically over the years.[8]

Jensen, a twelve-year-old boy said, *"I have the TV on from when I come home until dinner when I am usually doing my homework or being online, and then from after dinner until I go to bed. Mostly I watch shows that I have TiVo'd so I can stop them if something else is important or if I missed something on the show. If my mom and dad blocked all the shows that showed sex, there would pretty much be nothing left to watch but sports."* His seventeen-year-old sister, Jana, echoed his feelings: *"Every show I watch, except maybe* American Idol *and* Deal or No Deal *has sex in it. And even those shows have people wearing sexy clothes."*

Teen Sexual Experience

All data point to the conclusion that teenage sex is quite common. One recent study reported that 47% of high school students had sexual intercourse before the age of eighteen, with 7.4% before the age of thirteen. Of these, 14% had four or more sex partners before graduating high school.[9] Statistics show that nine hundred thousand teenage girls get pregnant each year, and 35% of American girls have been pregnant at least once by the age of twenty. Three million teens get STDs each year, approximately one-fourth of those who are sexually active.[10]

In generations past, "sex" typically meant intercourse. This generation does not agree. Several studies of fourteen- to fifteen-year-olds reported that oral sex was considered different and much more acceptable than vaginal sex. Based on many studies of teen sexuality, it is clear that teens do not view oral sex as sex. In study after study teens report that by just having oral sex, they were less likely to have a bad reputation, their actions were seen as more acceptable to their peers, and they felt less guilty than if they had intercourse.[11] Both Oprah Winfrey and Katie Couric[12] have hosted television shows where they discussed "rainbow parties" with parents and teens, and they were featured on an episode of CSI. Girls, each wearing a different shade of lipstick, have oral sex with boys, leaving them with a rainbow on their penises. A fifteen-year-old high school student explained why these parties didn't mean that you were having sex: *"You know, it's just a lot of fun. It's sort of like a game. It doesn't mean anything to anyone and it's not like you are going out with a guy. That means a lot more. I would never sleep with someone at a party. That's something that you only do when you are going out with a guy regularly."* When asked about how kids found out about these parties she told me, *"One cool thing is that if someone is having a party they just put a note on their MySpace and all their friends know about it."*

Although rainbow parties may not be springing up in your community, oral sex has become an important part of teen life. According to a *New York Times* article, "Oral sex has, undoubtedly, become part of many teenagers' sexual repertory."[13] In fact, research by the U.S. Department of Health and Human Services indicates that among fifteen- to sixteen-year-olds, one in ten sexually active boys and girls have had only oral sex.[14]

Other forms of teen sexuality—such as "hooking up" and "friends with benefits"—have become part of teen culture. According to the *New York Times Magazine*, "The term [hooking up] itself is vague—covering everything from kissing to intercourse—though it is sometimes a euphemism for oral sex, performed by a girl on a boy." Friends with benefits include "basically friends you hook up with regularly . . . it is not dating, it is just sex."[15] The article places the blame squarely on the media: "To a generation raised on MTV, AIDS, Britney Spears, Internet porn, Monica Lewinsky, and *Sex and the City*, oral sex is definitely not sex (it's just 'oral'), and hooking up is definitely not a big deal." Later in this chapter I pursue the major impact that the media has on teen sexuality.

Dating is another concept that has a vastly different connotation to adolescents today than it did just a generation ago. Perhaps this is best summed up in an article my seventeen-year-old daughter wrote for her high school newspaper.

> *"Going out and dating—two completely different terms. Dating is a preliminary trial period preceding going out, to confirm that two people are compatible. The difference being that if a girl 'goes out' with more than one guy at the same time, it is considered cheating. However, if the same girl were to date multiple guys at the same time, there would be no problem. To break it down for all those clueless guys out there—'dating' allows for one party to enjoy the company of multiple parties, whereas 'going out' signifies a committed relationship between a boyfriend and girlfriend."*

With the increase in teen sexual experimentation, and differences from previous generations in how tweens and teens view dating, sexuality, and opposite-sex relationships, parents are deeply concerned. One mother of a thirteen-year-old told me, *"I know that many of her friends are sexually active and I worry about how they may influence my daughter's choices. We have talked about this, and I have even read a book on teen sexuality, but I am just not sure that girls this young are really ready emotionally for sex."* This is a concern that I have heard from many parents and in the next section I explore these issues from what psychologists know about sexual development.

Developmental Sexual Growth

Development is both physical and psychological. It is important to examine how tweens and teens typically progress from the onset of puberty through adolescence in both arenas because in order to understand their behavior it is important to understand what is going on inside their bodies and their minds. Although each adolescent enters puberty at his or her own age—and girls do so earlier than boys—the process and milestones are similar. There are three main issues in sexual development: (1) gender identity, (2) sexual orientation, and (3) physiology. Although gender identity and sexual orientation may seem, on the surface, to be the same process, they are not. Gender identity incorporates decisions by the adolescent about his or her association with characteristics of each gender. Tweens and teens do not naturally develop gender identity based on their "physiological" gender. Instead, according to Erik Erikson, the foremost authority on identity development, each teen must determine whether to embrace more masculine personality traits or more feminine ones, or perhaps adopt a style combining the two.

In contrast, sexual orientation identity is where the adolescent deals with issues concerning who he or she is attracted to and plans to pursue for a possible romantic relationship. In the past, sexual orientation identity was not a major part of an adolescent's sexual development, because until recently homosexuality or bisexuality was considered aberrant behavior. However, as discussed later in this chapter, this has now become a very important developmental issue that is impacted by online social networking.

Finally, biological or physiological maturation involves the release of hormones that trigger puberty. This can begin as early as seven years old or as late as thirteen and can take anywhere from eighteen months to six years to complete. If you are amazed that puberty can begin so early, a recent study in the journal *Pediatrics* found that half of African American children and 15% of Caucasian preteens begin puberty by the age of eight.[16] Although there is no known cause for this trend toward early puberty, experts point to four possible culprits. First, fat cells produce a protein that promotes puberty. Given that we are experiencing an epidemic of childhood obesity where there are more fat cells than needed by the body to maintain weight, it is not surprising that this is one possible explanation. Second, some scientists point to the fact that animals raised for food are often injected with growth hormones to stimulate faster growth so that they can be brought to market more quickly. These growth hormones, consumed in meat eaten by a child, can trigger earlier development of puberty hormones. Third, chemical pollution has been linked to early puberty, a theory supported by research showing that urban children mature faster than rural children. Finally, there is some striking evidence indicating that when the home environment is less cohesive and has more adult-child conflict, hormones are released earlier than in children raised in happier homes.

Regardless of the age of onset, puberty brings forth fairly typical changes. On the average, the period from age nine to age twelve is where most teens begin to experience the physical changes of puberty. Psychologically, boys and girls typically experience the following between the ages of nine and twelve:

- More curiosity about their bodies
- Beginning interest in dating, often preceded by "crushes"
- General modesty and shyness about their physical changes
- Questioning how they compare to their peers
- Pressure to conform to family expectations of their new "adult" status
- Use of sexually related language, particularly among peers
- Interest in media portrayals of sexuality
- Romantic and sexual fantasies
- Curiosity about orgasms and perhaps experimenting with masturbation
- Learning about sexuality from family first, then the media and peers.

In the early high school years, roughly from ages thirteen to sixteen, adolescents experience more pronounced psychological changes, including:

- Heightened interest in personal attractiveness as a "sexual" being
- Increased pressure by peers to experiment sexually
- Heightened sexual fantasies
- Beginnings of sexual orientation exploration
- Worries about being "normal" sexually compared to peers
- Falling in and out of love
- First sexual experimentation
- Gathering information about sexuality from peers first, followed by the media and then family.

Finally, in late high school, seventeen- and eighteen-year-olds experience more adult aspects of their sexuality:

- Intense feelings of love and passion
- Serious relationships with increased sexual experimentation
- Better sense of sexual orientation and sexual identity
- More ability to express feelings about sexuality and love

These changes continue through young adulthood with an expanded interest and reliance on peers and, more particularly, the media. In the next section I explore what psychologists have learned about the impact of television and other media.

The Medium *Is* the Message . . . at Least on Television

Nielsen's television ratings estimated that 6.6 million children ages two to eleven and an additional 7.3 million teens watched Justin Timberlake rip open Janet Jackson's blouse during the 2004 Super Bowl halftime show. For weeks after, the scene was played and replayed in slow motion on the Internet. This episode was seen by psychologists as marking a milestone in the appearance of sexuality, as it appeared without warning, unlike the sexuality portrayed on normal nighttime television.[17]

As discussed in the beginning of this chapter, television is a major media outlet used by tweens and adolescents. The National Longitudinal Study of Adolescent Health, the largest, most comprehensive study of adolescents funded by the federal government, found that those teens under sixteen who had not yet had sexual intercourse and who watched more than two hours of television a day were more likely to initiate sex within one year than those who watched fewer than two hours.[18] So, what is the impact of, say, a twelve-year-old, consuming upwards of three or four hours of television per day, much of it depicting sexuality, mostly in the privacy of his or her bedroom and mostly alone at night? Dr. Liliana Escobar-Chaves, who studies the impact of the media on adolescent sexual attitudes and behavior, found that adolescents who watched more than average amounts of television behaved sexually as if they were nine to seventeen months older than those who watched only average amounts of television.[19] What this means, according to her findings, is that a couch potato twelve-year-old behaves sexually like a typical television-watching fourteen- or fifteen-year-old. While the fourteen- or fifteen-year-old is most likely developmentally ready to deal with sexuality, the twelve-year-old is not.

For example, Marie, the parent of a thirteen-year-old daughter, told me: *"I am so worried about Marissa. Her TV is on all night while she is studying or talking on the phone with her friends. Now she wants to buy only very revealing blouses and put on makeup in the morning before school. On the weekends she hangs out with her friends at the mall, and another parent told me that the other day she saw the girls talking to some older boys. I have tried to restrict her TV time but she whines about how she is missing 'her shows' that everyone at school watches and talks about the next day. I told her that she was too young for makeup and she yelled at me that all her friends wore it and there was no way I could stop her. She told me that if I wouldn't let her put it on before school she would just do it when she got to school in the bathroom."* In a later talk I had with Marissa, she told me: *"My mom is nice and all but she is old fashioned and trying to ruin my social life and making me look like a baby to my friends. It is no big deal that I wear makeup, and meeting high school boys at the mall is what everyone does all the time. It's nothing serious, not like I am going to date any of them. But it is fun when they notice how sexy I look and talk me up."*

If, like Marie, you are concerned about the impact of television on your child's sexuality, your worries may be justified. Several decades of research on the impact of television on sexuality has demonstrated its undeniable effect on teens and young adults. Here is just a small sampling of conclusions:[20]

- Teens who watched more television dramatically overestimated the percentage of adolescents who have had sexual intercourse and initiate sexual activity earlier than those who watched less television.
- College students who watched one hour of an X-rated film with sexual violence showed increased acceptance of sexual infidelity and promiscuity.

- Teens who saw a movie about an unmarried couple having sex rated this behavior as less objectionable than peers who saw a movie about sex between a married couple.
- College students who watched *just nine minutes* of an R-rated movie showed more lenient attitudes toward rape.
- Teens who watched more sexual content on television had more negative attitudes about peers who were not sexually active.
- A study by the RAND Corporation showed that just watching television characters talk about sex had the same impact on teens' sexual behaviors and attitudes as watching them engaging in sexual activity.[21]
- Male adolescents who watched a television show starring sexy women in skimpy outfits were more likely to rate potential dates as unattractive.
- Girls shown television commercials about beauty products were more likely to rate physical attractiveness as important in getting a boyfriend.

This is not to say that television cannot have a positive effect on teen sexuality. For example, a Kaiser Family Foundation study examined the effect on teens of an episode of the television show *Friends*, where Rachel gets pregnant even though she and Ross used a condom. In discussing their problem, the writers had Rachel and Ross present information on condom failure rates, indicating that condoms are only successful at preventing pregnancy 95% of the time. The Nielsen ratings estimated that 1.67 million adolescents watched this episode and the researchers contacted a sample of 506 regular *Friends* viewers, both a few weeks after the episode and six months later. Nearly two-thirds of the teens recalled that condom failure was the cause of Rachel's pregnancy and one-third even knew the exact condom failure rate of 95%. As a result of this episode, 10% of the teens reported having discussed condoms with a parent or other adult. Teens who had this discussion were twice as likely to recall the condom information.[22] Additional studies of the positive impact of television have demonstrated that four factors can decrease the likelihood of adolescent intercourse: (1) parents who monitor their teen's activities and know what they are doing and with whom, (2) parents who are more educated, (3) parents who indicate a disapproval of sexual relations between unmarried teens and adults; and (4) having two parents in the home.[23]

Interviews with two different teens, Natalia and Brandon, demonstrate the positive and negative impact of television on sexuality. According to Natalia,

"My friends and I talk a lot about 'our shows' the next day. Since most of them show people having sex or talking about having sex, it is usually one of the first things anyone talks about. It's strange. I don't want to have sex until I meet someone and really fall in love, but sometimes we just talk about how stupid it is to stay a virgin when everyone is having sex. I don't mean every one of my friends, but everyone on TV."

Brandon presented a different view:

"My parents are pretty strict about what I can watch on television. Most of the time they make me TiVo it and then one of them watches it to make sure it isn't all about sex. Even if it is most of the time they let me watch it—well, except for the really raunchy ones—but they talk with me about it first or sometimes after. I know that most of my friends will disagree, but I think that there is too much sex on TV and it makes it way too easy to just figure that everyone is doing it so why not do it, too. I don't really want to 'save myself for marriage' but I don't just wanna jump into bed with everyone I meet like they do on TV."

Sexuality in Other Media

It is not just television that adversely affects teen sexual attitudes and activities. Other media, such as video games, movies, magazines, and music videos, provide sexual images that impact teens. For example, a study of U.S. teens showed that after being exposed to hardcore pornography, two-thirds of boys and 40% of girls wanted to try out some of the behaviors they saw. In fact, 31% of the boys and 18% of the girls did so within a few days.[24] Many parents are unaware that video games display graphic sexual images, even those expressly developed for a younger teen audience. A random sample of four hundred video games rated "T" for teens found that although 15% noted "sexual themes"—a guide for parents posted on all videos—the actual incidence of these themes was twice that number and nearly one in four T-rated games contain profanity and partial nudity.[25] When teenage boys play video games filled with scantily clad female characters depicted as sexual objects, they are more likely to objectify women, form negative stereotypes, and develop negative attitudes toward girls.[26]

Even reading teen magazines has been shown to negatively impact adolescent girls' body image and sexual attitudes and behaviors. One study, for example, found that girls who read teen magazines believed more strongly that girls need to be beautiful to attract a man and that it is acceptable for women and girls to be the objects of male sexual desire.[27] Magazines also impact boys, as shown in a study in which college males who were shown centerfolds from *Playboy Magazine* and *Penthouse Magazine* were found to be more likely to rate their girlfriends as less sexually attractive than before they viewed the magazines.[28] It is not just magazines such as *Playboy* that should concern parents. The average teen girl magazine contains eighty column inches per issue on sexual topics.[29]

Music videos are primarily focused on tweens, teens, and young adults, and many are highly sexualized. Research has shown that between 20% and 50% of these videos show sexual content with an average of ninety-three sexual situations per hour including eleven depicting intercourse and oral sex.[30] Several studies have linked music video viewing to sexual attitudes with the following findings: (1) teens who watched one hour of MTV were more likely to approve of premarital sex than those who watched a show without sexual content;[31] (2) those exposed to more degrading music videos were more likely to initiate sex than those who did not view those videos and were more likely to assert that it is acceptable that women are sexual objects and men are sex-driven pursuers of women;[32] and (3) girls who watched more than fourteen hours of rap music videos per week were more likely to have multiple sex partners and also more likely to have an STD.[33]

It is clear that tweens and teens are bombarded by sexual content and lawmakers have, for the past decade, attempted to protect children by enacting, or attempting to enact, laws and by providing money for programs that teach teens to stay virgins until marriage. In 1996 Congress passed the Communications Decency Act, which prohibited sending and displaying offensive materials to minors. It was struck down as unconstitutional by the Supreme Court. In 1998 they passed the Child Online Protection Act. The U.S. Supreme Court overturned it. In 2000 they passed the Children's Internet Protection Act and in 2006 the Deleting Online Predators Act, both designed to block access to sexual materials and social networking sites such as MySpace at libraries and schools. Given that most adolescents access the Internet from their bedrooms at home, these acts are ineffectual at best.

Congress and MySpace continue to pursue avenues to protect tweens and teens from online sexual predators. This may be an impossible task given the ease of online deception. As an example of this, a teenage girl in one of my research studies passed along a posting from "Troy" that she received on MySpace, as a way of showing me how sexual solicitations can appear quite innocent. As an aside, the girl told me that before she deleted his message she sent him a scathing e-mail telling him how disgusting he was and also forwarded the message on to the MySpace security department. Here is Troy's message. I have not cleaned up any of his language, so you can see how one might believe he was just a teenager out to have fun. There is no way to validate his age, but having spoken at length with Kurt Eichenwald, who wrote an exposé in the *New York Times* on online pedophiles, I would guess that he would tell me Troy was most likely an adult, trolling for photos to post and sell to other pedophiles.[34]

> "hi ok so im troy , and i know this might be a little wierd but please work with me haha , ok so me and my friend are super borredd and he had a bright idea of making a bet that he htought he could win , but he bet me fifty dollars and public imbarassment that he could get more than i oculd , and the bet is like this , were seeing who can get the most girls to send a picture of them in like, (you dont have to show your face or nething if you dont want to) a thong , or boyshorts , w/e your into wearing nowadays , and it would be really greatly appriecatied if you could help me out!! i will do like literally anyhting for you!!!
>
> Thanks—Troy"

Given the difficulties in protecting children from sexual media, lawmakers have tried to focus on educational programs to teach children about "appropriate sexual behavior." In 1996 Congress signed into law the Personal Responsibility & Work Opportunities Reconciliation Act. A portion of this act set aside $250 million for state-sponsored programs that advocated sexual abstinence outside of marriage as the only acceptable standard of sexual behavior for adolescents. Programs were established, funded, and evaluated, and teens were asked to take a "virginity pledge" to remain abstinent until marriage. At first, the education programs were touted as successes with proponents pointing to the decreasing rates of both teenage pregnancy and teenage births in the United States over the same time period. However, due to different approaches used for evaluation, it is difficult to make a sweeping comment about the effectiveness of abstinence-only programs. A summary of program evaluations in ten states reported, "Evaluation of these programs showed few short-term benefits and no lasting, positive impact. A few programs showed mild success at improving attitudes and intentions to abstain. No program was able to demonstrate a positive impact on sexual behavior over time."[35] Other studies have replicated these findings with results showing that (1) young people who took the pledge were one-third *less likely* to use contraception when they did become sexually active than their peers who did not take the pledge; (2) those who took the pledge *did not decrease* their rate of STDs; and (3) those who took the pledge were *more likely* to engage in oral and anal sex.[36] Overall, it is clear that teaching teens and preteens to abstain from sexual intercourse until marriage is most likely not the solution to counteracting persuasive media messages promoting or normalizing teen sexual activities.

Before dealing with what you can do to help your child develop their sexual identity, it is important to talk about psychologists' findings on why the media has such a strong impact on teen sexuality.

Psychological Theories

Three major psychological theories have been formulated to explain how and why the media's depiction of sexual themes might impact adolescent sexual behavior. Each has its merits and each suggests possible ways of assisting children in developing a healthy sexual identity.

#555   11-13-2011 7:22PM
Item(s) checked out to Thomas, Andrea Ju

TITLE: Social networking
BARCODE: 00000002444260
DUE DATE: 12-04-11

TITLE: You are not a gadget : a manifest
BARCODE: 00000002374576
DUE DATE: 12-04-11

TITLE: Me, MySpace, and I : parenting th
BARCODE: 00000002298472
DUE DATE: 12-04-11

Social Learning Theory

Based on decades of research with animals, children, and adults, Dr. Albert Bandura of Stanford University developed social learning theory, which has a wealth of data to support its assertions that we learn through a combination of personal direct experience and indirect or vicarious experience by watching others learn. For the former, social learning theory says that we continue to display behaviors when we have been reinforced for doing so, and we discontinue behaviors when we have been punished for them. These are the core ideas behind behavioral psychology, although both reinforcement and punishment are often greatly misunderstood. Reinforcement does not necessarily mean a "reward," nor does punishment imply spanking. Both have other, more effective ways to promote learning. I discuss choices of reinforcers and punishers at the end of this chapter, but first let me address how children learn how to behave through modeling.

A major tenet of social learning theory is that behaviors are learned through observation of what happens when others perform a behavior. A child sees someone perform an action, pays attention to whether that action was reinforced or punished, and then decides whether it makes sense to perform the same action. Although much of this research has focused on how children model aggressive behaviors, the theory is easily applicable to modeling sexual behaviors. According to RAND scientist Dr. Rebecca Collins, "Exposure to the social models provided by TV also may alter beliefs about the likely outcome of engaging in sexual activity. Social learning theory predicts that teens who see characters having casual sex without experiencing negative consequences will be more likely to adopt the behaviors portrayed."[37]

In a classic study, Bandura exposed preschool children, ages three to six, to models exhibiting either aggressive or nonaggressive behaviors. The experiment took place in a playroom that had a variety of interesting toys. In the center of the room was a Bobo doll, which is an inflated toy that is about the height of a preschool child, but has a sand-filled bottom so that it stands up and when struck falls down and rights itself. The child sat in a chair in one corner while an adult sat in a chair in the opposite corner. In one condition, the adult would get up, strike the Bobo doll repeatedly and yell at it for about ten minutes. Another group of children watched an adult play with the toys nicely and not hit or yell at the Bobo doll. Regardless of the initial adult's behavior, another adult would take the child to a second playroom with another Bobo doll, as well as aggressive toys (rubber hammer, dart guns) and nonaggressive toys (tea set, crayons, dolls). The child was then left alone to play with the toys for twenty minutes while Bandura watched from behind a two-way mirror and recorded the number of aggressive behaviors.

Bandura found that the boys and girls both exhibited more verbal and physical aggression when they had seen the adult strike and yell at the Bobo doll, with boys showing more physical aggression than girls, but all children exhibiting the same amount of verbal aggression. Both boys and girls who saw the adult being aggressive with the doll were more physically and verbally aggressive than those who saw an adult playing nicely. These results were even more dramatic when a boy saw an aggressive male model and a girl saw an aggressive female model.

Using the same paradigm, Bandura added a feature showing a vid-eotape of aggressive behavior. In this study, the children who saw the "live" model beating up the doll were more aggressive than those who saw the videotaped version, but the videotaped-version group was still more aggressive than a control group that saw no aggression, suggesting that children are capable of modeling television aggression. Another interesting study showed three versions of the film, one in which the adult hitting the doll was rewarded, another in which he was punished, and a final one in which nothing good or bad happened to the adult. Children who saw the adult aggressor being rewarded (reinforced) and those who saw nothing happen to the adult were more likely to beat up the Bobo doll than those children who saw the perpetrator punished, demonstrating the power of seeing the consequences of aggression.

In studies extending the Bobo doll research into actual televised content, researchers found that children who watched a violent show were more willing to hurt another child than were children who watched a nonviolent show. This was particularly true for boys, who were more affected by violent shows, while girls were only slightly affected. In addition, when the children were later allowed to play together, those who had viewed the aggressive program were more likely to play with weapons and aggressive toys than the children who watched the nonviolent show. Similar studies have validated these results time after time. In essence, violence begets violence and reinforced violence leads to even stronger violence.

Social learning theory has been applied to a wide variety of behaviors including the impact of imitating media-viewed sexual behaviors. Bandura's model makes it clear that seeing actors having sex—or even talking about having sex—with positive consequences, will likely convince the teenager that sexual activity is a normal, healthy activity.[38]

Cognitive Schema or Script Theory

When you walk into a restaurant you probably have a very clear idea of what will occur. First, you will be seated and given menus. Next, you will order and so on. If, for example, you were served food before you ordered you would be confused and wonder how that happened. This is because you have a "script" that tells you what to expect in a restaurant.

Scripts are specialized types of "schemas," first introduced by Professor Jean Piaget, the famous Swiss psychologist, to explain how infants learn. In his theory, children are born with a few schemas for reflex reactions, such as sucking milk during nursing. When a child is exposed to any situation in the world, Piaget said he or she must decide whether this situation is the same as an existing schema or warrants a new schema. Building new schemas embodies learning for the child and sets guidelines of how to act. A script is simply a schema that sets out events in a particular order.

Tweens and adolescents develop "sexuality" scripts that, as shown in the studies mentioned earlier, are shaped in part by the media. One study, for example, found that virgin girls, who believed that their favorite actresses portrayed high levels of satisfaction engaging in or talking about sex on the screen, felt less satisfied that they were virgins. In fact, the more sexual media content teens consume, the less satisfied they are with their first sexual experience. After all, the actors they love all have great sexual experiences in their TV shows and movies, and these viewings build a script about what to expect during sexual relations. Just like being served food before ordering, the teen gets confused when she expects a great first sexual experience and it is not. It simply wasn't supposed to be that way, according to the script.

Janica, an eighteen-year-old high school senior told me: *"I realized that I carried around a lot of preconceived notions about the world that I got from television. When I saw The Bachelor pick his bride and they were all so happy, I felt warm all over and then very sad because I just don't feel that way about my boyfriend and we have been together for eighteen months. I felt like I had to break up with him until I talked to my friends who told me that that was crazy. We love each other, but it is unrealistic to expect that love to be like we see on television. My best friend Kira told me that she heard that the bachelor and the woman he chose didn't really like each other enough to be together and all that 'love' they showed on the show was not real. Sometimes it is hard to tell what is real and what is fake on TV and in movies. I guess I have to learn not to let all that stuff change or shape how I feel."* Janica presents a perfect example of how media-created scripts can affect how people see the world.

Cultivation Theory

A third psychological theory that explains how we learn about sexuality is cultivation theory, first introduced by Dr. George Gerbner at the University of Pennsylvania. Cultivation theory arose out of a concern that television was not necessarily affecting children right after they watched a show, but rather, it had a cumulative effect over time. For example, if an eight-year-old boy watches violent cartoons or plays violent video games every day after school, this will eventually lead him to manifest more violent behavior himself. Gerbner contends that this is a slow, subtle process that can affect both people who consume lots of media and even those who consume much less.

Cultivation theory has vast implications for how the media affects sexuality in adolescents. Estimates are that on television alone, adolescents view fourteen thousand sexual references, innuendoes, and behaviors *per year*. That does not include movies, music videos, the Internet, or magazines. By the time a child reaches the age of ten he or she has seen so much sexual media content that sex appears to be natural, acceptable, and even commonplace. It was of little surprise when twelve-year-old Briana told me, *"Some of my friends are having sex with their boyfriends. It is no biggie. One of my older friends, I can't tell you who, has a 'sex buddy' who she can call any time and he will come over.*

They don't talk or anything—they just have sex. I don't really see what's wrong with that, but my friend's mom would freak. Come to think of it, mine would too if she knew I hung around with her."

Taken together, these three theories provide a strong framework for understanding teen online sexual behavior. No single theory is correct and my perspective is that sexual behavior is most likely a combination of all three processes. One such scenario would be as follows. A child watches thousands of hours of television, many depicting sexual content, by the time he or she reaches the teenage years. In those years, the teen has built up a plethora of scripts about sexual behavior that have been carefully and slowly cultivated over the years. Upon reaching puberty, and developing the natural, intense interest in sexuality, as described earlier in this chapter, our teen sees sex on television, in the movies, on rock videos, on the Internet, and consciously or unconsciously begins to imitate that behavior as a result of social learning. It is hardly surprising to me that teenagers have no problem exposing themselves on MySpace, participating in sex at a younger age, and having a cavalier attitude toward sexuality and sexual experiences. Those views have been cultivated, scripted, and imitated since childhood. This does not mean that you cannot influence your teen's view of sexuality. I firmly believe that you can, and I will show you how to help your children develop a healthy attitude toward sexuality in a world replete with sexual images beckoning them to join in. Before doing so, however, there are two more areas where cyberspace has impacted teen sexuality—cybersex, and exploring feelings about sexual orientation.

Cyberspace and Sexuality

Cybersex

Cybersex is where two people, connected through the Internet—usually using IM or chat—send messages intended to sexually arouse the other person. As reported in *Clinical Psychiatry News*, a research study reported that cybersex, particularly among middle school boys, is becoming pervasive.[39] Although there is not much research on cybersex among teens, some researchers have found that perhaps as many as one-third of adults engage in this activity. In one study, Dr. Al Cooper discovered that 17% of adults showed signs of Internet sexual compulsivity in that they could not stay away from engaging in cybersex.[40] The following quote is a good definition of what Dr. Michael Ross describes as the ability to "type without doing and do without being":

> "Part of its attraction is that sex has also become, through the Internet, 'fast'—it can be likened to take-out versus a sit-down meal. The advantage of the Internet is that it is able to be engaged relatively anonymously, and, in the case of cybersex, without having to leave the house and at any time of the day or night. Snacking at the sexual smorgasbord for cybersex is as easy as having a candy bar while sitting at the computer. Thus, while previously sexual contact with another person was limited largely to the 'eat out' or 'fast food' variety, cybersex has added a new possibility of having sex that is less lonely than masturbation."[41]

One way to understand cybersex behavior is through how it impacts identity formation. Erik Erikson defined late adolescence as a struggle between isolation and intimacy. What better way to address that struggle, in a safe, anonymous environment, than to engage in cybersex? While we have no figures on the number of teens who are involved in sexual activity on the Internet, we do know, from one study, that 90% of nine- to nineteen-years-olds have viewed pornography on the Internet.[42] While some of this porn exposure is intentional, a recent national study found that one in three teens and tweens have been exposed to pornographic pictures and videos unintentionally.[43]

Sexual Orientation

Online social networking has also greatly impacted the number of teens who are openly declaring their homosexuality or bisexuality. The Gay-Straight Alliance, a youth-led club on many middle school and high school campuses, was founded in 1998 to help gay, lesbian, bisexual, and transgendered teens deal with issues concerning their gender identity and sexual orientation in an environment with peers and straight allies. The popularity of GSA is no surprise given the U.S. Department of Health and Human Services study that found that 4.5% of boys and 10.6% of girls ages fifteen to nineteen had had same-sex contact, and this is just the number reported about a topic that is considered sensitive and private to many teens.[44]

The average age of teens "coming out" is just over thirteen, compared to the '90s when teens came out between fourteen and sixteen years of age, and certainly younger than decades before, when teens did not dare reveal their homosexuality until they were adults.[45] Until recently, gays were portrayed by the media as societal outcasts suffering from a mental disorder, but the appearance of regular, positively portrayed gay characters on popular television shows and in movies is changing that. This dramatic change in acceptance was highlighted in a Gallup poll that found that 54% of the American population finds homosexuality acceptable, compared to 38% in 1992.[46]

For teens, questioning their sexual orientation usually starts before their teenage years. As they reach their midteens, they realize that they are different from their peers, often feel guilty about their feelings, worry about responses from their family and friends, and feel that they have to hide their feelings at the risk of being teased and harassed. GSA clubs have helped this process, but nowhere are gay teens more welcome than on the Internet. There are numerous online Web sites and chat rooms devoted to gay teens. MySpace alone has more than fifty thousand groups centered on gay issues where teens can post questions, make comments, or simply remain in the background and observe how other similar teens handle their lifestyle.

Just listen to Guillermo, a sixteen-year-old who had known he was gay since he was eleven:

> "I felt like a loser at school like I had a big Q for queer pasted on my chest and like everyone was looking at me and laughing. A friend showed me a couple of chat rooms where kids like me could talk and that made all the difference. I made some incredible friends, some who I visited across the country and others who I have never met. They were all so helpful in helping me come out. I guess I came out online and that made it easier to come out in RL ['real life']. Now I have a MySpace page and where it says 'Sexual Orientation' I am happy to check 'GAY.' In my profile, in the 'About Me' section, I wrote about my coming out online and I got some great comments back, mostly from people sharing their stories about how being on MySpace or Facebook has helped them come out."

Clearly, sexuality is a major part of tween and teen development, and the media are feeding them a substantial, constant sexual media diet through television, movies, video games, magazines, and the Internet. From a psychological perspective, this inundation can have strong negative behavioral and attitudinal implications for teens, including earlier sexual experiences, negative body images, harsh sexual attitudes toward others, and the pursuit of cybersex and pornography. Efforts by lawmakers and social abstinence programs have not successfully protected your children, so it is up to you to use proactive parenting to help your children develop a healthy sexual identity. Here are some suggestions of what you can do to make this happen.

Proactive Parenting for the MySpace Generation

Controlling Television

In the Kaiser Family Foundation study mentioned earlier in this chapter, 63% of parents expressed a great deal of concern that their children are exposed to too much sex and violence on television. Even teens agree, with three out of four admitting that television influences the sexual behavior of their peers.[47]

The first issue here is the amount of television your teen watches. The American Academy of Pediatrics recommends that children watch *fewer than two hours of television per day.* Given that children spend hours every day watching television, both directly and in the background, your tween or teen will most likely laugh at you or nod agreement and then figure out a way to watch as much as he or she wants. Besides, it is not the amount of television watched, but rather the content on the television that is more important. I truly believe, however, that it is ineffective simply to restrict your child from watching anything that has sexual content. The same goes for using a television V-Chip to restrict what your child watches on television. As June told me: *"My mom won't even let me watch shows like* Friends *or* Survivor *because they talk about sex so I just have Desiree, my best friend, TiVo them for me and I watch them at her house while we are 'doing homework.'"*

In nearly every study of sex on television, the impact on negative behaviors and attitudes is greatly reduced if parents do the following. First, monitor what your teen watches, not necessarily to ban certain shows, but just to be aware of what is on the screen. Second, discuss what your teen saw on the show. For example, if you know that she watched *The Bachelor* ask her to tell you what went on during the show. Listen for mentions of sex or avoidance of the topic. Ask her directly if they showed any sexual contact or made sexual comments; remember, there is no difference in the impact of viewing sexual contact and hearing sexual comments on sexual behavior. Discuss these issues in a nonjudgmental and nonthreatening way. Your goal is to be aware of what media is affecting your teen and to be prepared to help him or her understand the meaning at an appropriate developmental level.

Third, as often as possible, watch television with your teen. If, like many teenagers, he or she has TiVo'd shows, pick one that you think might have sexual content and watch it together, and then talk about it. You do not have to watch for hours on end. One great aspect of TiVo is that you can pause and rewind the show to have time to talk or to pay attention again to what was being said and done. This is a golden opportunity to share time with your teen and also to attend to how he or she is handling sexual content on television. It is also important to point out to teens that the portrayal of sex on television is, at times, quite inaccurate compared to sex in the real world. Often television characters are shown having sex with no physical or psychological consequences. That is, sadly, not typical reality for teenagers. Talk about protection, or the result of the lack thereof.

Having *The Big Talk*

When I turned twelve my parents gave me a book called *Finding Yourself.* I think it was put out by the American Medical Association and was chock-full of drawings and technical explanations . . . and said nothing that would help me deal with what I was feeling about sex and girls. They gave it to my sister and then passed it on to my brother and somehow, mysteriously, we found it years later and gave it to my brother at his bachelor party.

My parents were avoiding *the big talk*; you know, the one about sex that most of us dread and avoid. A lot of parents I talk with just assume that the sex talk was taken care of by the mandatory health class in seventh grade. Nope. Teens get most of their information about sex from peers and the media. On the list, school health class is somewhere about 999th. What we do know is that *the big talk* does not have to be one big talk. According to nearly all specialists, you should start offering information about sexuality at a young age and continue to talk about the same material at appropriate physical, emotional, and psychological levels of development. Research shows that the more often parents and adolescents talk about sex in a positive and nonjudgmental way, the fewer sex partners and the less frequent sexual activity the teen will have. Here are my thoughts and advice:

1. Begin talking about human bodies at an early age—even as young as four or five—using words that the children will understand. Only answer questions they ask. Don't worry, as they get older they will ask more questions.

2. Even if you feel uncomfortable, act as though it is the most natural thing in the world to talk about sex.

3. As the children grow, say less and listen more. They will ask questions about what they want to know when they are ready.

4. Remember that your ideas about dating and sex are very different from theirs. Ask, don't assume. Research shows that parents who are more supportive and less judgmental when talking about sex have children who take fewer sexual risks.

5. Try to maintain a sense of humor. That doesn't mean laughing. Just try to keep the talking upbeat and positive.

6. Talk about your own discomfort right from the start. If you tell them how uncomfortable you are talking about sex, then they will feel better about their discomfort.

7. Talk about birth control as soon as you get an inkling that your teen is "in love" or any of your teen or preteen's friends are dating. Despite popular myth, talking about birth control does not make kids want to have sex. Research shows that teens whose parents discussed birth control *before the teen was sexually active*

were three times more likely to use effective methods and half as likely to have sex.[48]

8. Talk about other consequences of sexual activity, including emotional ramifications and STDs. If you don't know, don't guess. Go online with your teen and look up information about anything you are not sure about.

9. Do not try to make sweeping rules and pronouncements about your teen's sexual expression. Research shows that having too many strict rules about sex actually leads to more sexual activity.[49]

10. Do not try to instill guilt. Again, parents who use guilt as a tool to repress sexual expression end up with children who have more, not less, sexual activity.

11. Finally, let your child know that you are there, available and supportive. Don't make it difficult and stressful to talk. Make it easy and common. The more often you talk, the more often your teen will talk with you spontaneously.

Sexual Predators

Common Sense Media reported in 2006 that 85% of parents felt that among all forms of media, the Internet posed the greatest risk to their children. Although data show that in spite of media reports to the contrary, sexual predators are very rare, parents still worry about this possibility.[50] As an aid to parents, the FBI has published *A Parent's Guide to Internet Safety*, which can be found online at http://www.fbi.gov/publications/pguide/pguidee.htm. At this writing, the FBI Web site provides the following information for parents in describing individuals who attempt to sexually exploit minors.

> "Some of these individuals gradually seduce their targets through the use of attention, affection, kindness, and even gifts. They listen to and empathize with the problems of children and gradually lower children's inhibitions by slowly introducing sexual context and content into their conversations. Parents and children should remember that a computer-sex offender can be any age or sex and the person does not have to fit the caricature of a dirty, unkempt, older man wearing a raincoat to be someone who could harm a child."

Although I believe that these occurrences are indeed rare, and that the data show that teens are quite adept at effortlessly handling "come-ons" from strangers, it is important to recognize signs for teens who are susceptible to such seemingly innocuous, yet predatory behavior. The FBI says to be particularly aware of the following:

- Your phone bill includes calls to and from people you do not know.
- Your teen gets mail and gifts from people you do not know.
- Your teen talks about new "friends" you do not know and when you ask about them the answers are evasive.
- Your teen makes plans to meet or visit someone whom you do not know.
- Your teen turns off the computer monitor or quickly switches screens when you walk in the room.

What should you do if you suspect your adolescent is potentially the victim of a sexual predator? First and foremost, you should talk openly and calmly with your teen about your concerns. Do not turn this talk into a confrontation. Your tween or teen may not even understand that his or her "friend," who is so understanding and kind, may be someone who is acting inappropriately.

Second, make sure that you set rules that allow you to examine what your teen is doing on the computer. Avoid the temptation to sneak around and check out the computer when you child is not around. Instead, talk openly about your concerns and make an agreement that as the parent you have the right to look at any e-mail sent to or received from people you do not know. Go through your child's e-mail and contact list with him and have him explain who each person is and how he knows that person. Do the same for your teen's friends list on MySpace or any other social network site. If you are not convinced, ask to see any e-mail correspondence between them. If your teen has deleted all his communications, that should raise a red flag, and you and your teenager may need to contact the person together.

Third, establish that you have the right, at any time, to view any instant message conversation or anything at all on the computer screen. This is tricky because, as I have mentioned, teens have their own language to alert people that they are being monitored. Feel free to insist that you are allowed to scroll back through any IM conversation so you can see what is being discussed. One concern here is that teens often have conversations that are not sexual, yet might be embarrassing. Once you establish trust between you and your teen, be willing to listen if he says that he would rather you not read his IM, not because he is talking to an unknown "friend," but because he and his known friends are having a private conversation.

Most parents I interviewed echoed the sentiments of Marie, who said: *"I know that my fourteen-year-old daughter is doing things on the computer that I do not approve of, but every time I come into her room, the computer screen is on her schoolwork. The few times I have mentioned that I thought something was going on she got incensed and accused me of being a snoop. I am not sure what to do because I really don't know enough about computers to tell if she is doing anything to keep me from seeing what is going on."* Marie is typical of many of us who are not as computer savvy as our children. I gave Marie three pieces of advice. First, tell your daughter that if you suspect that she is shutting down screens or switching screens when you walk in the room, there will be consequences that will involve losing computer privileges (more about this later). Second, have your daughter or someone else who is knowledgeable about computers show you the following: (1) how to shut down a screen quickly, (2) how to access the "history" function, which lists all Web sites that have been visited, and (3) how to do anything else to disguise what she is doing online. It is best to have your teen show you this, but if she balks, tell her that noncooperation is not going to work in her favor in the long run, and have someone else show you these computer skills and more. It is important that your teen understand that you will be monitoring what she is doing whether or not she likes it, and it will be easier if she cooperates. I am not saying that all tweens and teens are deceptive. In fact, from my experience, it is not the norm. Remember, however, that you are striving to set rules and guidelines that are both parent-centered and child-centered, meaning that you consult with your teen but you set the rules based on those discussions. If you take a "give-and-take" attitude about these rules, this process will go much more smoothly.

My third piece of advice for Marie is to move the computer from her teenager's bedroom to a common area. When her daughter gets upset about this—which she will—my first and second pieces of advice may work better. Use this as a last resort and a consequence of specific behaviors. You don't have to move the computer forever; after all, they are portable. Perhaps you can make an agreement that the first infraction results in three days of the computer being moved and each additional violation of your rules increases that by three more days. It should take only one or two times to ensure her cooperation.

One thing to avoid are "parental controls" available through Internet Explorer and from some Internet service providers (ISPs) such as AOL. These are *supposed* to control access to specific Internet activities including Web sites, IM, and e-mail. However, for every new control created, there are a dozen Web sites devoted to getting around the controls. Besides, in the long run, it is much smarter to use appropriate parenting tools rather than attempt ironclad controls and/or subterfuge. You will feel better, your teen will feel better, and, in all likelihood, your controls will work better.

Although my research and that of others shows that Internet sexual predators are not as common as many people think, there have been enough tragedies to warrant special attention. The story below is a work of fiction. However, it still gives me a chill whenever I read it. Read it to your children, if only so they will see how easy it is for someone online to be deceptive.[51]

Shannon could hear the footsteps behind her as she walked toward home. The thought of being followed made her heart beat faster. "You're being silly," she told herself, "no one is following you." To be safe, she began to walk faster, but the footsteps kept up with her pace. She was afraid to look back and she was glad she was almost home. Shannon said a quick prayer, "God, please get me home safe." She saw the porch light burning and ran the rest of the way to her house. Once inside, she leaned against the door for a moment, relieved to be in the safety of her home. She glanced out the window to see if anyone was there. The sidewalk was empty.

After tossing her books on the sofa, she decided to grab a snack and get online. She logged on under her screen name ByAngel213. She checked her Buddy List and saw GoTo123 was on. She sent him an instant message:

ByAngel213: Hi. I'm glad you are on! I thought someone was following me home today. It was really weird!

GoTo123: LOL You watch too much TV. Why would someone be following you?

Don't you live in a safe neighborhood?

ByAngel213: Of course I do. LOL I guess it was my imagination cuz' I didn't see anybody when I looked out.

GoTo123: Unless you gave your name out online. You haven't done that have you?

ByAngel213: Of course not. I'm not stupid, you know.

GoTo123: Did you have a softball game after school today?

ByAngel213: Yes and we won!!

GoTo123: That's great! Who did you play?

ByAngel213: We played the Hornets. LOL. Their uniforms are so gross! They look like bees. LOL

GoTo123: What is your team called?

ByAngel213: We are the Canton Cats. We have tiger paws on our uniforms. They are really cool.

GoTo123: Did you pitch?

ByAngel213: No I play second base. I got to go. My homework has to be done before my parents get home. I don't want them mad at me. Bye!

GoTo123: Catch you later. Bye

Meanwhile, GoTo123 went to the member menu and began to search for her profile. When it came up, he highlighted it and printed it out. He took out a pen and began to write down what he knew about Angel so far.

Her name: Shannon

Birthday: Jan. 3, 1985

Age: 13

State where she lived: North Carolina

Hobbies: softball, chorus, skating and going to the mall

Besides this information, he knew she lived in Canton, because she had just told him. He knew she stayed by herself until 6:30 P.M. every afternoon until her parents came home from work. He knew she played softball on Thursday afternoons on the school team, and the team was named the Canton Cats. Her favorite number "7" was printed on her jersey. He knew she was in the eighth grade at the Canton Junior High School. She had told him all this in the conversations they had online. He had enough information to find her now.

Shannon didn't tell her parents about the incident. She didn't want them to make a scene and stop her from walking home from the softball games. Parents were always overreacting and hers were the worst. It made her wish she were not an only child. Maybe if she had brothers and sisters, her parents would not be so overprotective. By Thursday, Shannon had forgotten about the footsteps following her. Her game was in full swing when suddenly she felt someone staring at her. It was then that the memory came back. She glanced up from her second base position to see a man watching her closely.

He was leaning against the fence behind first base and he smiled when she looked at him. He didn't look scary and she quickly dismissed the sudden fear she had felt. After the game, he sat on a bleacher while she talked to the coach. She noticed his smile once again as she walked past him. He nodded and she smiled back. He noticed her name on the back of her shirt. He knew he had found her.

Quietly, he walked a safe distance behind her. It was only a few blocks to Shannon's home, and once he saw where she lived he quickly returned to the park to get his car. Now he had to wait. He decided to get a bite to eat until the time came to go to Shannon's house. He drove to a fast food restaurant and sat there until it was time to make his move.

Shannon was in her room later that evening when she heard voices in the living room. "Shannon, come here," her father called. He sounded upset and she couldn't imagine why. She went into the room to see the man from the ballpark sitting on the sofa. "Sit down," her father began, "this man has just told us a most interesting story about you." Shannon sat back. How could he tell her parents anything? She had never seen him before today!

"Do you know who I am, Shannon?" the man asked. "No," Shannon answered. "I am a police officer and your online friend, GoTo123."

Shannon was stunned. "That's impossible! GoTo is a kid my age! He's fourteen. And he lives in Michigan!" The man smiled. "I know I told you all that, but it wasn't true. You see, Shannon, there are people online who pretend to be kids; I was one of them. But while others do it to injure kids and hurt them, I belong to a group of parents who do it to protect kids from predators. I came here to find you to teach you how dangerous it is to talk to people online. You told me enough about yourself to make it easy for me to find you. You named the school you went to, the name of your ball team and the position you played. The number and name on your jersey just made finding you a breeze."

Shannon was stunned. "You mean you don't live in Michigan?" He laughed. "No, I live in Raleigh. It made you feel safe to think I was so far away, didn't it?"

She nodded. "I had a friend whose daughter was like you. Only she wasn't as lucky. The guy found her and murdered her while she was home alone. Kids are taught not to tell anyone when they are alone, yet they do it all the time online. The wrong people trick you into giving out information a little here and there online. Before you know it, you have told them enough for them to find you without even realizing you have done it. I hope you've learned a lesson from this and won't do it again. Tell others about this so they will be safe too?"

Shannon nodded and said: "It's a promise!"

I interviewed Dr. Kimberly Mitchell, Research Professor at the Crimes Against Children Research Center at the University of New Hampshire, and Dr. Stephen Russell, Associate Professor of Family Studies and Human Development at the University of Arizona. Here is what they had to say:

Q: Is exposure to sexual material on the Internet for today's teen any different from exposure to, say, *Playboy Magazine* for boys growing up in the '60s and '70s? If so, do you feel that it may be harmful to adolescent sexual development?

Mitchell: I would say that exposure to sexual material today is different than it was before the Internet. Today, teens have instant access to millions of different pornographic images, ranging from still images, as one would find in a *Playboy Magazine*, to extremely violent images or clips. While some of this exposure is voluntary, much is not. This degree of unwanted exposure may be a new phenomenon, since prior to the Internet there were few places youth frequented where they might regularly encounter unsought pornography. While there is evidence that most youth are not particularly upset when they come across pornography on the Internet, some youth could be psychologically and developmentally unprepared for unwanted exposure, and online images may be typically more graphic and extreme than pornography available from other sources. Exposure to online pornography may have reached a point where it is normal among youth Internet users, particularly teenage boys.

Q: From your two studies five years apart, do you feel that teens have gotten better at dealing with sexuality on the Internet?

Mitchell: There is some indication that over the past five years, teens have gotten better at dealing with sexuality on the Internet. Over the five years there was a significant decline in the percentage of youth who said they went to chat rooms, from 56% to 30%. Similarly, we also saw a decline in the percentage of youth who said they talked online with someone they did not know in person, from 40% to 34%. These two activities are strongly related to increased risk for online sexual solicitation and, as such, are often a focus of prevention messages about Internet safety. This suggests that some of these Internet safety messages are reaching youth and they are adjusting their behavior accordingly.

Q: What impact do you see, either positive or negative, that MySpace has on teen exposure to sexual materials and sexual solicitations?

Mitchell: Starting in early 2006, there was considerable publicity about the potential dangers of social networking sites, which have become increasingly popular with adolescents. Fears among parents, child advocates, and law enforcement seem to have arisen particularly from the amount of personal information youth post online at such sites. Media stories have suggested that predators could use the information youth post about their plans and activities to identify, locate, and stalk youth. Nonetheless, a close perusal of media stories suggests that online molesters have not changed their tactics with the advent of social networking sites. Online molesters do not appear to be stalking unsuspecting youth, but rather they continue to seek youth who are susceptible to seduction. In addition, findings from our study suggest that maintaining online blogs or journals, which are similar to social networking sites because they often display considerable amounts of personal information, is not associated with greater likelihood of aggressive sexual solicitation (i.e., solicitation that moves or threatens to move offline) unless youth also interact online with people they do not know in person.

Q: Given the prevalence of sexual material online, what advice can you give parents to help their teens reduce that exposure and deal with it in a developmentally appropriate way?

Mitchell: Filtering, blocking, or monitoring software is effective in lowering the risk of unwanted exposure and reducing wanted exposure among youth Internet users. Attending a law enforcement presentation about Internet safety appears to reduce unwanted exposure as well. Youth may pay more attention or give more weight to information provided by law enforcement. Also, simple presentations that provide specific information about how to avoid online pornography may be particularly effective when aimed at a problem like unwanted exposure, which in most cases does not seem be an outgrowth of hard-to-change youth characteristics or behaviors. Finally, parents should not assume that simply relying on these methods will keep their children safe 100% of the time. Talking with their children and being frank about the dangers of the Internet, as well as how youth behaviors themselves may impact their safety, is extremely important.

Q: How do you feel that allowing teens to express their sexuality online can affect their view of sexuality in the physical world?

Russell: Clearly the online world probably has cons that outweigh the pros—in general, when considering most youth. The versions of sexuality that are accessible, and the ways sexuality gets framed, are not always the most optimal and healthy. On the other hand, for some youth (particularly marginalized young people), there is the possibility of getting support and feedback that isn't possible in most places, for most youth, in person.

Q: In what ways do you see the media, including television, music, etc., in general impacting teen sexuality?

Russell: I think it makes these multiple sexualities possible in a way that was never possible before. It exposes young people to possibilities that are beyond the realm of their immediate families and communities. How can it not impact teen sexuality?—at minimum, it changes the ways that contemporary young people think about sexualities, if not their actual behavior.

Q: In what ways does the Internet make it easier for homosexual and bisexual teens to "come out?"

Russell: Well—that's just it. It is a possibility that simply didn't exist before—which in itself offers transformational (as well as dangerous) opportunities. Why is it easier? Because teens can test the waters on people for whom the stakes are lower—we know that they come out to friends, siblings, and parents (in that order)—working their way up to the most important people in their lives. Online life allows young people to experiment with their gay/bi identities in ways where the risks are fairly low.

Q: What can parents do to help their children handle the steady "sexual media diet" they receive?

Russell: *Talk* about it. Get online and learn about it. Set limits for what is permissible online . . . actually set limits to use of the computer and Internet.

Chapter 7

Just a Few More Minutes, Mom

◆

"I don't know what happens, but I think I am going to just check my e-mail and to see who is on IM and next thing I know it is three hours later."

—Dwayne, age 17

◆

"He has no sense of time. I ask him to get off the computer and fifteen minutes later he is still on. I have to tell him three or four times and then threaten to turn off the computer until I can get him off and to go to bed."

—Dwayne's mother

◆

"The use of the Internet can definitely disrupt one's academic, social, financial, and occupational life the same way other well-documented addictions like pathological gambling, eating disorders, and alcoholism can."

—Dr. Kimberly Young, Director of the Center for Online Addiction and Professor at St. Bonaventure University[1]

◆

How can you tell if someone is "addicted" to the Internet? This is quite a controversial topic in psychology. Dr. Kimberly Young, author of *Caught in the Net: How to Recognize the Signs of Internet Addiction and a Winning Strategy for Recovery*,[2] cautions that "Everyone's situation is different, and it is not simply a matter of time spent online. Some people indicate they are addicted with only twenty hours of Internet use, while others who spend forty hours online insist it is not a problem to them. It is more important to measure the damage your Internet use causes in your life."[3] With this in mind, in Table 7.1 (on pages 154–155) you will find Dr. Young's "Parent-Child Internet Addiction Test" (IAT). Take a few minutes and complete the test, considering only the time your child uses the Internet for nonacademic purposes when answering.

After you have answered the questions, add the numbers at the top of the IAT for each response. Here is Dr. Young's assessment of your child's total score:

20–49 points: Your child is an average online user. He or she may surf the Web a bit too long at times, but seems to have control of his or her usage.

50–79 points: Your child seems to be experiencing occasional to frequent problems because of the Internet. You should consider the full impact of the Internet on your child's life and how this has impacted the rest of your family.

80–100 points: Internet usage is causing significant problems in your child's life and most likely your family. You need to address these problems now.

If your child's score is in one of the latter two groups, go back to the test itself and look at all those answers that were "often" or "always." Pay attention to what your child is doing that indicates potential Internet addiction. We will touch on this more, later in the chapter.

How prevalent is Internet addiction? In a recent study of mine, 18% of all teen MySpacers were addicted to the Internet based on the addiction test score.[4] Little research has been done with adolescents, but the numbers seem to indicate that around 10% to 20% of teens are highly addicted to the Internet, with perhaps another 30% to 40% being moderately addicted.[5]

Even though being online longer does not necessarily mean that a person is "addicted," my research found that addicted teens were on MySpace twenty-one hours per week compared to nonaddicted teens' ten hours per week. Other research with adolescents has shown similar results, with addicted users spending upwards of fifteen hours per week on the Internet.[6] According to my research, addicted teens had more online friends, were more depressed, had lower self-esteem, and gave out more personal information on their MySpace page. Parents of addicted teens were more likely to adopt a parenting style with few rules or boundaries and were less likely to place any specific limits on MySpace usage.[7]

What Are the Signs of Internet Addiction?

Following is a list of fourteen signs of potential Internet addiction. Note that not all Internet addicts show all of these signs. *If your teenager shows even five of these signs, it is time to be concerned.*

- Denial and lying about the amount of time spent on the Internet
- Lying about what he or she is doing on the Internet
- Excessive fatigue
- Changes in sleep habits, such as getting up early or staying up late to be on the Internet
- Academic problems, including slipping grades, missed or poor assignments, lower test scores
- Declining interest in outside hobbies
- Spending less time with offline friends
- Loss of appetite and a need to finish meals quickly to get back on the computer; may include frequent requests to eat meals while on the computer
- Hostility and irritability when asked to stop using the computer
- Deliberately breaking rules about computer use
- Losing track of time while on the Internet
- Always saying "Just one more minute and I will be off the computer"
- Spending less time with family and friends
- Rushing to check e-mail or IMs as soon as he or she enters the house

Table 7.1 Parent-Child Internet Addiction Test (IAT)

Question	Not Applicable or Rarely (1)	Occasionally (2)	Frequently (3)	Often (4)	Always (5)
1. How often does your child disobey time limits you set for online use?					
2. How often does your child neglect household chores to spend more time online?					
3. How often does your child prefer to spend time online rather than with the rest of your family?					
4. How often does your child form new relationships with fellow online users?					
5. How often do you complain about the amount of time your child spends online?					
6. How often do your child's grades suffer because of the amount of time he or she spends online?					
7. How often does your child check his or her e-mail before doing something else?					
8. How often does your child seem withdrawn from others since discovering the Internet?					
9. How often does your child become defensive or secretive when asked what he or she does online?					
10. How often have you caught your child sneaking online against your wishes?					

11. How often does your child spend time alone in his or her room playing on the computer?

12. How often does your child receive strange phone calls from new "online" friends?

13. How often does your child snap, yell, or act annoyed if bothered while online?

14. How often does your child seem more tired and fatigued than he or she did before the Internet came along?

15. How often does your child seem preoccupied with being back online when offline?

16. How often does your child throw tantrums with your interference about how long he or she spends online?

17. How often does your child choose to spend time online rather than doing once enjoyed hobbies and/or outside interests?

18. How often does your child become angry or belligerent when you place time limits on how much time he or she is allowed to spend online?

19. How often does your child choose to spend more time online than going out with friends?

20. How often does your child feel depressed, moody, or nervous when offline, which seems to go away once back online?

Internet addiction is so prevalent that psychologists are lobbying to include an Internet Addiction Disorder (IAD) in the next Diagnostic and Statistical Manual of Mental Disorders (DSM-V), which psychiatrists and psychologists utilize to identify mental disorders.[8] Someone demonstrating *three or more of the following eight symptoms* in a twelve-month period would be considered to be suffering from IAD:

1. A need for increased amounts of time on the Internet to feel satisfied, or feeling less satisfied with continued use of the Internet for the same amount of time.
2. Symptoms of withdrawal developing within days to one month after reduction of Internet use, including anxiety, agitation, obsessive thinking about the Internet, dreams about being on the Internet, and typing finger motions when not online.
3. Disruption of social, familial, and occupational activities.
4. Being on the Internet longer than intended.
5. Persistent desire or unsuccessful efforts to cut down on Internet use.
6. A great deal of time spent on activities related to Internet use, including downloading music and programs, organizing material, etc.
7. Neglect of important familial, social, occupational, or recreational activities due to Internet use.
8. Continuing to use the Internet despite knowledge and awareness of its negative consequences.

Using these criteria, I suspect that many of our adolescents will be labeled with this addiction. Whether or not IAD is accepted, it is clear that Internet addiction is rampant.

Why Is the Internet So Seductive?

According to Dr. Sherry Turkle, a leading expert on human-computer interaction, the computer itself has what she calls "holding power." Unlike television, which is a passive activity during which the watcher has little control over the content other than changing channels, much computer use is quite active, giving the user considerable control.

Computer gaming, Internet surfing, e-mailing, and IMing, for example, all provide the user with continual command over the computer, directing all actions through the keyboard and the mouse. This explains why a "couch potato" is different from a computer addict; it is the difference between being a passive observer and an active controller.

Being in control provides the person a form of positive reinforcement. From decades of research with children and adults, behavioral psychologists have found that when an action is positively reinforced it increases in frequency. So the teen, sitting for hours and controlling his or her computer environment, is getting the equivalent of a steady stream of M & Ms as positive reinforcers. Each action produces a positive response, which then encourages more similar actions. It's no wonder that parents are having tremendous difficulty dragging their teens off the computer.

Several other factors make the Interent ripe for addiction. First, it is easy and convenient to access. Second, the anonymity and disinhibition of the Internet that I discussed earlier makes it safe to do and say nearly anything with few consequences. This means that the Web surfer, feeling free behind the screen, is continually gaining positive reinforcement from Internet activities. More reinforcement yields more of the activity, which can lead to addiction. Third, there is an accelerated intimacy on the Internet, where people meet and become best friends within days, if not hours. This is obviously tremendously reinforcing and leads to more time spent talking to your new best friends.

Time spent online is also distorted. An hour online seems like only minutes. It's not uncommon to go online for "just a minute" and find that several hours have passed. Dr. Kimberly Young refers to this phenomenon as a "Terminal Time Warp," in which the user is in a state that is similar to being hypnotized.[9] Research on video game playing, an activity that very often leads to a disruption in time perception, atttibutes the intensified focus as a combination of psychological absorption and flow. Psychologists define psychological absorption as providing total attention, including a commitment of all perceptual systems (sights and sounds), motor responses, and brain power to a single task. The gamer's brain is completely absorbed, making it hard for him to break away. Flow theory, developed by Dr. Mihaly Csikszentmihalyi, is a feeling of enjoyment, focused attention, engagement, and time distortion when fully engaged in an activity. Csikszentmihalyi describes this feeling of being "in the flow" or "in the zone" as "being completely involved in an activity for its own sake. The ego falls away. Time flies. Every action, movement, and thought follows inevitably from the previous one, like playing jazz. Your whole being is involved, and you're using your skills to the utmost."[10]

The Internet also provides a sense of escape or separation from real life. What they don't have in real life, they can obtain online. Feeling miserable or lonely? Just go online and you have hundreds of friends. Unhappy with who you are? Go online and become someone else. For the adolescent, it is an easy way to feel good that is not so easily obtained in the real world.

Finally, the Internet provides a means of control that most likely does not exist in the teenager's real world. You can be or do anything that you want online with no one standing over your shoulder ready to limit you. You can go anywhere, any time, without worrying about borrowing the car or getting mom to drive you. You can meet interestng people all over the world (the Internet truly is a "global community") and be what and who you want to be. The bottom line of control is that if you are not happy with some aspect of your Internet life, simply go away, re-create yourself, and start over again.

If your tween or teen is addicted to the Internet, there may be some negative consequences. Research with adolescents has shown decisively that Internet addiction can lead to the following:[11]

- Increased depression
- Decreased self-esteem
- Loss of real-world friends
- Increased obsessive-compulsive behaviors
- Increased hostility
- Increased nervousness and irritability
- Increased aggressiveness
- Increased impulsivity
- Increased emotional volatility
- Increased suicidal ideation

No wonder Internet addiction is being considered as a category in the Diagnostic and Statistical Manual of Mental Disorders.

Some psychologists have likened Internet Addiction Disorder to Attention-Deficit Hyperactivity Disorder, in that they share common characteristics. ADHD is a controversial diagnosis that afflicts children and teens through symptoms such as hyperactivity, forgetfulness, mood shifts, poor impulse control, and distractibility. Research on adolescents diagnosed with ADHD has shown that in addition to the above-listed symptoms, ADHD children tend to be hyperfocused in some situations, need continual stimulation, have difficulty with self-monitoring, and may be compensating for poor social skills. All of these characteristics closely ressemble addictive behaviors. Regardless of how it is labeled, Internet addiction can be a serious problem with adolescents and the symptoms need to be heeded.

As soon as people began to show symptoms of Internet addiction, psychologists began to pose theoretical explanations for the behavior. Although theories are not necessarily definitive, several provide interesting perspectives on this issue and also suggest possible interventions. Three such theories—psychological gratification, operant conditioning, and social cognition—are particularly interesting in their unique, but overlapping, perspectives.

Psychological Gratification

This theory explores how people obtain positive emotional responses leading to a fulfillment of personal desires. One research study by Indeok Song, Dr. Robert LaRose, Dr. Matthew Eastin, and Dr. Carolyn Lin identified seven major forms of Internet gratification, including:[12]

1. Virtual Community—finding people online who are interesting, developing online romantic interests, meeting new friends, and interacting with a whole world of potential friends.
2. Information Seeking—gaining information about products, news, sports, community, and health.
3. Aesthetic Experience—discovering and enjoying multimedia aspects of online life, navigating interesting Web pages, and immersing oneself in graphics and new features.

4. Monetary Compensation—purchasing products, finding bargains, saving money.
5. Diversion—having fun, feeling relaxed, entertained, and excited.
6. Personal Status—getting up to date on technology, improving personal prospects.
7. Relationship Maintenance—getting in touch with friends (new and old), getting through to someone who is hard to reach by other means.

Although these data were collected from university students, it is my belief that several of these "gratifications" are relevant to a younger MySpace Generation, specifically Virtual Community, Relationship Maintenance, Aesthetic Experience, and Diversion. When I asked fifteen-year-old Marcha why she likes MySpace, she responded, *"I get to talk to friends who moved away and I haven't seen since elementary school, plus it is just fun to make my MySpace page look cool with graphics and music and stuff."* In my own studies, 86% of MySpacers spent at least an hour a week working on their home page and nearly half tinkered with it for two or more hours a week. This qualifies as an "aesthetic experience" gratification. Here are some typical comments from other teens when asked what they like best about MySpace. From the viewpoint of this theory, it is easy to see what gratifications are being met.

- *"It gives me the ability to stay in touch with friends, without the need for instant messaging and e-mailing. And it lets me know a little more about them, and their friends."*
- *"Finding people I haven't seen in years."*
- *"I can see how everyone from high school is doing and I can talk to my friends and see pictures of them all the time."*
- *"The ability to upload music and display video . . . FOR FREE!!!"*
- *"It's just something to do for fun when I am home. There is enough stuff on MySpace to just hang out and check stuff out."*

Operant Conditioning

Behavior and consequences are the key components of operant conditioning. Made famous by Professor B. F. Skinner's work with rats and Professor Edward Thorndike's earlier research with cats, and then used extensively in research with children and adults, operant conditioning rests on the principle that following a behavior with a positive consequence increases the behavior (positive reinforcement) while a negative consequence (punishment) decreases the behavior. Based on these concepts, Internet behavior can be viewed as a sequence of mostly positive reinforcement of pleasurable behaviors. Spending time online brings positive consequences such as new friendships, fun games, and interesting Web sites, which, in turn, increases the desire to be online more. Like Skinner's rats that got their cheese at the end of traversing a complicated maze, Internet surfers are continuously getting their "cheese" through online activities.

Another feature of operant conditioning is called a "Discriminative Stimulus" or S^D. The S^D is an environmental event or condition that provides a cue for performing a specific (previously reinforced) behavior. The S^D is essentially what occurs directly before the behavior, often called an "antecedent." A glance at the computer can be a powerful S^D, reminding the teen of an urgent need to log on to MySpace. Just thinking about MySpace can be an S^D. For the Internet addict, anything that is remotely related to an online experience can act as an S^D, which then leads to positive reinforcement, further strengthening the power of the S^D. With this process, it is easy to see how an adolescent can build up an urgent need to be online, which can only be satisfied by being online increasingly more often.

Social Cognition Theory

While operant conditioning does not pay attention to what the person is "thinking," this model, popularized by Dr. Albert Bandura of Stanford University, addresses behavior changes as a function of both behavior and cognition or thinking. Social cognition theory rests on three major cognitive concepts—self-regulation, self-efficacy, and self-reactive outcome expectations—and "habit strength," which is the behavioral result of reinforcement or punishment. Self-regulation is the ability to monitor one's own behavior in terms of its impact on self and others. Self-efficacy is a belief in one's own abilities, and self-reactive outcome expectations are the behavioral or psychological rewards expected from a behavior. Social cognition theory is depicted in Figure 7.1.[13] Although this may appear somewhat complex, it is a statement about how Internet use—particularly Internet abuse—is a multilayered interplay between these four factors, plus a person's psychological state of mind. Figure 7.1 shows that the person's "psychology" influences how well that person regulates behavior and his or her expected rewards, which then combine with the other components to predict Internet usage. Internet addiction, as seen in social cognition theory, is then influenced directly or indirectly by a person's cognitions, reinforced behaviors (habit strength), and psychological state. When a person is depressed or lonely, this would directly affect their ability to regulate behavior and their expected outcomes (usually negative), which would then increase the habit of being on the Internet. All of these factors then combine to produce excessive Internet usage, which can lead to addiction.

These three theories—psychological gratification, operant conditioning, and social cognition—can provide insight into potential addictive behaviors. As a parent, it is important to attend to issues from all three theories and ask the following questions: In terms of psychological gratifications, in what ways is my child getting positive enjoyment from the Internet? Is it from communication and affiliation needs? Simply having fun? Enjoying the multimedia graphics and music? Or feeling personally enhanced in ways not available from real life? If the answer is "yes" to any of these, it may be important to question why it is taking excessive Internet use to obtain these positive

Figure 7.1 Social Cognition Theory Model of Internet Use

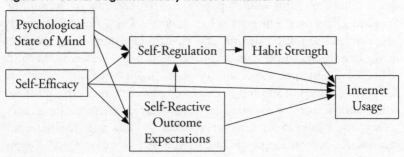

emotional responses. Discuss with your teen whether there are other ways that the same benefits might be gained, such as through sports, hobbies, after-school clubs, or other activities that do not involve the computer.

Effects of operant conditioning are more difficult to identify. Watch your teen to see what discriminative stimuli seem to prod him or her to get on the computer. When being on the computer seems so important, see if you can identify anything that might have happened to stimulate that need. Don't worry if it is not obvious, as many antecedents are internal. If it seems appropriate, ask your teen why he or she felt a "need" to get onto the computer at that moment. Don't be frustrated if the answer is "I don't know." Many discriminative stimuli are subconscious.

Finally, it is critical to pay attention to the features of social cognition theory. Starting at the left side of the figure on the previous page, ask yourself if there are any internal psychological factors that might be driving your adolescent to Internet addiction. Pay attention to issues of depression and loneliness, plus the other factors listed earlier as they have been identified as by-products of Internet addiction. Next, look at your teen's ability to self-regulate. Again, this is a factor associated with ADHD and a major feature in social cognition theory. Can he or she stop being on the Internet when requested, or does it seem to take a crowbar to get your teen away from the screen. Finally, it is important to try to ascertain what benefits or positive psychological gains your child expects from Internet use, including self-reactive outcomes from social cognition theory, as well as psychological gratifications and positive reinforcers mentioned earlier.

Looking at predictions from the three theories can teach us a lot about what to observe in our children's behavior. In addition, go back to the fourteen signs of Internet addiction presented earlier in this chapter and see how many fit your teen. The bottom line is that the first step in dealing with Internet addiction is being alert and observant to see what might be driving your teen's addictive behavior. Once you have found the precursors, then you will be better able to talk to your teen about changing those behaviors.

Dealing with Computer Addiction through Proactive Parenting

There are several strategies for helping an adolescent who either is already addicted to the Internet or may be showing the signs discussed earlier in this chapter. First, try proactive parenting. Use the information presented in this chapter to anticipate factors that might possibly lead to computer addiction and nip them in the bud. For example, where is the computer that your adolescent uses? If it is in his or her room, that may be a precursor to Internet addiction. Many Internet addicts change their sleep habits to be online more when others are online. With MySpace and online gaming, for example, there are always people all over the world available 24/7. Jeremy's mom described how she found out about her fourteen-year-old's addiction. *"One night, around 3:30 A.M., I couldn't sleep because I kept hearing a sort of tapping sound coming from down the hall. I grabbed a baseball bat and crept outside my door and down the hall until I realized that it was coming from Jeremy's room. When I opened the door, there he was, typing away on the computer and smiling to himself. I realized that he had seemed a bit overly tired lately and I just chalked it up to lots of homework since he seemed to have to be writing papers on the computer all afternoon and evening. It shocked the heck out of me to think that he had been doing this middle-of-the-night thing probably for months."*

Yelling at Jeremy and taking away his computer is not the answer. The first step is to recognize that like many teens, he has been given pretty free rein to use a computer with Internet access in his bedroom, under the assumption that he is doing schoolwork. There are two choices for solving this part of the problem. If you have a den or common area, move the computer there. Set up the computer in an area that won't disrupt normal traffic flow. If that is not possible, then you need to set up an "open door policy" for Jeremy's room. Whenever he is on the computer, the door must be open.

Regardless of whether you move the computer or use an open door policy, you should set up ground rules as follows:

1. You, the parent, have the right to look at your teen's computer screen at any time. And your child needs to know this and to agree to this stipulation if he or she wants to use the computer.
2. Looking at the computer screen means that you can see what Web pages are on the screen, view Web pages previously visited, read instant messages, read e-mail messages, view chat room transcripts, etc. It means you have complete access to anything and everything your child is doing and has done since sitting down at the computer. This can be a bit tricky because teens know way more about how to disguise what they are doing than parents. I recommend that you get your teen to show you how to read the "history" file on the Web browser. Each browser is different, but you can always click on the "Help" menu at the top of the screen and type the word "history" into the search box and it will show you how to read the history file. You should also set up your browser to keep this list for at least three weeks. To do this, once again use the Help menu to search for history; a help section will specify how to set the number of days the history is retained.
3. You must actually stop by the computer and take a look at what your teen is doing at least once a day in the beginning of this process. After that, it is enough to do it on a random basis.
4. Let your teen know that you are aware he or she may be tempted to close screens quickly upon your approach or clear the history or even switch to a different Web browser. See my later explanation of Behavioral Consequences for tips on proactively handling this potential situation.
5. If you suspect that your teen is doing something to hide activities, you will need to move to "Reactive Parenting Strategies," which I discuss next.

Reactive Parenting Strategies

If you suspect that your adolescent has crossed over the line and is possibly addicted to the Internet or MySpace, it is time for reactive parenting. This is where you should recognize that you must intervene to help your child. First, the tendency to simply remove the computer or disconnect the Internet connection will be overwhelming. This would be a major mistake as it will antagonize your child and just encourage him or her to get creative and figure out how to get online elsewhere. One twelve-year-old who was prohibited from going online at home would visit her friend when her friend's mom was at work. With no parental supervision, this girl could gleefully surf the Internet outside her own parent's control. Don't forget that your kids are Internet savvy. If there is a way around your restrictions, they will find it. The best bet for reactive parenting is to try one or more of the following strategies:

1. Stipulate what activities must be accomplished before your child gains Internet access. This may include homework, chores, or anything your child seems to neglect in order to go online.

2. Set a timer to limit Internet time. I recommend that you allow the child a sufficient amount of time, say an hour, to play on the Internet. To do this, you should buy an inexpensive minute minder clock—one of those white clocks with numbers from zero to sixty on the dial, which you turn to set the time before it winds down and rings (quite loudly). Set it for an hour and when it rings, immediately set it for five or ten more minutes, and tell your teen that when it rings again, he or she must be off the computer. My suggestion is that for every hour on the computer the teen spend from thirty to sixty minutes doing something off the computer. If they do not follow through, you will need to move on to the next steps.

3. Create a behavioral contract. This is a document where you stipulate: (1) expected behavior or behaviors and (2) *positive and negative consequences* if the behavior is or is not performed. I prefer a two-sided list with the behaviors you desire on the left and the consequences on the right. For example, if you want your child to be off the computer after one hour of use, your contract might look like that shown in Table 7.2.

Your behavioral contract can include as many behaviors as need be, but each behavior must always have a positive and negative consequence. We are too ready to punish children for misbehavior, but not

Table 7.2 Sample Behavioral Contract for Internet Behavior

Behavior	Positive Consequence	Negative Consequence
Be on the Internet for sixty minutes and then do something off the computer for thirty minutes	You get an extra sixty minutes of computer time on the weekend	You are not allowed to use the Internet for the rest of the day

very adept at reinforcing them for good behavior. I also recommend that you phrase the behavior in a positive direction and make it as specific as possible. Note that I could have put "Get off the computer in an hour," or "Don't stay on the computer too long," instead of framing it as a positive behavior with clear limits. Children respond well to clear behaviors and consequences. In fact, they crave them, although they may not understand that they do.

Once you have figured out that your child has a problem, it is important to pay attention to his or her moods. Expect that as soon as you start instituting some of these suggestions you are going to see a change in mood, and it will not be for the better. Anticipate hostility, aggression (particularly against other family members or objects), depression, and even tears and pleading. Use these moods in setting up your behavioral contract. If you want your child to be happy and smile, then you can make that a behavior that has positive and negative consequences. It may sound silly, but it works.

In your behavioral contract, it is important to make the positive and negative consequences reasonable. That means they are neither too excessive nor too punitive. A trip to Disneyland is too excessive and actually will not work once the trip is done. Grounding for a week will also not be effective in the long run, although it may initially seem to work. Interestingly, consequences that are based on activities (more computer time, later bedtime) work better than tangible reinforcers such as ice cream or a toy. And they don't cost anything, either.

One major issue parents grapple with is the constant arguing with their teens about spending too much time on the computer. Although it is tempting simply to remove the computer and Internet access, this is not a good solution. As Sherry Turkle pointed out, most kids are not even aware of how time flies when they are online. Try this experiment: When your teen goes on the computer write down the start time, and when he stops (or you make him stop) write down the stop time. Now, ask him to tell you how long he thought he was online. My guess is that he will radically underestimate his Internet time. This is Kimberly Young's "Terminal Time Warp" in action. Do this on a regular basis to help your teen get a better sense of online time. With this feedback in mind it will be easier for him to moderate his own online time. It may be advisable to have your teenager keep an Internet time diary where he writes down the time he begins and ends each computer session. Over time this will help in management of online versus offline time.

Finally, being online nearly always supplants other offline activities such as sports, visiting with family and friends, reading, or even sharing meals. Your teen may have forgotten how to spend time offline. If so, you will need to sit down with him or her and draft a list of potential offline activities so that when that minute minder rings, there is a list of alternative activities taped to the computer. Without this list, it will be easy simply to replace being online with another media activity like playing a video game. You can even list these alternative activities in the behavioral contract so that they are part of the plan. Remember, your goal is to help your Internet addicted child find his or her way back to the real world. Using these ideas will help get you there. The rest is up to you.

I interviewed Dr. Kimberly Young about Internet addiction. Here is what she had to say:

Q: Given that teens are spending huge amounts of time on MySpace, are they addicted to it or are they just being kids and hanging out in cyberspace?

Young: It depends. Certainly time online is not the variable to diagnosing compulsive use of the Internet. One needs to assess the extent of use as it impairs one's ability to function in other areas of their lives such as school performance or social activities.

Q: In your opinion, what is it about social networking that can be so addicting?

Young: That has always been the case. From the time I started studying Internet addiction in 1994, chat rooms and MUDs [multi-player, online computer games] were the most addictive applications (over pornography). So MySpace and Facebook are more geared toward teens and children and are like an electronic journal (replacing the old diaries).

Q: Compared to five years ago, why are we seeing more adolescent computer addiction?

Young: I think the biggest reason is the advancement in technologies. Five or ten years ago computers were still not in schools, or schools were just putting in the technology. Now children have greater access, and with greater access come more opportunities to become addicted.

Q: What would you do to help a teen addicted to MySpace who came to your clinic?

Young: It depends on the situation. Clinically, it is important to evaluate all the contributing factors. Does the child suffer from depression or anxiety problems? What type of activities has the child neglected because of the computer? How has the computer impacted the child's life? What are the typical computer habits of the child? Now you can start to get a picture of what role the computer plays and how this has specifically impacted that child.

Q: What should parents do to help their teens who are potentially addicted to the Internet?

Young: Treatment involves the family at every level. I work mainly with parents to learn how to help their children set better timelines and get involved in other offline activities. All parents get a copy of

"What Parents Can Do" to help them develop a plan to help their son or daughter.

Here's Dr. Young's guide:[14]

What Parents Can Do, guide by Dr. Kimberly Young

If you suspect your son or daughter may show signs of being addicted to the Internet, a carefully planned approach needs to be developed.*

- ◆ **Present a united front**—In a two-parent household, it is critical that both parents take the issue seriously and agree on common goals. Discuss the situation together and if necessary, compromise on your desired goals so that when you approach your child, you will be on the same page. If you don't, your child will appeal to the more skeptical parent and create division between you.

- ◆ **Assign an Internet time log**—Tell your child that you would like to see an accounting of just how much time they spend online each day and which Internet activities they engage in. Remind them that with television you can monitor their viewing habits more easily, but with the Internet you need their help and cooperation to become appropriately involved. Put them on the honor system to keep the log themselves for a week or two to build trust between you. If they balk at this idea or clearly lie in their log, you are likely dealing with their denial of addiction.

- ◆ **Set reasonable rules**—Many parents get angry when they see the signs of Internet addiction in their child and take the computer away as a form of punishment. Others become frightened and force their child to quit cold turkey, believing that is the only way to get rid of the problem. Both approaches invite trouble—your child will internalize the message that they are bad; they will look at you as the enemy instead of an ally; and they could suffer real withdrawal symptoms of nervousness, anger, and irritability. Instead, work with your child to establish clear boundaries of limited Internet usage. Perhaps an hour per night after homework will fit, or a few extra weekend hours. Stick to your rules and remember that you are not simply trying to control him or her—you are working to free him or her of a psychological dependence.

- **Make the computer visible**—Move your child's personal computer out of his or her bedroom and into the more visible kitchen or dining area. You do not want to stare over his or her shoulder every minute he or she is online, but by coming near the area now and then in your normal home activities you send the message that the Internet is not something he or she can use on the sly. If your child needs privacy to write a paper on the computer, allow him or her to move it back to the bedroom temporarily, but keep the modem in your possession so you will know when they go online.

- **Support, don't enable**—Parents often fall into an enabling role with an Internet-addicted child. They cover up or make excuses for their children when the children miss school or fail to meet deadlines. In the name of keeping peace they give in to their children's demands when the children complain loudly. If your child does rebel against your intervention efforts, let the first storm subside. Acknowledge their feelings—it must not be easy for them to feel that you are tugging at their only lifeline—but stick to your goals. Validate them for any effort they are making to work with you. Remind them that other kids have had problems with the Internet and that they found a new way, and that you support them in making these difficult changes.

- **Use outside resources when needed**—If your child is unable to moderate his or her Internet usage and the initial problems persist, along with new hostility in your relationship with them, it's best to seek outside help. You might visit a local alcohol and drug treatment program to gather more information about addictions. School counselors can also help alert you to your child's behavior at school. Ultimately, family therapy may be your best bet to help guide your child's recovery, address family strife, and heal wounds old and new.

* Used with permission from the Center for Internet Addiction Recovery at www.netaddiction.com.

Chapter 8

MySpace and Your Family

◆

"She comes home, rushes through her chores, tells me she has no homework and then jumps on MySpace. I didn't realize what was going on until she brought home four Cs, a D, and one F on her report card."

—Mom of a fourteen-year-old girl

◆

With their own computer, Internet access, video games, cell phone, iPod, and a dozen other gadgets, tweens and teens today have to leave their rooms only to go to school. Many spend more hours using technology in their rooms than they do in the classroom. Granted, some of this technology time is used for homework, but the vast majority is spent technologically multitasking.

By the time children hit adolescence, parents play second fiddle to friends and activities. I remember being about sixteen years old and chuckling at a chart in *Mad Magazine*. The diagram listed ages on the left, beginning at birth, and on the right pictorially ordered important people in the child's life. At birth, for example, a picture of a mother was first, followed by one of a father, and then the pediatrician. By the age of two, the parents were followed closely in influence by the child's siblings. By the early tweens, a best friend had assumed the most important position, followed by other friends, while mom and dad had fallen down the list. Although tongue-in-cheek, this visual depiction is actually quite accurate according to developmental psychologists.

Spending more time with friends and less time with parents is normal. But we know that much "friend time" is now spent conversing on the Internet. What is the impact of this on family relationships? In 1995, a research team from Carnegie Mellon University started a unique project in which they gave home computers and Internet access to families who had never had them and tracked their use and impact over several years. Initial results found that in spite of the Internet being a vehicle for social interaction, these Internet users experienced a drop in communication with close friends and family.[1] Two years later, after gathering more information, the authors now found that their earlier results were most likely a product of the "newness" of the Internet and that use of the Internet now had a positive impact on social relationships.[2] Recent studies by the Pew Internet & American Life Project have concurred that Internet users are actually more likely to visit with friends and family than those who do not go online.[3]

These studies were all performed before the appearance of MySpace and its overwhelming impact on adolescents. Now, instead of just surfing the Internet and sending e-mail, teens are actively involved in constant social interaction, often with many friends simultaneously. What impact does this have on the family? In my research, parents felt that time on MySpace interfered with family time, schoolwork, outdoor activities, and chores.[4] Here are some comments by parents of MySpace teens:

- *"He doesn't ever get his homework done before midnight because he is always on MySpace. Even if I try to get him off, he sneaks back on."*
- *"When I call him for dinner he takes forever to come downstairs. Sometimes I have to yell three or more times and send his sister up to get him. Even then he scarfs down his food and rushes back upstairs."*
- *"I am worried that he never has any friends over to play anymore. He tells me that it is easier to talk to them on MySpace, but that's not 'real' friendship at all."*

Other parents have told me that they are concerned about specific MySpace activities and how they affect their family. One parent of a thirteen-year-old boy told me, *"I worry about him making inappropriate contacts and giving out too much personal information that would allow someone to find our house."* Another mom told me, *"I found out that she posted information about her sweet sixteen party on MySpace and a whole bunch of kids who were not invited showed up and starting causing problems. My husband tried to get them to leave and then had to call the police. Needless to say, her party was a disaster."*

Nearly every parent I've worked with over the years has echoed similar sentiments. More time on the computer equaled less time spent on family activities. This leads to reduced family communication, which is a precursor of family conflict. Family cohesion, which is the emotional bonding that family members have with each other, depends on shared activities, supportive behavior, and affection. Research shows that less time spent together leads directly to less family cohesion. In contrast, when family cohesion is strong, children manifest higher school achievement, fewer behavior problems both at home and in school, reduced episodes of truancy, and less chance of dropping out of school.[5]

During adolescence family interaction is already reduced, which makes any further decline all the more problematic. One study of adolescents showed that increased time on the computer is strongly related to reduced family time. Interestingly, this result depended on the type of computer activity. When the computer was used for educational purposes, family cohesiveness was not affected by teens spending more time online; when it was used for social purposes, family interaction was affected negatively.[6] In addition, although television watching also reduces family time, its impact on the family pales in comparison to the impact of computer use on family time.

Family troubles are among the most common issues facing psychologists. Many derive their training and expertise from family systems theory. Let's first take a look at some aspects of that theory and then see how it can help us understand the impact of MySpace on the family structure.

Family Systems Theory

Family systems theory has been applied to situations such as teens spending too much time on the Internet to explain why and how families function poorly and what can promote family interaction. One of the central tenets of this theory is that families organize themselves to perform the tasks of daily life while, at the same time, accommodating the needs of their members. A family systems approach begins with the principle that we must look at the family as a whole, but realize that it is more than the sum of its parts. Technology has created problems for family systems as the parts—the parents and children—are often enmeshed with technology. Adolescents spend much of their time glued to the screen, which drastically reduces time available for family interaction. Parents, on the other hand, believe—but in reality mostly hope and pray—that the computer is being used for schoolwork.

Family systems theory, as it pertains to the use of technology, focuses on seven major concepts—hierarchies, dyads, triangles, boundaries, differentiation, homeostasis, and communication. Although each is important in its own right, there are complex interactions between them in which a change in one part of the system has ripple effects that impact all parts of the family.

Each family is composed of hierarchies, which are ways of organizing members in terms of influence and power. Mom and dad should form the top hierarchy with the children on lower rungs. However, when it comes to technology, the hierarchy is turned upside down. MySpacers, born amid technology and raised on the Internet, know decidedly more about technology than their parents. So, when it comes to family functions surrounding technology, the hierarchy is reversed, with the kids at the top and the parents below. This creates a situation ripe for family discord as it places the family power structure out of balance.

Dyads, or groups of two people, are an important element of this theory, as well. In family systems theory the focus is not on the individual, but rather on the interactions between family members. In a family of two parents, plus a son and a daughter, for example, there are only four individuals, but there are six dyads: mother/father, mother/son, mother/daughter, father/son, father/daughter, and son/daughter. Each dyad also forms a hierarchy of sorts, with one member having power over the other.

Whenever two dyad members have a problem with each other, they will often "triangle in" a third family member as a means of stabilizing the dyadic relationship. For example, if two children are having a disagreement, a parent will enter into the situation, forming a triangle to calm the situation, provide a solution, and restabilize the dyad. But just having functioning dyads does not necessarily ensure family cohesion. The other components, particularly boundaries, are important to establishing a healthy family system.

Boundaries are a critical component of a family system. Psychological boundaries, which are invisible, but based on relationships between people, prescribe what is part of a family system and what is not. Individuals also have "identity boundaries" that distinguish between what is part of that person's personality, needs, interests, and beliefs, and what is not.

For a family, boundaries separate the group from other groups by distinguishing between members of the family and others not in the family. In essence, boundaries specify a "family identity." Note that this is a broad definition of family, which means it can include people other than parents and children. To complicate matters, dyads also have boundaries, distinguishing what is part of the pair's identity and what is not. For example, mom and dad have their own boundaries that set them apart from other family members. These include intimacy, sexuality, and private matters that are not shared with others. According to Dr. Mark Dombeck, a family system expert:

> "Ideally, a family system (consisting of parents and children) will have a particular shape that works to help ensure the mental and emotional health of its members. Each parent needs to be able to trust the other parent and feel secure in their mutual bond. The parents need to identify themselves as parents and function together to coordinate their children's upbringing. Parents need to keep some information away from children (such as information about their sexual relationship, or worrisome information such as the state of family finances, etc.), but be sure to communicate other information clearly (such as their love for their children). Children ideally need to be allowed an age-appropriate amount of autonomy, but not allowed to have so much autonomy that they feel neglected or not also reigned in when that is necessary. Most families decidedly don't manage to do all of this perfectly, but many do manage to pull off enough of these goals to make it work."[7]

Boundaries establish bonds between family members. Equally important, each family member needs to possess his or her own sense of self, separate from other family members. This is called differentiation. At the same time that mom is her own person, she must also be a member of dyads with each family member and form a sense of dyadic identity. In the family there is a continual struggle between separateness and togetherness that makes the entire system dynamic and changing at every instant. Each family member is challenged to be both an individual person and at the same time connected to their family members in a compatible, mutual relationship. It is a delicate dance and, as we shall see, technology has an insidious way of creating difficulties.

Finally, the entire family system is held together in a delicate balance called homeostasis. As you may know, in biology the term homeostasis refers to the manner in which an organism regulates its internal and external environment to maintain a constant condition that allows it to function optimally. It does this through a continual series of adjustments of its internal environment to changes in both its internal and external worlds. In a family, the internal world is each person's individual sense of self or identity while the external world consists of other family members plus outside influences. Homeostasis is a never-ending process that allows the family to function over time amid myriad individual and group struggles both from within and without.

Communication is what drives the family system. Healthy communication among dyads creates a sense of homeostasis by allowing members to maintain their independence while functioning as a member of the group. Poor communication works to upset the homeostatic boundaries and create conflict, which then leads to dysfunction. The term "dysfunctional family" simply reflects one that is out of homeostasis.

Technology and the Family System

With these details about family systems theory in mind, let's take a look at what happens when technology enters the system. Janet, a single mom of three boys, ages eleven, fourteen, and seventeen, told me that her greatest family struggles concerned the Internet. Janet had one computer for the boys, located in the oldest one's bedroom, and another in her bedroom, which was available for everyone to use. In our interview, Janet told me how technology had created rifts in her family.

"Freddy, my oldest, has his own computer that he got from his dad when he started high school. From day one he was on it all day long, mostly playing video games since I had not allowed him to get an X-Box or any other game system. His dad and I disagreed about this but I finally gave in as long as he did his homework first before he started playing games. When Mikey turned thirteen he started nagging me that he needed a computer. I told him to share with his brother and we had a long family talk about this. We even drew up a schedule of when he could use Freddy's PC but every time he tried to use it Freddy had some excuse about how he was right in the middle of the game or he was doing his homework. I finally decided that I had to get another one but didn't want to put it in Mikey and Benny's room, because I worried that Benny was too young and might get hooked, too. So, even though I really didn't need a computer myself, I put it in my room in the corner with a desk. What a mistake! It got so bad that I had to scream and yell at Mikey nearly every night to get off the machine so I could go to bed. The final straw was when he acted like I wasn't even in the room and I had to actually yank the plug out of the wall. He was so mad at me that he didn't talk to me for a week. He refused to eat with us and wouldn't do his homework. Just sat in his room and moped. I was so upset that I screamed at all three of them for an hour and told them all that there was no more computer use for a week until we got it all figured out. Freddy immediately called his dad who called me all pissed off and threatened to take me back to court for endangering his children."

Janet is in the midst of a family crisis. In terms of family systems theory, there are several salient issues going on simultaneously. First, there are some dyadic relationships that are out of balance—Janet and her ex-husband, Freddy and his dad, Freddy and Mikey, and Mikey and his mom. In fact, as you might guess, this computer issue probably affected all ten possible dyads if you count Janet's ex-husband in the mix.

Janet was also facing other family systems issues. These include hierarchies, triangles, boundaries, differentiation, homeostasis, and communication.

Clearly the computer had turned the family hierarchy upside down. Janet felt like she was no longer in control, but rather that her children had assumed power with respect to the technology of the computer. Another parent of a nine-year-old girl told me, *"I am amazed at how Annie's fingers seem to fly across the keyboard. The few times I have tried to understand what she is doing she looks at me like I am a zombie from some horror flick. I pretty much stay away from the computer when she is on and if I am on and there is something I need her to do she just reaches over my shoulder, taps a few keys and walks out. She is my computer guru and it seems a bit strange."* Annie is not unique. I remember hearing a story from a fellow professor about how he had some trouble with his computer and went to an online support site that offered a chat conversation with an expert. Someone named Damon told him what to do and after fixing the problem my friend asked him how he got into this field. Damon said he did it on the side for extra money and when my fellow professor asked what he did for a living, Damon paused for a moment and said, *"Nothing. I go to middle school."* That was quite an eye opener. Our children have grown up with technology and it is as natural to them as the air we breathe.

With respect to triangles, Freddy created one by inviting his dad to join the argument with his mom. In this case, the triangle not only did not help smooth out the dyadic relationship, but it also created more problems between Janet and Freddy. In addition, by adding their dad to the dyad of Freddy and Benny, ostensibly to solve the problem of the computer in their room, they formed another dysfunctional triangle.

The computer problem also disrupted boundaries for Janet and her family. It is most likely that the family identity included only Janet and her three sons. By reintroducing the dad (and ex-husband), this boundary was disrupted, causing clear problems between all parties. However, there are other identity boundaries that may have been encroached upon, including the boys' privacy in their room. Each boundary "violation" increased the chance for family disharmony.

The children each had their own identity that fostered their all-important "separateness" in the family structure. Freddy's separateness was impinged upon when Janet offered the other children use of his computer. Then Janet threatened the differentiation of the other boys when she placed the computer in her room, rather than in theirs. Finally, Janet most certainly sacrificed her own separateness when she decided to lodge the second computer in her bedroom. All in all, togetherness appeared to be lost amidst an attempt for each boy and Janet to assert his or her own identities.

There is no doubt that, as a result of the growing computer crisis, family balance was out of sync. In this situation, although nobody was in the wrong, none of the participants were blameless in upsetting familial homeostasis. Rather than lay blame, however, we must look instead at what the family can do to regain their sense of equilibrium.

Finally, family communication was complex and problematic. The kids were not talking to their mom. Janet was so angry that she was making decisions without consulting the kids, and, to top it off, the children included their dad in the communication loop, which now infringed on his outside communication with his ex-wife. Overall, the breakdown in communication was a major family systems issue.

What Can You Do?

1. Develop a Healthy Parenting Style

Dr. Diana Baumrind, a clinical and developmental psychologist at the University of California, Berkeley, and other researchers[8] identified four major parenting styles—authoritarian, indulgent, authoritative, and neglectful.[9] The differentiation between these parenting styles centers on two issues: how demanding the parent is of the child and how warmly the parent relates to the child. Demandingness refers to how parents set limits and rules and their expectations for their children to comply with those rules. The second dimension, warmth, indicates how responsive parents are to their children's emotional and physical needs.

Authoritarian parents are demanding and not necessarily warm in relating to their children. They are also parent-centered, meaning that they demand obedience to all of their rules and they set the rules with no discussion or questioning. Violation of the rules results in punishment, which is often quite severe. Successful behavior is rarely or never addressed, and reinforcements are few and far between for these children. Contrariwise, indulgent parents are child-centered and permissive. They allow their children to function without many rules and even those rules are allowed to be broken. Limits are rare, but when they are established, it is usually with the agreement of the child. In essence, indulgent parents attempt to set up a lifestyle where there are no hassles or confrontations between their child and themselves.

Authoritative parents are also child-centered, but they are also demanding. They do set clear limits for their children, but those limits are often discussed and negotiated with each child. These parents both expect their children to follow the rules and enforce the rules they establish, although the consequences of violations tend to be much less extreme than those meted out by authoritarian parents, usually involving discussion rather than severe physical or verbally abusive punishments. These parents also focus on the positive, reinforcing successes in a consistent fashion. Finally, neglectful parents are neither demanding nor responsive to their child. They have no rules and basically let their children know that they would prefer not to be bothered with day-to-day issues and problems.

Children who live under different parenting styles have different psychological outcomes, both in the short and long term. For example, children of authoritarian parents tend to do moderately well in school and rarely exhibit behavior problems. However, they often have poor social skills, reduced self-esteem, and moderate-to-high levels of stress and depression. Children of indulgent parents are more likely to evidence behavioral problems at school and at home. They often do not do very well in school, but they do exhibit high self-esteem, fairly good social skills, and lower levels of depression. Children of neglectful parents fare the worst in all areas. They have behavioral problems, low self-esteem, and depressive symptoms, and do not have many successful social interactions. The children who are most psychologically healthy are those with authoritative parents. These children tend to be more independent and socially responsible, and are mostly friendly, outgoing, and cooperative. They also tend to have higher grades in school, few behavioral problems at home or at school, and are even, according to several studies, less likely to smoke cigarettes or try drugs. However, as I mentioned earlier, keep in mind that "authoritative" does not mean that there are no rules. In fact, authoritative parents do set clear rules and limits on their children's behavior. They do so, however, in a way that includes their children in warm, emotionally supportive way.[10]

In a comprehensive study of over four thousand fourteen- to eighteen-year-olds, Dr. Susie Lamborn found 32% of the teens reported their parents were authoritative, 37% were neglectful, 15% were authoritarian and 15% were indulgent. In a follow-up study of these adolescents one year later, Lamborn discovered that "Differences in adjustment associated with variations in parenting are either maintained or increase over time. However, whereas the benefits of authoritative parenting are largely in the maintenance of previous levels of high adjustment, the deleterious consequences of neglectful parenting continue to accumulate." In Lamborn's research, children with authoritative parents were the most psychologically healthy in all measured aspects, when compared with other parenting styles that either lacked warmth and responsiveness (authoritarian), limit-setting and rules (indulgent) or both (neglectful).[11]

Similarly, I have also looked at how parenting styles affected MySpace teens, and the following results emerged:[12]

- Adolescents with authoritative parents felt that they had the most parent-teen intimacy.
- Adolescents with authoritative parents were more socially confident.
- Adolescents with authoritative parents were more attached to their parents, trusted their parents more, and had better communication with them.
- Authoritative parents were better at setting limits and monitoring their teenagers.
- Teens with indulgent parents spent fifteen hours per week on MySpace, compared to those with neglectful parents (eleven hours per week), authoritative (nine hours per week), and authoritarian parents (six hours per week).

Clearly, parents can make a lasting impact on their children simply by following an authoritative—not authoritarian—parenting style. Remember, good authoritative parenting requires clear limits and boundaries. However, those boundaries are mutually agreed upon and infractions are discussed, rather than harshly penalized. This does not mean that a parent cannot punish an errant child. It simply means that the punishment should not involve physical force or verbal abuse and should fit the level of misbehavior. Punishment can and should be a learning experience so that the child is aware of the parental expectations and the consequences of rule violations.

Based on my interview with Janet, my guess is that she was trying her best to be an authoritative parent. Her family meeting when Mikey wanted a computer was an excellent authoritative parenting strategy: it allowed the children to have input while still giving her the final say on where the computer would be housed and how it would be used. With very little evidence it is difficult to determine Janet's ex-husband's parenting style, but his actions suggest that he is most likely an indulgent parent who caters to his children's needs. Having parents with different parenting styles is not unusual, and children can develop healthy relationships with both as long as the parents communicate how and when they will set limits with their children and do so in consultation with the entire family. This is quite difficult, but not impossible, when parents are living in two separate homes. Janet and her ex-husband need to keep the children's best interest at heart and modify their parenting styles to place emphasis on setting clear, consistent boundaries concerning computer use.

2. Set and Maintain Behavioral Limits

A recent study by the Annenberg Public Policy Center indicated that although two-thirds of parents report they have imposed time limits on computer use, only one-third of their children report that their parents enforce those rules.[13] In one of my studies, nearly half the parents reported that they set limits on MySpace use, but half of their children said that those limits were not implemented. This means that the vast majority of teens and adolescents are on the Internet without any limits on the time they spend online or on the Web sites they visit.[14]

What are reasonable limits on Internet behavior? Although there is no absolute answer to this question, my experience working with parents tells me that the following suggestions can help:

- Homework and household chores need to be completed before any computer use. If the computer is needed for homework, that work must be completed prior to any "fun" activities that are not related to schoolwork.

- Internet use should be apportioned so that adolescents do not spend large chunks of time online. One to two hours at a time is a good start. I also recommend that for whatever time limit you set, there must be a "technology break" of half that time before returning online. For example, if you allow your teen to stay online for two hours, then he or she must take a one-hour break with no technology. Encourage outdoor activities or visiting with a friend (live, not online), playing a game, or reading a book. Just make sure that this time does not involve technology, which means no television, no video games, and even no telephone.

- Allow your teen to earn extra computer time. As you can probably tell from other chapters, I am a strong believer in positive reinforcement. This is a golden opportunity to employ this approach to its fullest extent. I am sure that there are extra chores or behaviors that you want your teen to do. Set up, in advance, a plan so that the teen can earn rewards. For example, if your teen is having difficulties finishing homework assignments in a timely fashion, you can set up a system where he or she can gain points for completing tasks. Finishing homework in, say, one hour, might earn three points. Finishing in ninety minutes might earn one point and so on. The best way to do this is to sit down with your teen and discuss all the behaviors you wish to happen. You can even add in some tasks that he or she already does to ensure that some points will be obtained easily. Next, develop your cache of reinforcers, which, of course, will include extra computer time. Now, *and this is critical*, through discussion with your teen, figure out how many points each behavior is worth (tasks that take longer or perhaps are more important to you, should earn more points) and how many points need to be attained to accrue extra online time. This is helpful because you will reward your teen for good (positive) behavior. For example, "Make your bed before going to school" is preferable to a more negative formulation, such as, "Don't leave your bed messy when you go to school," because the latter focuses on the *negative* and you are looking for an increase in the *positive*. It is also important that the behaviors are not long-term behaviors. It will not help to say "Get at least a B in each class," because that goal is too far away. You can, however, try something more short term and specific such as, "Get at least a B on your history test this Friday." Consider making a chart and using a point system—such as shown in Tables 8.1 and 8.2—both of which help promote these ideas, and place the chart in a conspicuous location so that your teen (and even other family members) can see progress and accomplishment.

- There are four other things that you *must* do to make this point system work. First, do not, under any circumstances, remove points for bad behavior. The punishment is built into the system. Bad behavior already means no points, which translates into missed rewards. Second, do not include expensive items on your reward chart, because they do not work well. What works best are activity rewards (getting to do something your child chooses) or inexpensive items. Third, within limits, your child should be allowed to use his or her accumulated points at any time. Stipulate, in advance, any constraints, such as being able to use computer time only on the weekends, or not staying up late to use the extra time. The point system only works if you are straightforward and clear from the outset. Set up the rules and make sure that everyone understands them. However, don't worry if you forget something. You and your teen can always make adjustments when necessary. Fourth, and most important, whenever your teen does one of the behaviors on the chart add his or her points as soon as possible and provide additional positive social reinforcement. For example, if he takes out the trash without being asked, put the points on the chart and tell him something like "Great job! I really appreciate it that you did it without me asking," or "Your taking out the trash really helped me out today. Thanks a lot." Vary what you say, but it is best to compliment the behavior (not the person) and also tell him how wonderful it made you feel.

Janet's children would definitely benefit from a point system in which the rewards include "earning" computer time. This takes the pressure off Janet to determine who gets to use the computer and for how long. The point system would be most successful if both Janet and her ex-husband could invoke it together as a unified parental pair, but

Table 8.1 Sample Weekly Point System Chart

Behavior	Mon	Tues	Wed	Thur	Fri	Sat	Sun
Take out the trash without being asked. (1 point)							
Make your bed before going to school. (1 point)							
Brush your teeth and get ready for bed by 9:00 P.M. (1 point)							
Wash the car on the weekend (2 points)							
Take care of or pick up your brother when asked (2 points each time)							
Total Points							

Table 8.2 Sample Point System Reward Chart

Rewards	Points Needed
1 hour extra computer time	15
1 hour later bedtime on weekend	30
Tickets for you and a friend to see a movie	45
A music download of five tunes	45

if that is not possible, children are very adaptable and can learn different behavior at each parent's home.

3. Find Computer Uses that Are Positive for Everyone

Research has shown that using the computer and Internet for educational purposes increases family cohesion. If your teenager is more technologically savvy than you, find some information that you need and have him or her show you how to obtain it. Let your teen show off by whipping through the computer screens. Let her wow you with her technological abilities. Don't forget to positively reward her for this, too. Family decisions are made all the time. Include your children and let them help you obtain information online. When we wanted to adopt a dog, we all went online and looked at different breeds, found a chart listing the most intelligent dogs, and even e-mailed questions to breeders. When the e-mail responses started coming back we all got to share in the excitement. The Internet is also particularly helpful with medical issues. Whenever possible, ask your kids to search the Internet for what you need. This is also a good opportunity to teach them how to assess the validity of online information. Health data from WebMD, for example, is more likely to be accurate than information from someone's personal Web site.

These are just some simple suggestions you can use to enhance the family system. They are general strategies and will be effective in dealing with any of the other issues I cover throughout this book. For example, the point system can be quite effective if you are dealing with the issue of Internet addiction by making your child "earn" computer time that helps you monitor and control their ventures into cyberspace. None of these parenting suggestions is rocket science and if you just think about what keeps your family in and out of balance, I am sure that you will come up with others that work equally well. Just remember, the goal is to maintain homeostasis by providing clear boundaries that encourage both togetherness and separateness.

I interviewed Drs. Kerby Alvy and Matthew Eastin on how technology has affected the family system. Dr. Alvy is founder and Executive Director of the thirty-three-year-old parenting education organization, the Center for the Improvement of Child Caring. He is an internationally respected authority on parenting and parent education and has written many books on these topics. One of the center's latest efforts to assist parents in raising children effectively is its *Parenting the Net Generation Project*. Dr. Eastin is a professor in the advertising department at the University of Texas. Focusing on youth, he has done extensive research on the adoption and impact of new media, including the influence of parenting styles and mediation techniques. Here is what they had to say:

Q: What issues do you see impacting today's family, with adolescents spending two to four hours per day on the Internet, and how do you see parents dealing with those issues?

Alvy: The first issue is to determine if spending time using the Internet is having a negative impact on the abilities and opportunities for teens and parents to interact and bond together. That is a serious issue, even though developmentally this is a time that teens need to be connected to peers for their growth and identity formation. It is also important, for their development and harmony in the home, for teens to have time with their parents. There are some ways you can relate to that concern via the Internet. Parents and teens can go online together and use some of that time to interact and bond. They can play games together or challenge each other to find topics on the Internet, and use these experiences as opportunities for parents to interact with teens. It is in many ways their domain and to be able to interact over their domain in enjoyable ways for both is a pretty neat thing to do. This is a way to help teens when they go into their cybercocoons.

Another time-related issue for parents to be concerned about is that while their teens are absorbed online, they are not moving around and getting any exercise. There is reason to believe that this amount of sedentary time is contributing to the current obesity epidemic. Here parents could have the teens take exercise or movement breaks. Also, setting some rules about usage can be a good opportunity to teach responsible behavior, especially if there are consequences for breaking the rules, such as losing access for a week. The power of the use of technology in the lives of teens also creates a situation where the use of the technology can be made contingent on teens adhering to other family rules, like curfews and doing their chores.

There is also the issue of how parents talk to their teens about the use of the Internet, cell phones, and the violence that is so pervasive through the media. How do you talk to your kids about these issues? The conversations need to be productive and not be seen as imposing your will on their domains. It is very important that parents develop and use good communication skills in relating to the content and the amazing amount of information and opportunities to interact over electronic media. This is basic child-parent communication. It is a matter of content and issues you are discussing with your children. So part of rearing a child, who, in this day and age, is so connected to the Internet and other technology, is through basic human relations communications.

Another issue with the Internet has to do with where the computer is located in the home. I think the combined wisdom of people who have studied the impact of the Internet and its many dangers is that it is probably wise for parents to position the computer and access to the Internet in a more public place rather than in the bedrooms of their teens, if, indeed, their teens have their own bedrooms. Even though parents are not around all the time when their children are on the computer, having the computer in a public place makes it less of a private undertaking, and the teen knows that parents are concerned about what he or she is doing and viewing online. Having the computer in a public area of the home makes it easier to interact with kids over what they are doing and make sure that they are staying safe.

One final issue is multitasking that so many teens do all the time—simultaneously watching television, using the Internet to complete homework assignments, e-mailing, text messaging, listening to music—they go from one media to another at nano-speed. This is fascinating, but indications from research are that by doing homework while watching TV or talking to peers, detracts from the ability to focus on matters that require concentration including academic work that they can do online. If they are doing this homework while they are also on MySpace and e-mail and IM, there is some indication that it is going to detract from their ability to give the proper concentration to high-level thinking. One suggestion is to work with teens and let them know that this simultaneous multitasking could interfere with their developing or refining the skills and habits that are needed for life success. Parents can help their teens to organize themselves and learn to do work in sequence, not simultaneously. For example, work on a school paper for hour, then spend ten minutes e-mailing and fifteen IMing. Get them into the habit of doing work in sequence and their performance may even improve.

Eastin: Time. We only have so many hours to spend with family, and the more time youth spend online results in a possible displacement effect. That said, time online is most likely just replacing (displacing) time with other media such as television, movies, and so forth. Other than family time, adolescents need to be careful that their online life does not replace time with "real" or offline friends. This is not to suggest that online contacts are not meaningful, but rather, most of us work with people offline, and thus, social skills needed to function in such environments will still be important.

Q: What do you feel parents can do to preserve healthy family functioning in the age of the Internet?

Eastin: Talk to your kids! In an age where content is moving faster than we can co-view, talking and instilling values in youth will be paramount. Simply, parents need to make their child's online activities part of the family offline environment. This will allow parents to understand and perhaps take part in their child's online world. Simply, make online activities as common a conversation as the weather or what's going on at school.

Q: How can parents help their children grow socially while much of their socializing is now done online?

Alvy: Today's families are facing both unprecedented learning opportunities and unprecedented safety hazards as a result of their children's extensive use of modern technologies and media. The potential for enhancing knowledge and personal growth through such exposure, and especially through Internet use, is tremendous. So too are safety hazards such as identity theft, sexual predators, cyberbullying, sharing of private information, and online addiction. These are all "social" issues and parents need to be aware of them and work with their children to ensure that they are safe. It is not enough to assume that just because they are more cyber-literate that they are capable of dealing with these social issues. Parents need to recognize that their input is critical in helping children develop socially while they are living in their cybercocoons for sizable amounts of their days.

Eastin: This is going to be an ongoing issue in the future. Parents will be best served by talking to their children and encouraging their children to have offline social interactions. Yes, it sounds corny, but sleepovers, pizza parties, and so on, will give teens a chance to unplug. Additionally, take your child to work, or at least, adult functions. Let your children see that the future is less like *The Jetsons* and more like *Friends*.

Q: Dr. Alvy, you have been involved in promoting positive parenting for nearly forty years. What new challenges do you see for parenting the net generation?

Alvy: I see that in addition to the ones we have spoken of that evolve around the use of modern technologies, and the customary challenges of the teen years, there are two interrelated challenges that particularly affect this generation of teens and their parents—the HIV/AIDS and STD epidemic, and early participation in adult sexual behavior. Technology and the media exacerbate these challenges with their emphasis on being sexy and foxy. So these are not unrelated to the ones we have been speaking about. Hence parents also need and deserve education and training in how to cope with these modern phenomena.

Q: In what ways do parenting styles affect what teens do online both positively and negatively?

Eastin: I believe talking with children is the best route to teaching good online values. Who to trust, what type of information is *always* off limits, and how to speak with others (depending on who they are) will be key for digital youths entering an online era when youth are the creators of content, values, and policies. Further, talking will take the mystery out of online activities. Besides most likely being educational, talking about what children are doing and with whom they are interacting, will allow parents better to understand the life their child is living online. The age-old excuse of being helpless because their kids know more is just not going to cut it. Just as with past media such as television and video games, parents need to take responsibility for their children's online actions—talking to them is a first step.

I also believe we will see a continued rise in electronic tracking. If used with caution, electronic monitoring could be a great mediation technique that allows parents to monitor (not spy) their children's online activity. That said, violating privacy expectations could have a negative effect—forcing adolescents to cloak their online life from snooping parental eyes.

Chapter 9

Hate Mail

◆

"First she was IMing me any time I was on. I didn't know her but she was a friend of a friend and needed someone to talk with. Then she was posting stuff on my bulletins and got mad at me when I didn't put her on my Top 8, so I did. But then she found out how to get into my MySpace page and put a picture of her and me up that she Photoshopped from two pics and then finally, when I blocked her, she made an I HATE JACKSON page on MySpace. It made me sick and I couldn't sleep trying to get her to stop doing it. I didn't want to but after two weeks of this, I had to report her to Tom."

—Jackson, age 17, Plano, Texas

◆

"Cyberbullying involves the use of information and communication technologies such as e-mail, cell phone and pager text messages, instant messaging, defamatory personal Web sites, and defamatory online personal polling Web sites, to support deliberate, repeated, and hostile behaviour by an individual or group, that is intended to harm others."

—Bill Belsey, President, Bullying.org, Canada[1]

◆

Being bullied on the Internet hurts just as much as being bullied at school. For an impressionable adolescent already struggling with teen angst, Internet bullying can be brutal and emotionally debilitating. Instead of happening on the playground, it happens in the teen's home and can go on twenty-four hours a day.

I spent quite some time talking with Anne Collier, codirector of BlogSafety.com, and Nancy Willard, president of the Center for Safe and Responsible Internet Use, about cyberbullying. Both have been vocally active on a national level, meeting with influential groups about this issue. We discussed the fact that there are many different types of cyberbullying, which are summarized here:[2]

1. Sending unwanted, mean, vulgar, or threatening e-mail messages, text messages, or IMs.
2. Posting sensitive, private information about another person.
3. FLAMING (typing in all capitals, which is construed as yelling) in chat rooms, IMs, or e-mails.
4. Altering photos and posting them on a Web site.
5. Spreading gossip or rumors online.
6. Impersonating another by creating a MySpace page and posting a fake profile in order to make the person look bad.
7. Excluding someone from discussions by blocking them.

As an example of cyberbullying, let's consider Marie, a fourteen-year-old high school freshman, who was being bullied by a classmate. As she tells it, *"She kept IMing me and telling me I am ugly, and my mom just told me to block her so I did, but then she sent me e-mails that were even more nasty. My mom told me not to read them but I had to see what she was writing. I answered the first few, trying to find out why she was doing this and then I stopped. When I didn't write back, she sent me about fifty messages in one day with all sorts of scary stuff about how she was gonna kick my ass at school cuz I dissed her, which I didn't. I was just trying to get her to stop. Finally, mom made me and her go tell the principal, but I made him promise to just talk to her and not suspend her. Finally, she stopped sending me e-mails but my best friend told me that she nominated me for the Biggest Fag contest that someone posted as a discussion group from my high school. I still don't get it but my mom says that I have to feel sorry for her rather than be mad at her."*

Marie is not alone. Dr. Robin Kowalski and her colleagues have reported that approximately one in four or five middle school students have experienced cyberbullying. Girls were slightly more likely to be attacked than boys. More than half of the eleven- to thirteen-year-olds knew someone who had been harassed online.[3]

Online bullying and harassment are on the rise. A study by Crimes Against Children Research Center compared the results from two national Youth Internet Safety Surveys (YISS) of ten- to seventeen-year-olds five years apart (2000 to 2005) and found that the amount of harassment had increased 50% over five years, from 6% to 9%. In addition, this report found that the percentage of these children and teens harassing others increased from 14% to 28%.[4] In my own studies, although only 11% of the teens reported being harassed, 57% of parents and 34% of teens told me that they were concerned about harassment on MySpace.[5] The fact that teen and parent concerns about harassment eclipse the reported incidence indicates that this is an issue that needs to be addressed.

Harassment includes being sent mean, nasty messages; being threatened with bodily harm; name-calling (including racial slurs); and having others tell lies about you on the Internet. According to my research and that of others, most harassed teens handle the problem appropriately by telling the person to stop, blocking the harasser from their MySpace site, ignoring him or her, or reporting the incident to an adult.[6] However, this does not mean that cyberbullying is not a problem; because of its cruel and sensitive nature, it is precisely the type of Internet experience that teens may be hesitant to report.

It's not surprising that the most common perpetrator is a schoolmate or a friend. We can all remember times when we were younger and kids at school teased us or bullied someone we knew. Now, with the Internet, this bullying has taken on a new dimension. One-third of the girls and half of the boys I interviewed in a recent study were bullied by someone the teen did not know.[7] The following table, from a Clemson University study,[8] sheds some light on what type of misery is being spread and how it is accomplished. Note that these figures add up to more than 100% because cyberbullying is most often done in a variety of ways, using multiple electronic means. Clearly, Cyberbullies use many tools to hurt someone else in many different ways. The most common place is through instant messages, with other means providing fewer instances.

Of course, there are many reasons why teens harass other teens online. First, technology allows the harasser to be invisible. Even if your teen

Table 9.1   Cyberbullying of Middle School Children

How Is the Person Bullied?	Girls	Boys
Teased in a harmful way	88%	72%
Told lies/spread false rumors about	73%	65%
Used screen name/username to impersonate	52%	40%
What Type of Communication Tool Is Used?		
IM	78%	61%
On Web site	39%	26%
E-Mail	38%	29%
Chat Room	34%	39%
Text Message	23%	26%
Who Does the Cyberbullying?		
Another student at school	63%	60%
Friend	54%	60%
Stranger	31%	50%
Family member	11%	29%

knows the perpetrator, being "behind the screen" provides a sense of anonymity. Interestingly, in the same way a shy teenaged boy may find it easier to break the ice with a girl online rather than in person, an angry teen can make nasty comments online that would be uncomfortable to say face-to-face. One sixteen-year-old summed it up this way: *"A friend sent a really bad message to me even though he lives next door, I guess it makes people feel brave enough to say anything."*

Second, when you say something nasty to someone face-to-face, you get to see the results of your actions. The person may cry, get upset, strike out, slink away, or have any number of visible negative reactions. In person, these reactions may invite an apology or an empathetic response. Online, however, there is no physical or verbal feedback. Without seeing or hearing the ramifications of online nastiness, it is much easier to bully someone, and to continue to do so, with no regard for the other person's feelings. Taken together, these first two examples provide a situation of "You can't see me; I can't see you," which makes cyberbullying all the easier and appealing, as explained by the theory of disinhibition discussed in chapters 3 and 4. Remember that disinhibition in this context means that you feel comfortable making comments online, or behind the anonymity of the computer screen, that you would not consider saying to someone face-to-face. When you talk online you are missing many cues that signal an emotional response, such as a pained expression or full-blown tears, so it becomes easier to make nasty, rude comments.

Third, although most cyberbullying starts out on a one-to-one basis through IM or e-mail, it often spreads to more public spaces. The cyberbully now has a wider audience and is emboldened any time someone provides positive feedback. Douglas encountered a bully named "JuniperJumper" in a chat room, who took something Douglas said as an insult and started name-calling and flaming him. Suddenly, other people in the chat room joined in and started cheering him on and the attack escalated. Douglas exited the chat room, but the bully found him in other chat rooms later the same day and continued to harass him.

Bullying is an act of power and control. As such, the person doing the bullying feels powerful, which, in turn, provides an increase in the bully's self-esteem. This reinforcement then continues the bullying cycle, as he attempts to gain more positive feedback (for his negative behavior) and still more positive self-regard. He can rationalize it by asserting that it is just a game and "everyone does it," or by appealing to the Internet as a vehicle for "free speech." I have even heard some teens modify the Las Vegas ad campaign to "What happens online, stays online" as a way of justifying their right to bully.

Sadly, not all of those attacked end up telling an adult.[9] This is particularly disheartening given that the majority of those who are bullied are younger than sixteen. At this age, such an aggressive act can have a strong impact on a young boy or girl. Seeing messages that malign a teen's character can be overwhelming and create massive embarrassment. The wounds from an online assault can be even more devastating than those from a fistfight because they are hidden from sight. There are no black eyes or bruises to evoke sympathy. There are only hurt feelings and bruised psyches. Bullying can cause long-term psychological harm, including low self-esteem, depression, anger, school failure, and school avoidance. In more drastic cases, the victim can even contemplate suicide or violence against others as a means of relieving the emotional burden.

Although researchers are at the early stages of studying the impact of cyberbullying, live bullying has been studied extensively around the world. Long-term studies in Norway, Australia, Korea, and the United States have shown that this form of abuse has major effects on children.[10] In addition, most researchers admit that the online version may be more devastating psychologically. Online bullying is not time-limited. With teens being online large chunks of the time, there are ample opportunities to be harassed through IM, e-mail, and the like. Moreover, information on the Internet *stays* online—forever. All the bully has to do is write one scathing post online and it can haunt the teen every time he logs on to the Internet. It also appears from research that online bullying provides an easy opportunity for others to join in. Perhaps it is the anonymity, or maybe it is just a fun game, but one comment can lead to two, four, eight, and an explosion of nastiness and upset. The Internet is also a worldwide phenomenon, and there are countless people out there who have nothing better to do than to search out opportunities to feel better by lashing out and hurting other teens.

Similarly, research on schoolyard bullying has shown conclusively that the victims suffer from depression, low self-image, school maladjustment, chronic anxiety and fear, stomachaches, headaches, sleep problems, and more. A large, long-term study in Norway found that bullied middle school children were more prone to depression and negative self-image at twenty-three years of age, showing that bullying can have a long term impact.[11] Although the research on cyberbullies is relatively new, effects similar to "live" bullying have been found. In fact, if anything, the negative effects are more pronounced online.

Psychologically, the victim of bullying will most likely place the blame on himself or herself. Twelve-year-old Will told me he was hassled for a month by a sixteen-year-old that he met doing online gaming. *"I don't know what I did to piss him off. We were playing the game*

*and my character killed his. Every time I went online to play the game,
he was there. He seemed to have gotten a bunch of his friends and they all
tried to kill my character. I tried to ask them why they were doing this but
nobody would answer. I even apologized for offing his character, but that
didn't stop him. It was no fun anymore, so I left. It's too bad. I really liked
that game and I had been playing for a year or so and had gotten to know
many of the players. I kept thinking that they would yell at him and get
him to stop but maybe they thought it was my fault because no matter what
I did, they never stopped. They just kept getting meaner and meaner."*

In terms of the psychology of bullies themselves, research on schoolyard bullies reveals that they often tend to be more aggressive, have a
strong need to dominate, feel provoked even when not actually provoked, believe that aggression is the best solution to a problem, lack the
ability to see someone else's feelings, get satisfaction from injuring others, and typically do not have the mild anxiety level that keeps normal
kids from antisocial actions.[12] Bullies are often admired and well liked
when they are young, due to their physical strength. Usually in elementary school their popularity begins to wane as other students sense their
meanness. Often their first bullying begins in mid-to-late elementary
school and continues to escalate through middle school as their popularity wanes and they start hanging out with a tougher crowd. According to Dr. Melissa DeRosier, bullies are "clueless as to how little they
are liked. They are out of touch with what other kids think."[13]

Online, however, the bully appears to be quite "normal" with few,
if any, distinguishing negative characteristics. These aren't bullies who
are beating up kids for lunch money. Often these are just normal kids,
doing something that they justify as being harmless. I interviewed one
teen who told me that she had a boyfriend who was quite athletic and
strong, and that seemed to irk one of her school friends, an honor student who was lean, lanky, and not nearly as strong. This irked friend
also happened to have an immense crush on her. Online, he told her
he was going to beat up her boyfriend and even threatened when and
where he was going to do it. Offline, however, he hid at school and
stayed away from her and her boyfriend. Online he felt emboldened
enough to create the illusion that he was a tough guy.

What Can You Do?

Many of the following suggestions for helping a cyberbullied teen come from the excellent work by Anne Collier and Larry Magid at SafeKids. com and Nancy Willard at csriu.org or cyberbully.org. These Web sites are invaluable resources for keeping your teens safe on the Internet, in general, and on MySpace, in particular.

1. Be Proactive: Talk to Your Children *Before* They Get Bullied

Throughout this book I have stressed that it is important to talk to your children about what they are doing on the Internet. It is also critical that you help them anticipate that someone may say or do things that hurt their feelings and make them feel bad. Give them the examples from earlier in this chapter and tell them to be on the lookout for any of these attacks. It is important for you to be proactive, to the best of your ability, so you don't have to be reactive. As they say, the best offensive is a good defense. If you teach your children what might happen and what to do when it does, then they will be less injured emotionally if and when it does happen to them.

Teach your children strategies to stay safe in cyberspace. First, tell them never to give out passwords, even to their friends. Zeraldah, a twelve-year-old, gave her password to her friend Bettsee so her friend could log on to her MySpace account for her. A month later, when their friendship had soured, Zeraldah found that Bettsee had gotten on her MySpace page and *"she totally messed it up. She put up a naked picture of someone else and said that it was me and she made some nasty comments like I said them about my friends. I had to turn her in to Tom even though I really didn't want to and then he kicked her off MySpace. But I hear that she just got another account so I had to change my password."* Second, caution them against sending messages when they are angry. I recommend teaching them about the "twenty-four-hour cooling-off period." This means that they refrain from responding for twenty-four hours so they can calm down and think through what they want to say without the anger clouding their reply. Third, tell them that if there is anything that makes them the least bit uncomfortable, to come and alert you. Assure them that you will not punish them, because it is not their fault (although they probably think that it is). You just want to prevent them from getting hurt.

2. Help Them Understand Why They Are Being Bullied

Help your teen understand that the bullying is not about them; it is about the bully who is trying to control them. Since most kids have seen the damage a school bully can inflict, you can liken it to that level of brutality. Explain to them about how anonymity makes people bolder and nastier and how easy it is to escalate this type of attack. Make sure they understand that the bully's goal is to make another person feel bad, most likely out of his need to feel good.

3. Caution Them about Bullying Someone Else

It is easy to lash out at someone online. You need to talk, preemptively, to your children about this. Ask them to consider the following questions before they antagonize someone:

- How would you feel if the person said that to you?
- How would you feel if what you did was reported to your parents?
- How would you feel if what you did was reported to the school administration?
- How would you feel if what you did and said was reported in the newspaper?
- Would you be willing to say the same thing to the person's face?
- How would you feel if what you said was sent out all over the Internet for anyone to read and comment on?

Use these questions as a starting point for a discussion about their own online behavior.

4. Pay Attention to Your School's Acceptable Use Policy

Many schools require parents and children to sign a form called an Acceptable Use Policy (AUP) prior to starting school each fall. If you are like most parents, you simply go through the huge packet of information and sign and date it, reading only the important parts. The

AUP is important as it outlines what the school considers acceptable computer and Internet use and it should include a section on how students may not behave toward others online. This is an excellent opportunity to broach the topic. Don't just sign it and move on to the next form. Read it and talk about it before letting your child sign on the dotted line.

5. When to Be Reactive: What You Can Do If Your Child Is Attacked

Bullying most often occurs on IM, over e-mail, in chat rooms, or through Web sites or text messaging. The bottom line is that you need to gather as much information as you can about the perpetrator from online clues. If an IM is the vehicle, have your child copy all of the IM conversation and create a document. Include the date and time and make sure that you have the screen names of all involved. Then make sure that your child blocks the person from IMing. Clearly, being able to block someone, ignore that person, or even tell him or her to stop, helps lessen any potential psychological harm.

If bullying happens through an e-mail, save that message, plus any other messages from the same person, including their e-mail address and date and time it was received. Each e-mail contains a header, which includes valuable tracking information (e.g., the originating address). Figure out how to copy this information. If you are not technologically savvy, ask your child how to do it or find a friend who has the technological knowledge to help. Once you have the information, have your teen block this person by identifying the sender's e-mail address (or domain) as "junk mail," which will send it to a junk folder that you can have automatically emptied. Also make sure that your teen doesn't read the e-mail. It will only continue to hurt more.

Chat rooms are a popular location for name-calling. If your teen is being bullied in a chat room, make sure you copy the entire chat conversation with all screen names, dates, and times. Many chat rooms are moderated, but all have some type of hierarchical system. Report the conversation to the moderator and tell your teen to refrain from using that chat room. Often bullies will follow people through their screen names to other Web locations. As a last resort, your teen may have to change his or her screen name or e-mail address as a means of protection.

If the assault occurs through a Web site, make sure you print the offending information and the Web address. Contact the host of the site and report the problem. Most Web hosting services are happy to investigate and ban someone for such behavior. If the Web site has a unique name you can find out who is in charge of the Web site by using "Whois." Go to http://www.networksolutions.com/whois and type the domain name in the box. This will give you contact information for the registrant, the administrator, and the hosting Web service.

If the bullying is happening online it may have spread. Go to Google, enter your teen's first and last name in quotation marks and see if there are any Web sites where he or she is mentioned. If so, use the above tips to get the information and report it to the Web hosting service. You can also go to www.google.com/alerts and put your child's name in as an alert. If any Web site mentions his or her name, you will get an e-mail and a link to the Web site, which you can report if it is offensive.

If your child is the recipient of hurtful text messages, make sure you note the time, the exact message, and the caller's contact information. Contact the cell phone company and report it to them with all the above information so they can trace it. If the message is through the voice mail system, save it and forward it to the phone company. One interesting strategy to tell your teen to use if he or she gets an abusive phone call is to put the phone down and walk away for a few minutes. When the bully realizes that your teen is not there and his tirade is not upsetting his target, he will go away and probably won't try it again.

If the perpetrator is a fellow student, contact the school administration. Many schools can and will confront offenders and use the AUP to justify penalties. You may need to be insistent, as many schools have yet to recognize the severity of cyberbullying.

Again, cyberbullying can be psychologically devastating. If you follow the advice above you can help your teens stay safe and happy so they can enjoy the online world. The following Web sites are invaluable resources for keeping your teens safe on the Internet, in general, and on MySpace, in particular:

- SafeKids.com
- Center for Safe and Responsible Internet Use at csriu.org
- cyberbully.org
- NetFamilyNews.org
- StaySafe.org
- www.cyberbullyhelp.com

For the most part, the kids really are all right. You can help ensure that they are safe by practicing proactive and reactive parenting.

I interviewed Anne Collier, editor of NetFamilyNews.org, codirector of BlogSafety.com and coauthor of *MySpace Unraveled: What It Is and How to Use It Safely*, and Nancy Willard, Director of Center for Safe and Responsible Internet Use, and author of *Cyber-Safe Kids, Cyber-Savvy Teens: Helping Young People Use the Internet Safely and Responsibly*, about cyberbullying. Here is what they had to say:

Q: What impact has MySpace had on cyberbullying by teens?

Willard: MySpace, which is just one of a number of popular social networking sites, has likely led to an increase in cyberbullying. We do not have much data on this phenomenon, so the actual degree of impact is hard to assess. But it appears that the increase in reported cyberbullying incidents has coincided with the increased popularity of these sites. Social networking sites are places where many teens are seeking to establish an online "community." Unfortunately, for some teens this means engaging in harmful activities to establish their social status in the community. All bullying is grounded in the search for social status by teens who think that they gain in status by putting others down.

    Collier: I don't think MySpace has had much of an impact on cyberbullying, which certainly predated MySpace. MySpace and other social networks are just tools for cyberbullies, but attractive ones, I suppose, for bullies who want to impersonate peers by creating profiles about them.

Q: Kids have always been bullied by other kids at school. Why is cyberbullying so important? Is it different from schoolyard harassment?

Willard: I think we need to address the harm caused by all forms of bullying. Cyberbullying is simply a new means of engaging in cruelty. It is possible that the harm caused by cyberbullying is more significant than face-to-face bullying. Online communications can be very vicious. Cyberbullying can occur at all times, 24/7, not just at school. The harmful material can be sent to many people and can be difficult to remove. Cyberbullies can be anonymous and can solicit the help of online "friends" who do not know the target. This means that the target will not know whom to trust. And there is a strong teen norm that it is not appropriate to tell adults what is happening online.

Collier: Yes, it's different from schoolyard harassment. In fact, it augments the problem because of the anonymity the Internet allows. It is also different in that gender and physique are irrelevant, whether via social networks, e-mail, instant messaging, or texting on phones. Girls can bully just as easily as boys can in cyberspace, and they certainly do. UK educators will tell you mobile-phone-based cyberbullying has become a significant problem in their country, where the vast majority of kids and teens have their own phones.

Q: What is your number one piece of advice that you would give kids about what they can do to prevent cyberbullying?

Willard: Actually, I have three pieces of advice on preventing cyberbullying: Don't put information online that others can use to hurt you. Look at how you are communicating to make sure you are not putting others down. Pick your friends carefully—Life's too short to waste your time trying to be friends with mean people.

Collier: Don't respond. Experts tell us bullies are usually trying to get a reaction—don't give them that. Also, it's not your fault! For useful tips see the two articles, "Bullying & cyberbullying: Samantha's story" (available at: http://www.netfamilynews.org/nl051021.html#1) and "Samantha's bully-proofing tips" (available at: http://www.netfamilynews.org/nl051028.html#1).

Q: What advice can you give adolescents on how to deal with cyberbullying once it has occurred?

Collier: Get help from a parent, guardian, or other adult you trust. By all means don't keep it to yourself. You deserve support.

Willard: If you are a target of cyberbullying, the most important thing is not to retaliate—keep your hands off the keyboard until you are calm enough to respond intelligently. Make sure you save the evidence. Then decide whether this is a situation you can resolve yourself or whether you need to ask an adult for assistance. You could try a few steps to resolve the situation and if these steps do not work, then talk with an adult. Appropriate responses to cyberbullying range from asking or demanding the cyberbully to stop, leaving the environment, filing a complaint with the site or service, having your parents write a letter to the parents of the cyberbully, talking with the school, or even consulting an attorney or calling the police.

Q: What advice would you give parents about discussing cyberbullying with their children both before and after it happens?

Willard: Parents should talk with their children about the importance of being kind online—and also discuss all of the guidance I provided above in preventing and responding.

Collier: I'd send them to Nancy's guidebook, "A Parent's Guide to Cyberbullying & Cyberthreats," which can be found at http://cyberbully.org/docs/cbctparents.pdf.

Chapter 10

Proactive Parenting
Teaching Your Children to Look Both Ways in Cyberspace

◆

"Indeed, there is no clear distinction between life as lived in real space and in cyberspace; one social sphere is now a natural and complementing extension of the other. This is often difficult for adults to comprehend, given they: (1) have not grown up with Internet-based socializing and therefore are not naturally predisposed to it, and (2) use the Internet to supplement their lives as lived in real space. Discomfort and unfamiliarity, then, has seemingly contributed to some degree of frustration, confusion, and panic when observing youth culture's complete surrender to the novel technology of MySpace."

—Drs. Justin Patchin and Sameer Hinduja[1]

◆

"We didn't have a childhood online. This is a very alien experience. So we don't know how to guide our children as they go into a world that wasn't part of our childhood experiences."

—Dr. Henry Jenkins, Codirector of the Comparative Media Studies Program at the Massachusetts Institute of Technology[2]

◆

"Parents are saying that through IMing, cell phones, voice mail, and e-mail they don't know who their kids are talking to. It's hard to be a parent."

—Dr. Jeffrey Cole, Director of the Center for the Digital Future at the University of Southern California[3]

◆

The reality is that your children are going to live in a virtual world. With MySpace, YouTube, instant messaging, e-mail, iPods, texting, video games, and more media than they can possibly consume, children spend a large portion of their time online. In my research, they spend two to three hours per weekday and three to four hours per weekend day on MySpace alone.[4] A recent study tracking adolescent online use between 2003—before MySpace—and 2006 found that teens increased their weekly online time from twenty-one hours to nearly twenty-seven hours, which means that they are spending almost *four hours per day* in their virtual worlds.[5] Their friends live online and they need the opportunity to learn and grow socially. If teen life is online, then your teen is going to be online.

But your children also need to be safe in cyberspace, and making sure of that involves two kinds of parenting—proactive and reactive. Just as you teach your five-year-old to look both ways before crossing the street, and you grab his hand if he starts ahead without looking, you must teach your tweens and teens to do the same in cyberspace. You must teach your children how to be safe, and if they are doing something online that you feel might be harmful, then you need to confront the problem.

As a Baby Boomer or Gen X parent, you may feel that you have a good handle on the Internet. After all, you use it for your job, you know how to Google, and you are no novice when it comes to computers and the Internet. In spite of your expertise, you may be simply visiting the Internet in the same way you would visit a somewhat familiar foreign country. You log on to the online world, and you surf the Internet; but you are different from your kids. They own the Internet and they live it, literally 24/7. It is their life, and when they are not on MySpace, they are playing video games or texting their friends. Most likely, they are doing everything at the same time. Many years of talking on the phone or watching television while doing their homework have made them multitasking whizzes. Statistically, according to a national Kaiser Family Foundation study, adolescents today spend more time using media than attending school or sleeping.[6]

The Zandl Group, one of America's foremost consumer trends experts, has studied key teen consumer trends for more than a decade.

A look at their most recent observations provides a striking glimpse of the MySpace Generation.[7] Ten years ago, a teen's identity was defined by the opinions of his school classmates.[8] Now identity is displayed on MySpace pages.[9] For today's tweens and teens, connectivity is key, but the ways they connect have changed. Telephone calls replaced face-to-face communication. Then came e-mail, now replaced by MySpace bulletins, cell phones, text messaging, and IMing. Gone are the days that teens had a fixed, home-based entertainment center. Portability is in. Laptops, iPods, and cell phones travel with them to create their own roving TechnoCocoons. Sports stars—the role models of the '90s—are out as more teens turn to the entertainment arena for their heroes. Reading is passé. Creating is fashionable. From MySpace to YouTube, from blogging to Web pages, they are artists displaying their lives online.

According to Zandl, teens are more family-centered than their Gen X predecessors. They value their parents' opinions and look to them for advice. According to a recent national study, 71% of teens see their parents as their main role models and six in ten list a parent as their best friend.[10] Teens are less rebellious than those of previous generations as their parents allow them more freedom. According to the Zandl report, "Parents have become less strict, and are now less likely to impose curfews or even restrict teens' expression of style such as piercings or tattoos. Teens simply have less to rebel against."[11]

Another key trend is that teens are more independent, more future-oriented and more focused on pursuit of education and a career. As Alanna, a fifteen-year-old high school junior said, *"I am going to go visit colleges this Spring break even though I won't be applying for another year. I just feel that it is smart to get a sense of what colleges will be best for me and for my career goals. All my friends are doing their college visits, too. We talk a lot about going to college and what we think we want to major in. I want to be an astrophysicist and have been e-mailing professors at the schools I am visiting to set up private appointments."* High school students are being advised that a 4.0 grade point average is no longer a guarantee to get into the college of their choice, nor is a high SAT score. So teens are working harder, taking more advanced courses, and planning their careers beginning as early as freshman year in high school. This generation is more serious about their career goals than ever before.[12] And they are both easier and more difficult to parent.

Throughout this book I have stressed the importance of a dual approach to parenting. On the one hand, I believe that when problems arise, parents must deal with them immediately and decisively. This is what I call reactive parenting. On the other hand, I am a strong advocate of anticipating potential problems and taking action before reactions are needed. This is proactive parenting. Neither is better than the other. They are both part of a good parenting plan to help your children develop healthy values and lifestyles. The virtual world in which your kids reside demands both proactive and reactive parenting. Since proactive parenting precedes reactive parenting, I will first explore a model I call TALK—Trust, Assess, Learn, and "K"ommunicate.

TALK

Trust

Trust is critical in parenting, but even more so in the age of the Internet. It is so tempting to sneak a peek at your teen's computer when he is not around to see what he is up to. Technology makes it easy. Inexpensive programs such as NetNanny, CyberPatrol, or CyberSitter (rated among the top three) can help you limit Web sites your teen may visit, limit computer time, restrict IMing, scan e-mail for sensitive material, limit pornographic pictures, and block certain discussion groups.[13] According to a recent national study, more than half of parents use such filters.[14] I believe this is a mistake. Internet filters are akin to snooping in your daughter's room to find and read her locked diary. Many parents use them surreptitiously yet might fail to realize that MySpacers are amazingly adept at working around any Internet filter. They will go online and find a Web site that posts a "work around" to bypass the filter, or simply use someone else's computer without filters. Filters engender mistrust. In lieu of electronically monitoring your children's Internet use, I recommend that you work together proactively to understand what they are doing online. Open collaboration engenders trust.

Assess

Do you know what your tween or teen does in her time online? Have you seen her MySpace page? According to my research, the majority of parents are either unaware of or vastly underestimate their child's online behavior. I believe that gaining knowledge is half the battle. There are two ways of discovering your child's online behavior—directly and indirectly. The indirect method involves snooping, which can lead to conflict, while the direct way requires spending time with your adolescent and using a mediation technique called "co-viewing."[15] Co-viewing means that you spend time going online with your children. Ask them to show you their MySpace page, including comments, blogs, photos, and any other material they have there, such as quizzes and music.[16] Essentially, you are trying to get a sense of how they represent themselves online. Look at their list of friends, particularly those in the Top 8 and those who leave comments on their page. Ask about each one to learn whether they are school friends or online friends. Take time to click on the avatar—a picture that teen MySpacers select to represent themselves—next to their comments, and take a look at their pages.

Pay particular attention to personal information disclosure.[17] It is important to check their profile and any comments or blogs. These are the most likely sources of information disclosure. Many MySpace comments include specific information about the location of upcoming social events while others include phone numbers in their comments asking the MySpacer to call. Before you can check your adolescent's MySpace page, it is critical that you learn how to navigate MySpace, as well as how to perform basic online operations such as IMing.

Learn

If you do not already have a MySpace page, get your tween or teen to show you how to create one. Don't be afraid of how much your kids know. Be proud of them. Have them tell you what to do and then try it yourself. Your hands need to touch the computer keys and mouse. You need to make mistakes and have your teen tell you how to do it correctly so you can learn. I have already provided instructions on how to do this in chapter 4. Use those as guidelines, but ask your tween or teen to help. This is a good way to find out what he is doing and also a great way to begin a dialogue about online limits. According to Dr. Justin Patchin, "We encourage parents to sit with their kids to create a MySpace profile together. Teens can teach their parents about the technology and parents can talk to their kids about making responsible choices online. MySpace can be a way for parents to get closer to their kids."[18]

Although MySpace is a major force in adolescents' lives, teens also use other online tools that you should sample. Don't expect to become an expert. Just familiarize yourself with their world. IMing is a good example. Most kids use AIM as their IM tool, so set up an AIM username and practice IMing your child. If you aren't sure how to do this, have your teen help.[19] Also make sure you learn about the video games your teen is playing, if any, what television shows they are watching, and what other media they are consuming. Once you have learned a bit about your teen's electronic lifestyle, it is time to develop proactive communication tools to help them use these media in a healthy, rather than harmful, way.

"K"ommunicate

The most important tool for proactive and reactive parenting is communication. In earlier chapters I provided several examples of when and how you might spend time talking with your children. With single-parent and two-parent families in which the adults work, it is often difficult to find time to actually sit down and talk with your children. From my experience working with parents, I have discovered that if a mom or dad has an hour to talk with their teen, they try to cram in as many topics as they can and often end up frustrating themselves and their teen, and the talk often ends uncomfortably. Wilson, a thirteen-year-old MySpacer, told me about his family communication: *It's just me and my mom at home. My dad lives back east and I mostly see him during summer. My mom works until six and doesn't get home until close to seven. So, I have to come right home after school unless I can arrange in advance to go home with a friend after school. When she does get home she is usually really tired and sometimes grumpy. Even though she works hard she asks me about my day—school, friends, homework—and tries to have a conversation. But mostly she starts out just asking questions and then gets upset at the answers and often we get into an argument about homework or my grades or something and then she goes up to her room and I go to mine. I know it is hard on her but I just wish she didn't get so mad at me for little stuff.*" Wilson's relationship with his mother is typical of many teens I interviewed. She really wants to talk to her son and he really wants to talk with his mom, but there is so much information to share and so little time.

Fostering regular time with your family is a way to ensure that communication channels are open. Research shows that having dinner with your children is important in their development and their behavior. As noted earlier, children in families that eat together less often are more likely to display behavioral problems, try drugs, and do worse in school.[20] I am not suggesting that you eat together every night and the dinners have to take hours, but regular mealtimes are an excellent place where you can communicate about important issues. It is useful to create a regular routine that involves mealtime just as you would require a regular bedtime or other family rules. It's best to remove all outside distractions and let your children talk while you listen, sharing information with them about your own day and including them in household decisions. Use this as a time to supply as much positive reinforcement as possible for their choices and successes.

As part of your dinner conversation, remember to focus on complimenting the behavior, not the child. Saying "you did a great job on that math test" is much better than, "you are good at math." In a fascinating study, Dr. Carol Dweck of Columbia University, after an easy test, gave compliments about their specific performance to one group of fifth-grade children and more general ones about their intelligence to another group. After a difficult task, which all children failed, she again gave an easy test and discovered that the children who received reinforcements about their specific behaviors on the first easy test were more likely to score higher on the second easy test, while those who received more general comments about their intelligence were actually more likely to do worse on the second easy test. According to Dweck, "Emphasizing effort [a general, rather than specific reinforcement] gives a child a variable that they can control. They come to see themselves as in control of their success. Emphasizing natural intelligence takes it out of the child's control, and it provides no good recipe for responding to a failure."[21]

Whether you have time for family dinners or not, what is important is getting "face time" with your teenager on a regular basis to provide opportunities for communication. Face time can involve talking for a few minutes at bedtime; watching television together and discussing the show; spending time in the car without your teen being plugged into an iPod, using a Game Boy, or texting his or her friends; and scheduling short family outings, which can be as simple as getting an ice cream after dinner or playing a card or board game before bedtime. It is not communication and face time *quantity* that makes the difference. It is what you do with that time. It saddens me when I see a family out to dinner and the parents are talking while the kids are immersed in their TechnoCocoons. They are all missing a great opportunity to bond as a family.

In addition to enjoying the warmth of close family time, this is a good occasion to educate your children on how to handle themselves in cyberspace. Socialization is new to them so don't be afraid to bring critical media topics into your discussions, including meeting online strangers, divulging personal information in cyberspace, video game aggression, Internet addiction, online pornography, television content, and music lyrics. Don't discuss more than one of these sensitive topics at a time, and remember to talk about them in a nonjudgmental tone and take the time to listen to your children's impressions. Your real aim here is to create a comfortable space where your teens will be relaxed enough to open up with you about their concerns and fears.

Reactive Parenting

It is all well and good to try to anticipate problems but often that is simply not possible. We parents often find ourselves facing situations with our adolescents that concern and upset us. For example, you discover your teen has been talking with an older person online and they have made plans to meet.[22] The natural tendency when faced with a difficult situation with your adolescent is to institute a strong immediate punishment. Telling your teenager that he is "grounded for life" won't work.

In fact, any harsh verbal or physical punishment most likely will back-fire and your teen will find other ways around your restrictions. If you take away computer access, they will find other ways and places to go online. In my research nearly half the teens used computers at friends' houses in addition to school, the public library, and even on their cell phones while many parents were unaware of those access points.[23]

The trick to reactive parenting is using what is called the "least restrictive alternative" to determine limits and punishments. What this means is that you begin by instituting punishments that are less harsh and if they do not work you move to more severe restrictions in incremental steps. Starting with severe punishment rarely works. The best place to begin is by using mild social disapproval.

Mild social disapproval requires you to keep your cool and not yell or even speak loudly. When your teen does something you do not approve of or think is potentially harmful, you look them in the eye, tell them that what they did is not acceptable and inform them what will happen if they do it again. In general, it is best if you do not apply any limits or punishments at this time and consider this a warning of future restrictions. Two parts of this procedure are critical. First, your disapproval has to be done in a neutral manner. Your tone of voice must be calm, your face needs to remain neutral and you must avoid any negative nonverbal cues such as balled fists, furrowed brow, and glaring eyes. If you lose your cool it will lessen the chance of the punishment working. Second, you must be clear about what will happen if the behavior recurs. This is sometimes difficult since you are reacting rather than being proactive. However, it is good to have in mind several layers of punishment ranging from mild restrictions to severe limitations. Start with fairly straightforward, mildly punitive restrictions, and if they fail to alter the behavior move to more restrictions.

Punishment works best under three conditions—immediacy, contingency, and consistency. Mild social disapproval should be applied immediately following the behavior, should be directly linked to the behavior, and should be applied consistently any time the behavior occurs. In fact, any punishment works best if these principles are applied. It is much less effective, for example, to tell a teenager, "Wait until your father gets home and then you will be punished." This lacks immediacy and makes it less likely that the punishment will be linked to the actual behavior. Similarly, punishing a teenager by saying something vague such as, "You have done bad things on the computer" is too general. Saying instead, "You spent too long on the computer after I told you to turn it off" is more specific; the punishment can then be made contingent on this specific misbehavior.

Consistency is the most difficult part of punishment. Listen to what Bernard, a seventeen-year-old high school senior, had to say about how his dad handled his excessive video game playing: *"At first he came down really hard and told me that I could only play video games when my homework was done and then only an hour a day during the school week and two hours on the weekend. But then he rarely checked on me at all. The first day he came in my room after an hour and turned off the game, but the next day he was busy on his computer and I got to play for three hours. Saturday he was gone playing golf and I stayed on the whole time and got off as I heard his car drive up."* Bernard's dad had good intentions, but needed to be more consistent in carrying out the restrictions to be effective.

Two other points are critical to consider when punishing a behavior. It is rather easy to see many behaviors as "punishable," particularly in reference to the Internet and technology. Remember, teens are hooked in most of the time and this is an important part of their socialization. It is important, I believe, to carefully pick your battles. For example, Andrew, a fourteen-year-old middle school student, commented that, *"My dad is just so rigid that I hardly get any time online. Last night at eight I told him that I had finished my homework and would like to check my MySpace messages until my bedtime at nine. He threw a fit and yelled at me that I was spending too much time online as it is. Heck, I have even told him that he could time me and I would be done in thirty minutes. We argued. He just seems to want to restrict everything I do even when what I am asking is very reasonable."* I believe that Andrew's dad would have been better served if he chose to give in to what was most likely a reasonable request and it would have made future limit-setting more effective. Your teen will be more likely to respond to your punishment and respect your authority if you choose to punish only those behaviors that are most bothersome to you and to let slide the little ones. Also be willing to compromise, and engage with them in an honest dialogue about discipline. You might ask their opinion about a suitable punishment. Most likely, it will be less restrictive than what you have in mind. Be willing to negotiate and find a middle ground. Teens are more responsive to punishment when they have a say in its severity and restrictions.

Punishment itself is rarely effective on its own. It does little good to punish your teenager for misbehavior if you fail to praise them for behavior you deem positive. Be vigilant about catching your teenager being good. When he does what you want, tell him you are happy. Reinforce the positive actions and compliment him on his good behavior. In all likelihood, as with ignoring cyberbullies, the bad behaviors will gradually disappear.

Regardless of whether you need to react or to be proactive, your general parenting style is an important moderator of how your children will react to punishment and restrictions. In chapter 8, I discussed four styles of parenting—authoritative, authoritarian, indulgent, and neglectful—based on two dimensions: (1) the amount of warmth, responsiveness, and parental involvement, and (2) the amount of control, strictness, and level of expectation. As explained there, children of authoritative parents model better overall behavior in all arenas, including school performance, socialization, self-esteem, general psychological health, and substance abuse. Being an authoritative parent means that you establish clear limits with your children with their input and consultation, adhere to those rules, and administer predetermined punishments—again with input from the children—in a warm, caring manner with as little anger and emotional upset as possible. In my own studies, as well as those of others, authoritative parenting led to more positive online behaviors.[24] Note that being an authoritative parent does mean that you set limits. Although I have covered many of these limits in earlier chapters, the following section presents the overall guiding principles of limit setting.

Setting Limits

Parents can easily set realistic limits for their cyberspace children in several ways, including: limiting their screen time, approving Web sites, monitoring screen content, positioning the computer in a common area, and monitoring their children's sleep patterns and school grades; parents can also monitor their own media behavior and model healthy media use. Let's talk about each of these options in turn.

1. Limit Screen Time

Screen time is any activity that is done in front of a screen, which includes the computer and the Internet, television, cell phones, video games, and portable music devices such as iPods. Research shows that more screen time during the school week results in poorer school performance.[25] Screen time limits should be realistic and not punitive. Personally, when I speak with parent groups, I recommend that screen time can only occur after homework and family obligations are completed, that it is limited to one to two hours per day, that it must be followed by some outdoor or social activities, and that additional screen time may be *earned* by good behavior.

2. Approve Sites They Visit

Tell your teens that you at least need to know which sites they're visiting to check that the sites are age appropriate and contain acceptable content. The most important thing to check is the age limit since sites with pornographic images or offensive language have visitors check a box indicating that they are old enough to view the content. Many teens lie about their age, and most sites have no way to verify that they are old enough. Similarly, MySpace has a fourteen-year-old age limit, and many teens skirt this limit either by lying about their age or indicating that they are ninety-nine years old. In my research, 16% of the MySpacers were *under fourteen*, so it is important for parents of tweens and young teens to make sure that they are old enough to join this social networking site.[26] Children younger than fourteen have other choices for social networking, such as Club Penguin or Disney Extreme Digital.[27]

3. Monitor Screen Content

Not all screen time is problematic. Make sure that you talk with your teenager about what content is and is not acceptable, including pornography, speaking with strangers, divulging personal information, playing overly violent or sexualized video games, and listening to music with degrading or sexual lyrics. You won't be able completely to restrict your teen and insulate him or her from questionable content, but you can discuss this proactively and stay aware of screen content by randomly observing your teen's screen behavior. Check video game box ratings, and sample the video's level of violence and sexuality for yourself.[28] Monitor IM conversations, or at least have an agreement with your teen that you have the option to view any IM chat, e-mail, or online material whenever you feel it is necessary. Make sure that you talk with caregivers and parents of any friends where your teen may have screen time, and coordinate monitoring of both time and content. Agree upon a prearranged set of consequences with your teen about what will happen if you find him or her viewing questionable screen content.

4. Position the Computer in a Common Area

In my research, and that of others, having a computer in the bedroom is directly related to more time spent online and more problem online behaviors.[29] To prevent this outcome, place the computer in a den or common area. If your only option is to place the computer in your teen's bedroom, maintain an open door policy that grants you the option to enter and view his or her computer activity at any time. Insist that if you enter the room and see screens switching, there will be consequences that you have set up in advance.

5. Monitor Sleep Patterns

Not all teens who spend hours in cyberspace display behavioral problems. A few easily monitored behaviors, however, may point to a need for proactive parenting. First, monitor your child's sleep habits. Lack of sleep or poor sleep habits could be a reflection of too much time spent using technology. Is your son or daughter difficult to wake for school? Does he or she fall asleep while doing homework? Does your teen rely on caffeinated drinks to stay alert during the day or to wake up in the morning? Does he or she take naps in the afternoon? Any of these are signs of potential over-involvement in the virtual world. If you notice these symptoms, you need to intervene proactively by setting a consistent bedtime and wake time that allow for at least seven hours of sleep per night. Instituting a consistent bedtime routine that is followed every night, removing technology such as a television or computer from the bedroom where the teen sleeps, and prohibiting caffeinated drinks after dinner is a good combination of steps.

6. Monitor School Grades

It is important to monitor your child's school progress diligently. Many schools are now putting grades online for parental access. Check to make sure that your teen's homework and test scores are not falling. This can be an indication of a potential problem with technology overuse.

7. Monitor Your Own Behavior

You need to set an example with your own personal media use. If you have the television on all day long, then it is not reasonable to restrict your teen's television viewing. If you are checking your e-mail and surfing the Internet at night after dinner, then you will find it difficult to effectively restrict your teen's online behavior. If you are always talking on your cell phone, how can you expect your teen to respond to your limits on his or her cell phone use?

8. Encourage Your Child by Modeling Good Behavior

"Do as I say, not as I do" is not a good parenting strategy. If you expect your teen to limit screen time, then you need to do the same, whether it is resisting plopping in front of the television and mindlessly flipping channels or monitoring your own online behavior. If you don't want your teen to text while you are having a conversation or family time, then don't answer your own cell phone during that time. If you don't want your teen watching certain television shows that you want to watch, TiVo them, and watch them when your teen is not home. If you want your teen to call you and tell you where he or she is at all times, then you should do the same. If you want your teen to spend more time socializing with the family, then it is your responsibility to make opportunities for that to happen. Unless you exhibit positive media behaviors, it is unlikely that your child will do so, no matter what limits and restrictions you place on him or her.

Parenting is not an easy job. Children do not come with an instruction manual. And when they are adolescents, the issues become more complex. This new generation presents a complex set of parenting challenges surrounding technology. Teens live in a virtual world, connect on MySpace, and multitask in ways that we, as parents, cannot fathom. Certainly, they are as different from us as we were from our parents, but the differences are unique due to the rapidly changing technological environment. Daily, it seems, a new virtual technology springs up and spreads through teen culture. Just look at YouTube, for example. It went from obscurity to commonplace in less than a year. Technologies that used to take tens of years to become mainstream now take months. This technological explosion makes parenting more difficult for this generation than any prior generation.

What Can You Do?

Practice both proactive and reactive parenting. To do this you need to listen to your children and create a comfortable enough home environment that encourages them to confide in you. Ideally you should try to get to a place where your children feel safe enough to use you as a sounding board to voice their fears and ambivalence, and draw on your experience as an adult to teach them to handle these situations on their own. You want to get to a place where they trust you enough to run problems by you and feel confident enough to resolve them independently.

Do your best to anticipate problems and establish rules before problems arise. When you must react, do so with a mild form of punishment and only escalate to harsher punishments if that fails. Above all, you must help your children learn acceptable virtual behavior by setting clear limits, modeling good media behavior yourself, and by providing praise and other positive reinforcements any time your teenager demonstrates positive media behavior. You may not realize it, but your children are telling you things all the time. What you hear depends on how closely you listen and how well you communicate. Their online world is different, new, and ever-changing. Use the proactive and reactive parenting skills introduced in this book to encourage your children to talk about what they are doing online so that you can help them make those experiences socially and emotionally healthy.

Finally, remember also that you are not alone. There are myriad available resources for dealing with any situation you and your child may encounter. Here are a few Web sites that provide valuable information for you to help raise healthy adolescents in their online world.

- www.isafe.org
- www.parenthood.com
- www.allianceforchildhood.net
- www.kids.getnetwise.org
- www.cybersmart.org
- www.netsmartz.org
- www.besafe.com
- www.protectkids.com
- www.webwisekids.com
- www.internetbehavior.com
- www.safeteens.com
- www.blogsafety.com
- www.commonsensemedia.com
- www.safefamilies.org
- www.wiredsafety.org
- www.netfamilynews.com

I interviewed Teri Schroeder, founder and CEO of iSafe, a worldwide leader in Internet safety education. Here are her thoughts:

Q: Why do you think that MySpace is so popular with adolescents?

Schroeder: One of the things that we have seen, particularly with areas like MySpace, is the fact that it gives students a lot of freedom. We really promote that but the problem is that when you look at exercising this freedom there is responsibility that goes along with it. We see this time and time again, particularly at these age demographics. Teens are really flexing their freedom muscles by making their own decisions. MySpace gives them lots of options, which are at their sole discretion, and they are making those decisions. They blog, talk, post pictures, promote themselves—all things that the Internet allows in term of accessibility.

Q: What recommendations do you have for parents on setting limits for media use including television, social networking, and video games?

Schroeder: I am a very big advocate of parents parenting in cyberspace as they do in real life. My recommendation for parents is that you need to parent no matter what the medium is, whether your kids are on a Web site such as MySpace, with a neighbor next door, or doing activities in their community. Parents need one set of rules with their child, regardless of whether or not that child is online. Many parents have a different set of rules with kids online than they do offline and this is confusing for both the parents and the kids. Kids online are doing the same things as they are in real life—socially communicating, making friends, buying things, looking at movies—all things that kids do in real life. For real life we have rules that regulate the teen's responsibilities and means of communication. To kids online, the line gets fuzzier because parents don't understand the Internet and have a whole different set of rules. So that in itself is a huge problem. A parent's job is to protect his or her child. Many feel their parenting skills are being challenged because of the technological media. They feel that they can't or are afraid to have those lines of communication with their sons or daughters. Parents need to disregard the fact that they don't understand "firewalls" or everything about MySpace. Whatever their rules are for making friends, going places, or buying things in the real world, those rules need to be the same in cyberspace. The flip side of that is that a lot of parenting is being taken out of the hands of parents because of the way the Internet functions. Parents say no, but kids have access with just a click of a button. Communication is the key. Talk with your son or daughter about these issues.

Q: What steps should parents take to help keep their teenagers safe in cyberspace?

Schroeder: The same steps that they would take to keep their sons or daughters safe in the real world. These conversations should be the same as the ones you have the first time you allow them to go to the mall with friends or go on a first date. As parents I hope we all have conversations about "stranger danger" with our children. We need to have those same conversations about talking to strangers online. Parents should not overreact when their teen does something wrong online. This creates a barrier between parent and child. The parent is saying to the child that he or she can have this technology and hands over the keys, and then does not have conversations about how to use it safely. If then the parent reacts to an online issue by taking away Internet access, this creates a barrier to future communication. Parents also need to become educated about the Internet. It is so important and they shouldn't be intimidated by the fact that it is "technology."

Q: How should parents teach their adolescents to behave online (i.e., what should be taught about language, sexism, and boundaries)?

Schroeder: Parents also need to talk about language use online, sexism, and boundaries just the same as they should do in real life. In real life, you have a talk about how when you dress or behave a certain way this is the message that you are sending to others. It is the same online. Kids have their identities online and how they want to be viewed. All kids have screen names. If a girl's screen name is "sexybabe14" what does that say about her? The same goes for language. If they would not say something to a classmate in the real world, then they need to think about not saying that online. Kids need to understand they have an identity online and it is important for parents to have a discussion about how their behavior affects that identity both online and offline. They should talk about how the teen views herself and how she wants to be viewed online. Kids need to know that how they portray themselves online can have consequences both now and down the road as they go on to college or jobs.

Q: How can parents monitor teen Internet use without invading their privacy or violating their trust?

Schroeder: There's a big difference between policing and protecting. If in real life you need to be the type of parent who has to check everything, because you suspect your child of some behavior like doing drugs or whatever, you might look in their closet or check their backpack. In cyberspace if you snoop and look at their activities online you are telling kids that you don't trust them, instead of establishing open lines of communication. Just like in real life, you need to talk to your kids. Parents should parent. If kids are getting gifts from strangers at the front door, are online instead of being in bed at night, or getting phone calls from people you do not know, it is time for a conversation. However, if a parent suspects that their child's safety may be at risk, they may have to look at the computer and find out what their child is doing. Some may say that this is an invasion of privacy and I hope that parents choose to communicate rather than snoop. So if an issue comes up such as your teen receiving gifts from someone they do not know, you need to talk about whether this is in their best interests. Pedophiles groom kids online. They isolate them and then take advantage of them. Parents need to understand that if there is a problem they need to go investigate it. However, they need to make sure that they don't make it worse. Parents and kids need honest, open communication about online activities just the same as they would have about offline activities.

Notes

Chapter 1: Living in a Virtual World

1 Greenfield, P., & Yan, Z. (2006). Children, adolescents, and the Internet: A new field of inquiry in developmental psychology. *Developmental Psychology, 42(3)*, 391–394.

2 These statistics can be found at the following Web sites:

> http://www.comscore.com
> http://www.un.org/cyberschoolbus/briefing/technology/tech.pdf
> http://www.rtnda.org/resources/wiredweb/text.html
> http://www.charlottesvillenewsplex.tv/station/misc/2305236.html
> http://www.imediaconnection.com/content/4547.asp
> http://www.usatoday.com/tech/news/2006-07-16-youtube-views_x.htm
> http://www.apple.com/pr/library/2007/04/09ipod.html

3 Toffler, A. (1980). *The third wave.* New York: William Morrow.

4 Roberts, D. F., Foehr, U. G., & Rideout, V. (2005). *Generation M: Media in the lives of 8–18 year-olds.* Menlo Park, CA: Kaiser Family Foundation. Retrieved from http://www.kff.org/entmedia/upload/Generation-M-Media-in-the-Lives-of -8-18-Year-olds-Report.pdf

5 Hallowell, E. M. (2006). *CrazyBusy: Overstretched, overbooked, and about to snap! Strategies for coping in a world gone ADD.* New York: Ballantine Books.

6 Lenhart, A., Madden, M., & Hitlin, P. (2005). *Teens and technology: Youth are leading the transition to a fully wired and mobile nation.* Washington, DC: Pew Internet & American Life Project Retrieved from http://www.pewinternet.org/ pdfs/PIP_Teens_Tech_July2005web.pdf

7 Rosen, L. D., Cheever, N. A., & Carrier, L. M. (2007). *The impact of parental attachment style, limit setting and monitoring on teen MySpace behavior.* Paper submitted for publication. Retrieved from http://www.csudh.edu/psych/The% 20Impact%20of%20Parental%20Attachment%20Style%20Rosen-Cheever -Ca.pdf. Rosen, L. D., Cummings, C., Albertella, M., Babcock, J., & Cheever,

N. A. (2007, May 3). *The MySpace generation: Adolescents living in a virtual world.* Symposium presented at the Western Psychological Association meeting, Vancouver, BC, Canada.

8   McNamara, M. P. (2006, June 13). *Teens are wired . . . and, yes, it's OK.* CBSNews .com. Retrieved from http://www.cbsnews.com/stories/2006/06/09/gentech/main1698246.shtml

9   Walsh, D., Gentile, D., Walsh, E., Bennett, N., Robideau, B., Walsh, et al. (2005, November 29). *Tenth annual MediaWise video game report card.* Minneapolis: National Institute on Media and the Family. Retrieved from http://www.mediafamily.org/research/report_vgrc_2005.shtml

10 Lenhart, A., Madden, M., & Hitlin, P. (2005). *Teens and technology: Youth are leading the transition to a fully wired and mobile nation.* Washington, DC: Pew Internet & American Life Project. Retrieved from http://www.pewinternet.org/pdfs/PIP_Teens_Tech_July2005web.pdf

11 2006 Teen Trend Study, by Harrison Group, reported in Olsen, S. (2006, December 7). *Teens and media: A full-time job.* CNET News.com: http://news.com.com/2100-1041_3-6141920.html

12 2006 Teen Trend Study, by Harrison Group, reported in Olsen, S. (2006, December 7). *Teens and media: A full-time job.* CNET News.com: http://news.com.com/2100-1041_3-6141920.html

13 Conti, N. D. (2007, August 8). Education 2.0: The best social networks for students. *Wired Magazine.* Retrieved from http://www.wired.com/software/webservices/news/2007/08/student_networks

14 Lenhart, A., Madden, M., & Hitlin, P. (2005). *Teens and technology: Youth are leading the transition to a fully wired and mobile nation.* Washington, DC: Pew Internet & American Life Project. Retrieved from http://www.pewinternet.org/pdfs/PIP_Teens_Tech_July2005web.pdf

15 Roberts, D. F., Foehr, U. G., & Rideout, V. (2005). *Generation M: Media in the lives of 8–18 year-olds.* Menlo Park, CA: Kaiser Family Foundation. Retrieved from http://www.kff.org/entmedia/upload/Generation-M-Media-in-the-Lives-of-8-18-Year-olds-Report.pdf

16 Becker, A. (2005). *TV watching is on the rise again: Study says more kids' rooms have TVs.* The Progress Report. Retrieved from http://www.progress.org/2005/tv02.htm

17 Rosen, L. D., Cheever, N. A., & Carrier, L. M. (2007). *The impact of parental attachment style, limit setting and monitoring on teen MySpace behavior.* Paper submitted for publication and retrieved from http://www.csudh.edu/psych/The%20Impact%20of%20Parental%20Attachment%20Style%20Rosen-Cheever-Ca.pdf. Rosen, L. D., Cummings, C., Albertella, M., Babcock, J., & Cheever, N. A. (2007, May 3). *The MySpace generation: Adolescents living in a virtual world.* Symposium presented at the Western Psychological Association meeting, Vancouver, BC, Canada.

18 Weil, M. M., & Rosen, L. D. (1997). *TechnoStress: Coping with technology @work @home @play*. New York, NY: Wiley, p. 129.

19 2006 Teen Trend Study, by Harrison Group, reported in Olsen, S. (2006, December 7). *Teens and media: A full-time job*. CNET News.com: http://news.com.com/2100-1041_3-6141920.html

20 Rideout, V., & Hamel, E. (2006, May). *The media family: Electronic media in the lives of infants, toddlers, preschoolers and their parents*. Menlo Park, CA: Kaiser Family Foundation. Retrieved from http://www.kff.org/entmedia/upload/7500.pdf

21 Roberts, D. F., Foehr, U. G., & Rideout, V. (2005). *Generation M: Media in the lives of 8–18 year-olds*. Menlo Park, CA: Kaiser Family Foundation. Retrieved from http://www.kff.org/entmedia/upload/Generation-M-Media-in-the-Lives-of-8-18-Year-olds-Report.pdf

22 Vandewater, E. A., Bickham, D. S., Lee, J. H., Cummings, H. M., Wartella, E. A., & Rideout, V. J. (2005). When the television is always on: Heavy television exposure and young children's development. *American Behavioral Scientist, 48,* 562–577.

23 Gellene, D. (2006, May 24). Teens who use cell phones most found to be sadder and less assured. *San Francisco Chronicle*. Retrieved from http://www.sfgate.com/cgi-bin/article.cgi?file=/c/a/2006/05/24/MNGVKJ12341.DTL

24 Lenhart, A., Rainie, L., & Lewis, O. (2001, June 20). *Teenage life online: The rise of the instant-message generation and the Internet's impact on friendships and family relationships*. Washington, DC: Pew Internet & American Life Project. Retrieved from http://www.pewinternet.org/pdfs/PIP_Teens_Report.pdf

25 Klauer, S. G., Dingus, T. A., Neale, V. L., Sudweeks, J., & Ramsey, D. *The impact of driver inattention on near-crash/crash risk: An analysis using the 100-car naturalistic driving study data*. Performed by Virginia Tech Transportation Institute, Blacksburg, VA, sponsored by National Highway Traffic Safety Administration, Washington, DC, April 2006, DOT HS 810 594- April 2006. Retrieved from http://www-nrd.nhtsa.dot.gov/departments/nrd-13/driver-distraction/PDF/DriverInattention.pdf

26 Partnership for Safe Driving: http://www.drivenowchatlater.com

27 Strayer, D. L., & Johnston, W. A. (2001). Driven to distraction: Dual-task studies of simulated driving and conversing on a cellular telephone. *Psychological Science, 12,* 462–466.

28 For a list of states and countries banning cell phones while driving visit cellular-news at http://www.cellular-news.com/car_bans/

29 Burke, M., Hornof, A., & Nilsen, E. (2005). High-cost banner blindness: Ads increase perceived workload, hinder visual search, and are forgotten. *ACM Transactions on Computer-Human Interaction, 12,* 423–445.

30 The ABCs of back-to-school sleep schedules: The consequences of insufficient sleep. Washington, DC: National Sleep Foundation, August 16, 2006. Retrieved from http://www.sleepfoundation.org/site/apps/nl/content2.asp?c=huIXKjM0Ix F&b=2424611&ct=3459755

31 America's sleep-deprived teens nodding off at school, behind the wheel, new National Sleep Foundation Poll Finds. Washington, DC: National Sleep Foundation, March 28, 2006. Retrieved from http://www.sleepfoundation.org/site/c.huIXKjM0IxF/b.2428023/k.8425/Americas_SleepDeprived_Teens_Nodding_Off_at_School_Behind_the_Wheel.htm

32 Wallis, C. (2006, May 19). The multitasking generation. *Time*. Retrieved from http://www.time.com/time/magazine/article/0,9171,1174696-1,00.html

33 Conti, N. D. (2007, August 8). Education 2.0: The best social networks for students. *Wired Magazine*. Retrieved from http://www.wired.com/software/webservices/news/2007/08/student_networks

34 Rosen, L. D., Cheever, N. A., & Carrier, L. M. (2007). *The impact of parental attachment style, limit setting and monitoring on teen MySpace behavior*. Paper submitted for publication and retrieved from http://www.csudh.edu/psych/The%20Impact%20of%20Parental%20Attachment%20Style%20Rosen-Cheever-Ca.pdf. Rosen, L. D., Cummings, C., Albertella, M., Babcock, J., & Cheever, N. A. (2007, May 3). *The MySpace generation: Adolescents living in a virtual world*. Symposium presented at the Western Psychological Association meeting, Vancouver, BC, Canada.

35 *Online world as important to Internet users as real world? USC-Annenberg Digital Future Project finds major shifts in social communication and personal connections on the Internet*. USC Annenberg Center for the Digital Future. November 29, 2006. Retrieved from http://www.digitalcenter.org/pages/news_content.asp?intGlobalId=212&intTypeId=1

36 *New national poll: The Internet now seen as #1 media concern for parents*. San Francisco: Common Sense Media. June 7, 2006. Retrieved from http://www.commonsensemedia.org/news/press-releases.php?id=23

Chapter 2: The MySpace Generation

1 Pierce, T. A. (2005, Winter). Violence in the news: Attachment styles as moderators of priming effects. *Journal of Media Psychology, 10*. Retrieved from http://www.calstatela.edu/faculty/sfischo/Violence_in_the_News.html

2 The American Psychiatric Association develops and publishes criteria for mental disorders in a book entitled *The Diagnostic and Statistical Manual of Mental Disorders*. The third edition of this manual—DSM-III—published in 1980, identified Attention Deficit Disorder, with two subtypes depending on whether the attention difficulties were a function of hyperactivity (ADD/H) or involved inattention without hyperactivity (ADD/WO). A revision of the manual in 1987 (DSM-IIIR) renamed the disorder Attention Deficit Hyperactivity Disorder (ADHD) asserting that the disorder must contain a hyperactive component. However, in 1994, the new DSM-IV maintained the name ADHD but divided it into three subtypes: Primarily Inattentive, Primarily Hyperactive/Impulsive, and

Combined Type. The diagnostic criteria are described in an excellent summary article at the PBS Web site: http://www.pbs.org/wgbh/pages/frontline/shows/medicating/adhd/diagnostic.html

3 Lindgaard, G., Fernandes, G., Dudek, C., & Brown, J. (2006). Attention Web designers: You have 50 milliseconds to make a good first impression. *Behaviour & Information Technology, 25(2)*, 115–126.

4 Rosen, L. D., Cheever, N. A., & Carrier, L. M. (2007). *The impact of parental attachment style, limit setting and monitoring on teen MySpace behavior.* Paper submitted for publication. Retrieved from http://www.csudh.edu/psych/The%20 Impact%20of%20Parental%20Attachment%20Style%20Rosen-Cheever-Ca .pdf. Rosen, L. D., Cummings, C., Albertella, M., Babcock, J., & Cheever, N. A. (2007, May 3). *The MySpace generation: Adolescents living in a virtual world.* Symposium presented at the Western Psychological Association meeting, Vancouver, BC, Canada.

5 In two research studies, 33%–38% of parents had not seen their teen's MySpace page and 44%–52% admitted they never or almost never visited their teen's MySpace page. Rosen, L. D., Cheever, N. A., & Carrier, L. M. (2007). *The impact of parental attachment style, limit setting and monitoring on teen MySpace behavior.* Paper submitted for publication. Retrieved from http://www.csudh.edu/ psych/The%20Impact%20of%20Parental%20Attachment%20Style%20Rosen -Cheever-Ca.pdf

6 Cooperative Institutional Research Program (2002). *The American freshman: National norms for fall 2001.* Los Angeles: UCLA. Retrieved from http://www .gseis.ucla.edu/heri/norms_pr_01.html

7 Cooperative Institutional Research Program (2002). *The American freshman: National norms for Fall 2001.* Los Angeles: UCLA. Retrieved from http://www .gseis.ucla.edu/heri/norms_pr_01.html

8 Roberts, D. F., Foehr, U. G., & Rideout, V. (2005). *Generation M: Media in the lives of 8–18 year-olds.* Menlo Park, CA: Kaiser Family Foundation. Retrieved from http://www.kff.org/entmedia/upload/Generation-M-Media-in-the-Lives-of -8-18-Year-olds-Report.pdf

9 National Sleep Foundation (2006). *2006 Sleep in America poll highlights and key findings.* Retrieved from http://www.sleepfoundation.org/atf/cf/%7BF6BF2668 -A1B4-4FE8-8D1A-A5D39340D9CB%7D/Highlights_facts_06.pdf. Additional information about this poll can be found at: http://www.sleepfoundation.org/site/ c.huIXKjM0IxF/b.2419037/k.1466/2006_Sleep_in_America_Poll.htm

10 van Duinen, H., Lorist, M. M., & Zijdewind, I. (2005). The effects of caffeine on cognitive task performance and motor fatigue. *Psychopharmacology, 180*, 539–547.

11 Roberts, D. F., Foehr, U. G., & Rideout, V. (2005). *Generation M: Media in the lives of 8–18 year-olds.* Menlo Park, CA: Kaiser Family Foundation. Retrieved from http://www.kff.org/entmedia/upload/Generation-M-Media-in-the-Lives-of -8-18-Year-olds-Report.pdf

Chapter 3: Real People in Virtual Relationships

1 Miller, M., Smith-Lovin, L., & Brashears, M. (2006). Social isolation in America: Changes in Core Discussion Networks over Two Decades. *American Sociological Review 71(3)*, 353–375. Quoted in Beck, A. (2006, June 23). Americans' circle of close friends shrinking. *Reuters*.

2 For further information on crowds and cliques, here are five references that provide excellent coverage of this topic: (1) Cole, M., Cole, S. R., & Lightfoot, C. (2005). *The development of children*. New York: Worth. Fifth Edition. (2) Coleman, J. S. (1962). *The adolescent society*. Glencoe, IL: Free Press. (3) Brown, B. B., & Huang, B. (1995). Examining parenting practices in different peer contexts: Implications for adolescent trajectories. In L. J. Crockett & A. C. Crouter (Eds.), *Pathways through adolescence: Individual development in relation to social contexts* (pp. 151–174). Mahwah, NJ: Erlbaum. (4) Brown, B. B. (1990). Peer groups and peer cultures. In S. S. Feldman & G. R. Elliott, *At the threshold: The developing adolescent*. (pp. 171-196). Cambridge, MA: Harvard University Press. (5) Garner, R., Bootcheck, J., Lorr, M., & Rauch, K. (2006). The Adolescent society revisited: Cultures, crowds, climates, and status structures in seven secondary schools. *Journal of Youth and Adolescence, 35(6)*, 1023–1035.

3 In her national sample of teens, Dr. Jane Wolak and her colleagues at the University of New Hampshire reported that 14% had made "close online friendships." Wolak, J., Mitchell, K. J., & Finkelhor, D. (2003). Escaping or connecting? Characteristics of youth who form close online relationships. *Journal of Adolescence, 26*, 105–119. Wolak, J., Mitchell, K. J., & Finkelhor, D. (2002). Close online relationships in a national sample of adolescents. *Adolescence, 37(147)*, 441–455.

4 Rosen, L. D., Cheever, N. A., & Carrier, L. M. (2007). *The impact of parental attachment style, limit setting and monitoring on teen MySpace behavior*. Paper submitted for publication. Retrieved from http://www.csudh.edu/psych/The%20 Impact%20of%20Parental%20Attachment%20Style%20Rosen-Cheever-Ca .pdf. Rosen, L. D., Cummings, C., Albertella, M., Babcock, J., & Cheever, N. A. (2007, May 3). *The MySpace generation: Adolescents living in a virtual world*. Symposium presented at the Western Psychological Association meeting, Vancouver, BC, Canada.

5 Valkenburg, P. M., Peter, J., & Schouten, A. P. (2006). Friend networking sites and their relationship to adolescents' well-being and social self-esteem. *Cyber-Psychology & Behavior, 9(5)*, 584–590. Peter, J., Valkenburg, P. M., & Schouten, A. P. (2006). Characteristics and motives of adolescents talking with strangers on the Internet. *CyberPsychology & Behavior, 9(5)*, 526–530. Valkenburg, P. M., & Peter, J. (2007). Preadolescents' and adolescents' online communication and their closeness to friends. *Developmental Psychology, 43(2)*, 267–277. Peter, J., Valkenburg, P. M., & Schouten, A. P. (2005). Developing a model of adolescent friendship formation on the Internet. *CyberPsychology & Behavior, 8(5)*, 423–430.

6 Rosen, L. D., Cheever, N. A., & Carrier, L. M. (2007). *The impact of parental attachment style, limit setting and monitoring on teen MySpace behavior*. Paper submitted

for publication. Retrieved from http://www.csudh.edu/psych/The%20Impact%20of%20Parental%20Attachment%20Style%20Rosen-Cheever-Ca.pdf. Rosen, L. D., Cummings, C., Albertella, M., Babcock, J., & Cheever, N. A. (2007, May 3). *The MySpace generation: Adolescents living in a virtual world.* Symposium presented at the Western Psychological Association meeting, Vancouver, BC, Canada.

7 Shiu, E., & Lenhart, A. (2004, September 1). *How Americans use instant messaging.* Washington, DC: Pew Internet & American Life Project. Retrieved from http://www.pewinternet.org/pdfs/PIP_Instantmessage_Report.pdf

8 Shiu, E., & Lenhart, A. (2004, September 1). *How Americans use instant messaging.* Washington, DC: Pew Internet & American Life Project. Retrieved from http://www.pewinternet.org/pdfs/PIP_Instantmessage_Report.pdf

9 Joinson, A. N. (1998). Causes and effects of disinhibition on the Internet. In J. Gackenbach (Ed.), *The psychology of the Internet (pp. 43–60).* New York: Academic Press.

10 Joinson, A. N. (2001). Self-disclosure in computer-mediated communication: The role of self-awareness and visual anonymity. *European Journal of Social Psychology* 31, 177–192.

11 Walther, J. B. (2007). Selective self-presentation in computer-mediated communication: Hyperpersonal dimensions of technology, language, and cognition. *Computers in Human Behavior, 23,* 2538–2557.

12 Goering, S. (2003). Choosing our friends: Moral partiality and the value of diversity. *Journal of Social Philosophy, 34(3),* 400-413.

13 Rosen, L. D., Cheever, N. A., Cummings, C., Albertella, M., Ruoti, H., & Rifa, J. (2007). *Seeking advice on the Internet: Who do we trust?* Unpublished manuscript.

14 Demir, M. (2004). *Friendship and happiness among adolescents.* Unpublished master's thesis. Wayne State University. Requena, F. (1995). Friends and Subjective Well-Being in Spain: A Cross-National Comparison with the United States. *Social Indicators Research, 35,* 271–288. Brendt, F (1995). Friendship Quality and Social Development. *Current Directions in Psychological Science, 11,* 7–11.

15 Rosen, L. D., Cheever, N. A., & Carrier, L. M. (2007). *The impact of parental attachment style, limit setting and monitoring on teen MySpace behavior.* Paper submitted for publication. Retrieved from http://www.csudh.edu/psych/The%20Impact%20of%20Parental%20Attachment%20Style%20Rosen-Cheever-Ca.pdf

16 Wolak, J., Mitchell, K. J., & Finkelhor, D. (2003). Escaping or connecting? Characteristics of youth who form close online relationships. *Journal of Adolescence, 26,* 105–119.

17 Boase, J., Horrigan, J. B., Wellman, B., & Rainie, L. (2006, January 25). *The strength of Internet ties.* Washington, DC: Pew Internet & American Life Project. Retrieved from http://www.pewinternet.org/pdfs/PIP_Internet_ties.pdf

18 Valkenburg, P. M., & Peter, J. *Adolescents' online communication and their closeness to friends.* Paper presented at the annual meeting of the International Communication Association, New York, NY. Retrieved from http://www.allacademic.com/meta/p11699_index.html

19 Cole, M., Cole, S. R., & Lightfoot, C. (2005). *The development of children*. New York: Worth. Fifth Edition.

20 Rosen, L. D., Cheever, N. A., & Carrier, L. M. (2007). *The impact of parental attachment style, limit setting and monitoring on teen MySpace behavior*. Paper submitted for publication. Retrieved from http://www.csudh.edu/psych/The%20Impact%20of%20Parental%20Attachment%20Style%20Rosen-Cheever-Ca.pdf.

21 Rosen, L. D., Cheever, N. A., Felt, J., & Cummings, C. (2007). *The impact of emotionality and self-disclosure on online dating versus traditional dating*. Submitted for publication. Retrieved from http://www.csudh.edu/psych/The%20Impact%20of%20Emotionality%20and%20Self-Disclosure%20on%20Online%20Dating%20versus%20Traditional%20Dating.pdf

22 Wolak, J., Mitchell, K. J., & Finkelhor, D. (2003). Escaping or connecting? Characteristics of youth who form close online relationships. *Journal of Adolescence, 26*, 105–119. Wolak, J., Mitchell, K. J., & Finkelhor, D. (2002). Close online relationships in a national sample of adolescents. *Adolescence, 37(147)*, 441–455.

23 Cox Communications and the National Center for Missing & Exploited Children (2006, May 11). *New study reveals 14% of teens have had face-to-face meetings with people they've met on the Internet*. Retrieved from http://www.missingkids.com/missingkids/servlet/NewsEventServlet?LanguageCountry=en_US&PageId=2383

24 Rosen, L. D., Cheever, N. A., & Carrier, L. M. (2007). *The impact of parental attachment style, limit setting and monitoring on teen MySpace behavior*. Paper submitted for publication. Retrieved from http://www.csudh.edu/psych/The%20Impact%20of%20Parental%20Attachment%20Style%20Rosen-Cheever-Ca.pdf

25 boyd, d. (2006, February 19). *Identity production in a networked culture: Why youth heart MySpace*. American Association for the Advancement of Science. St. Louis, MO. Retrieved from http://www.danah.org/papers/AAAS2006.html.

Chapter 4: Me, MySpace, and I

1 Quoted in Wright, S. H., (2006, May 24). *Experts discuss MySpace issues*. Boston, MA: Massachusetts Institute of Technology News Office. Retrieved from http://web.mit.edu/newsoffice/2006/myspace-0524.html

2 Murray, B. (2000). A mirror on the self. *Monitor on Psychology, 31(4)*. Retrieved from http://www.apa.org/monitor/apr00/mirror.html

3 Jenkins, H. (2006, May 30). *Discussion: MySpace and Deleting Online Predators Act (DOPA)*. Media Center, MIT. Retrieved from http://web.mit.edu/cms/People/henry3/myspaceissues.htm

4 Jenkins, H. (2006, May 30). *Discussion: MySpace and Deleting Online Predators Act (DOPA)*. Media Center, MIT. Retrieved from http://web.mit.edu/cms/People/henry3/myspaceissues.htm

5 Rosen, L. D., Cheever, N. A., & Carrier, L. M. (2007). *The impact of parental attachment style, limit setting and monitoring on teen MySpace behavior*. Paper submitted for publication. Retrieved from http://www.csudh.edu/psych/The%20Impact%20of%20Parental%20Attachment%20Style%20Rosen-Cheever-Ca.pdf

6 McConochie, R., & Solomon, D. (2003, September 23). *Children's media odys-seys: Kids' 6–17 evolving media mix.* Arbitron and MindShare. Retrieved from http://www.arbitronradio.com/downloads/PPM_Kids_Pres.pdf

7 Turkle, S. (1995). *Life on the screen: Identity in the age of the Internet.* New York: Simon & Schuster.

8 Turkle, S. (2004). Our split screens. In A. Feenberg & D. Barney (Eds.), *Community in the digital age: Philosophy and practice.* Lanham, MD: Rowman & Littlefield.

9 Thibaut, J. W., & Kelley, H. H. (1959). *The social psychology of groups.* New York: Wiley.

10 Joinson, A. N. (2004). Self-esteem, interpersonal risk, and preferences for e-mail to face-to-face communication. *CyberPsychology and Behavior, 7(4)*, 479–485. Joinson, A. N. (2001). Self-disclosure in computer-mediated communication: The role of self-awareness and visual anonymity. *European Journal of Social Psychology, 31*, 177–192.

11 Rosen, L. D., Cheever, N. A., Felt, J., & Cummings, C. (2007). *The impact of emo-tionality and self-disclosure on online dating versus traditional dating.* Submitted for publication. Retrieved from http://www.csudh.edu/psych/The%20Impact%20 of%20Emotionality%20and%20Self-Disclosure%20on%20Online%20Dating %20versus%20Traditional%20Dating.pdf

12 Suler, J. (2004). The online disinhibition effect. *CyberPsychology & Behavior, 7*, 321–326.

13 Suler, J. (2004). The online disinhibition effect. *CyberPsychology & Behavior, 7*, 321–326.

14 Jazwinski, C. H. (2001). Gender identities on the World Wide Web. In Chris-topher Wolfe (Ed.), *Learning and teaching* (pp. 171–189). New York: Academic Press.

15 Lenhart, A., & Madden, M. (2007, April 18). *Teens, privacy & online social net-works: How teens manage their online identities and personal information in the age of MySpace.* Washington, DC: Pew Internet & American Life Project. Retrieved from http://www.pewinternet.org/pdfs/PIP_Teens_Privacy_SNS_Report_Final .pdf

16 Goffman, E. (1959). *The presentation of self in everyday life.* Garden City, NY: Doubleday.

17 Bargh, J. A., McKenna, K. Y. A, & Fitzsimmons, G. M. (2002). Can you see the real me? Activation and expression of the "true self" on the Internet. *Journal of Social Issues, 58*, 33–48.

18 Bargh, J. A., McKenna, K. Y. A, & Fitzsimmons, G. M. (2002). Can you see the real me? Activation and expression of the "true self" on the Internet. *Journal of Social Issues, 58*, 33–48.

19 McKenna, K. Y. A., Green, A. S, & Gleason, E. J. (2002). Relationship formation on the Internet: What's the big attraction? *Journal of Social Issues. 58*, 9–31.

20 McKenna, K. Y. A., Green, A. S, & Gleason, E. J. (2002). Relationship formation on the Internet: What's the big attraction? *Journal of Social Issues. 58*, 9–31.

21 Rosen, L. D., Cheever, N. A., & Carrier, L. M. (2007). *The impact of parental attachment style, limit setting and monitoring on teen MySpace behavior.* Paper submitted for publication. Retrieved from http://www.csudh.edu/psych/The%20 Impact%20of%20Parental%20Attachment%20Style%20Rosen-Cheever-Ca .pdf. Correlations between being shy offline and finding it easier to make friends (r=.29, p<.001); finding it easier to be honest online (r=.31, p<.001) and self-esteem (r=.24, p<.001).

22 Cole, M., Cole, S. R., & Lightfoot, C. (2005). *The development of children.* New York: Worth. Fifth Edition.

23 Vogensen, A. C. (2003). Finding themselves: Identity formation and romantic styles in late adolescence (Doctoral dissertation, Clinical Psychology, The Wright Institute, Berkeley, CA, 2003). *Dissertation Abstracts International: Section B: The Sciences and Engineering, 64(3-B),* 1529.

24 Rosen, L. D., Cheever, N. A., & Carrier, L. M. (2007). *The impact of parental attachment style, limit setting and monitoring on teen MySpace behavior.* Paper submitted for publication. Retrieved from http://www.csudh.edu/psych/The%20 Impact%20of%20Parental%20Attachment%20Style%20Rosen-Cheever-Ca.pdf

25 boyd, d. (2006, February 19). *Identity production in a networked culture: Why youth heart MySpace.* American Association for the Advancement of Science. St. Louis, MO. Retrieved from http://www.danah.org/papers/AAAS2006.html. Donath, J., & boyd, d. (2004). Public displays of connection. *BT Technology Journal, 22(4),* 71–82. Retrieved from http://www.danah.org/papers/AAAS2006.html

26 Lenhart, A., & Madden, M. (2007, April 18). *Teens, privacy & online social networks: How teens manage their online identities and personal information in the age of MySpace.* Washington, DC: Pew Internet & American Life Project. Retrieved from http://www.pewinternet.org/pdfs/PIP_Teens_Privacy_SNS_Report_Final .pdf

27 Conti, N. D. (2007, August 8). Education 2.0: The best social networks for students. *Wired Magazine.* Retrieved from http://www.wired.com/software/ webservices/news/2007/08/student_networks

28 Lenhart, A., & Madden, M. (2007, April 18). *Teens, privacy & online social networks.* Washington, DC: Pew Internet & American Life Project. Retrieved from http://www.pewinternet.org/pdfs/PIP_Teens_Privacy_SNS_Report_Final.pdf

29 Goodstein, A. (2007). *Totally wired: What teens and tweens are really doing online.* New York: St. Martin's Griffin.

30 Rosen, L. D., Cheever, N. A., & Carrier, L. M. (2007). *The impact of parental attachment style, limit setting and monitoring on teen MySpace behavior.* Paper submitted for publication. Retrieved from http://www.csudh.edu/psych/The%20 Impact%20of%20Parental%20Attachment%20Style%20Rosen-Cheever-Ca .pdf. Parents and teens differed significantly on their concern that MySpace interferes with the following: schoolwork (parents: 28%; teens: 16%), family time (parents: 29%; teens: 9%), outdoor activities (parents: 34%; teens: 13%), and chores (parents: 30%; teens: 16%).

31   Lenhart, A., & Madden, M. (2007, April 18). *Teens, privacy & online social networks.* Washington, DC: Pew Internet & American Life Project. Retrieved from http://www.pewinternet.org/pdfs/PIP_Teens_Privacy_SNS_Report_Final.pdf

32   Comparable data can be found in Lenhart, A., & Madden, M. (2007, April 18). *Teens, privacy & online social networks.* Washington, DC: Pew Internet & American Life Project. Retrieved from http://www.pewinternet.org/pdfs/PIP_Teens _Privacy_SNS_Report_Final.pdf, and Hinduja, S, & Patchin, J. W. (in press). *Personal information of adolescents on the Internet: A quantitative content analysis MySpace. Journal of Adolescence.*

33   Rosen, L. D., Cheever, N. A., & Carrier, L. M. (2007). *The impact of parental attachment style, limit setting and monitoring on teen MySpace behavior.* Paper submitted for publication. Retrieved from http://www.csudh.edu/psych/The%20 Impact%20of%20Parental%20Attachment%20Style%20Rosen-Cheever-Ca .pdf. Overall, 43% of parents were not sure how many days per week their teenager visited MySpace and 36% were not sure how many hours per day they spent there.

34   Parents were concerned about the following potential problems on MySpace: sexual solicitation (65%), sexual materials (65%), sexual talk (63%), divulging personal information (62%), meeting online friends (60%), harassment (56%), Internet addiction (45%), lack of physical activity (44%), and social isolation (36%).

35   In three studies, 46% of teens reported that their computer was located in their bedroom.

36   Rideout, V., & Hamel, E. (2006, May). *The media family: Electronic media in the lives of infants, toddlers, preschoolers and their parents.* Menlo Park, CA: Kaiser Family Foundation.

37   In the Pew Internet & American Life Project, 64% of the parents claimed that they set rules about online time. Sixty-two percent said that they checked up on their children's Internet surfing habits. However, only 33% of the teens in that study said that their parents actually monitored them. An earlier Pew study found similar results with 61% of the parents saying they enforced limits but only 37% of their children concurring. My study showed that 46% of the parents claimed to have limits on computer use but only 25% of the adolescents said that their parents actually upheld the limits. And only 31% of the parents had limits on MySpace use with only 24% of them actually checking on their children's MySpace use. For a summary of how parents are monitoring their teens see, Lenhart, A., & Madden, M. (2007, April 18). *Teens, privacy & online social networks: How teens manage their online identities and personal information in the age of MySpace.* Washington, DC: Pew Internet & American Life Project. Retrieved from http:// www.pewinternet.org/pdfs/PIP_Teens_Privacy_SNS_Report_Final.pdf

38   Rosen, L. D., Cheever, N. A, & Carrier, L. M. (2007). *The impact of parental attachment style, limit setting and monitoring on teen MySpace behavior.* Paper submitted for publication. Retrieved from http://www.csudh.edu/psych/The%20 Impact%20of%20Parental%20Attachment%20Style%20Rosen-Cheever-Ca.pdf

Chapter 5: Virtually Exposed

1   Crosby, R. (2006, February 6). *Caught in the dangers of web. Are people putting too much information online?* MSNBC. Retrieved from http://www.msnbc.msn.com/id/11203148/

2   Herring, S. C., Kouper, I., Scheidt, L. A, & Wright, E. (2004). Women and children last: The discursive construction of weblogs. In L. Gurak, S. Antonijevic, L. Johnson, C. Ratlif, & J. Reyman (Eds.), *Into the blogosphere: Rhetoric, community, and culture of weblogs.* Minneapolis: University of Minnesota. http://blog.lib .umn.edu/blogosphere/women_and_children.html. Herring, S. C., Scheidt, L. A., Bonus, S, & Wright, E. (2004). Bridging the gap: A genre analysis of weblogs. *Proceedings of the 37th Hawai'i International Conference on System Sciences (HICSS-37).* Los Alamitos: IEEE Computer Society Press. http://www .blogninja.com/DDGDD04.doc. Dr. Susan Herring's publications can be found at http://www.slis.indiana.edu/faculty/herring/pubs.html

3   Rosen, L. D., Cheever, N. A, & Carrier, L. M. (2007). *The impact of parental attachment style, limit setting and monitoring on teen MySpace behavior.* Paper submitted for publication. Retrieved from http://www.csudh.edu/psych/The%20 Impact%20of%20Parental%20Attachment%20Style%20Rosen-Cheever-Ca.pdf

4   Ostrowski, A. (2003, May 30). Most bloggers are teenage girls. *The register.* Retrieved from www.theregister.co.uk/2003/05/30/most_bloggers_are_teenage _girls. Herring, S. C., Kouper, I., Scheidt, L. A., & Wright, E. (2004). Women and children last: The discursive construction of weblogs. In L. Gurak, S. Antonijevic, L. Johnson, C. Ratliff & J. Reyman (Eds.), *Into the blogosphere: Rhetoric, community, and culture of weblogs.* Minneapolis: University of Minnesota. http:// blog.lib.umn.edu/blogosphere/women_and_children.html. Lenhart, A., & Madden, M. (2005, November 2). *Teen content creators and consumers.* Washington, DC: Pew Internet & American Life Project. Retrieved from http://www .pewinternet.org/pdfs/PIP_Teens_Content_Creation.pdf

5   *AOL survey says: People blog as therapy. BusinessWire,* September 16, 2005. Retrieved from http://peopleconnection.aol.com/blogs or http://www.business week.com/the_thread/blogspotting/archives/document/AOL%20Survey.doc

6   Willard, N. E. (2007). *Cyber-safe kids, cyber-savvy teens: Helping young people learn to use the internet safely and responsibly.* San Francisco: Jossey-Bass.

7   Turkle, S. (1995). *Life on the screen: Identity in the age of the Internet.* New York: Simon & Schuster.

8   Huffaker, D. A., & Calvert, S. L. (2005). Gender, identity, and language use in teenage blogs. *Journal of Computer-Mediated Communication, 10(2).* Retrieved from http://jcmc.indiana.edu/vol10/issue2/huffaker.html

9   Shiu, E., & Lenhart, A. (2004, September 1). *How Americans use instant messaging.* Washington, DC: Pew Internet & American Life Project. Retrieved from http://www.pewinternet.org/pdfs/PIP_Instantmessage_Report.pdf

10 Boneva, B. S., Quinn, A., Kraut, R. E., Kiesler, S, & Shklovski, I. (2006). Teenage communication in the instant message era. In R. Kraut, M. Bryni, & S. Kiesler

(Eds.), *Computers, phones, and the Internet: Domesticating information technology.* New York: Oxford University Press. Retrieved from http://www.cs.cmu.edu/~kraut/ RKraut.site.files/pubs/Domesticating-PDFs/Ch14-Boneva-IMandTeens.pdf

11 Shiu, E., & Lenhart, A. (2004, September 1). *How Americans use instant messaging.* Washington, DC: Pew Internet & American Life Project. Retrieved from http://www.pewinternet.org/pdfs/PIP_Instantmessage_Report.pdf

12 Boneva, B. S., Quinn, A., Kraut, R. E., Kiesler, S., & Shklovski, I. (2006). Teenage communication in the instant message era. In R. Kraut, M. Brynin, & S. Kiesler (Eds.), *Computers, phones, and the Internet: Domesticating information technology.* New York: Oxford University Press. Retrieved from http://www.cs.cmu.edu/~kraut/ RKraut.site.files/pubs/Domesticating-PDFs/Ch14-Boneva-IMandTeens.pdf

13 Boneva, B. S., Quinn, A., Kraut, R. E., Kiesler, S., & Shklovski, I. (2006). Teenage communication in the instant message era. In R. Kraut, M. Brynin, & S. Kiesler (Eds.), *Computers, phones, and the Internet: Domesticating information technology.* New York: Oxford University Press. Retrieved from http://www.cs.cmu.edu/~kraut/ RKraut.site.files/pubs/Domesticating-PDFs/Ch14-Boneva-IMandTeens.pdf

14 boyd, d., & Heer, J. (2006, January 4–7). Profiles as conversation: Networked identity performance on Friendster. *Proceedings of the 37th Hawai'i International Conference on System Sciences (HICSS-37),* Kauai, HI: IEEE Computer Society.

15 Rosen, L. D., Cheever, N. A., & Carrier, L. M. (2007). *The impact of parental attachment style, limit setting and monitoring on teen MySpace behavior.* Paper submitted for publication. Retrieved from http://www.csudh.edu/psych/The%20 Impact%20of%20Parental%20Attachment%20Style%20Rosen-Cheever-Ca.pdf

16 Rosen, L. D., Cheever, N. A., Felt, J., & Cummings, C. (2007). *The impact of emotionality and self-disclosure on online dating versus traditional dating.* Submitted for publication. Retrieved from http://www.csudh.edu/psych/The%20Impact%20 of%20Emotionality%20and%20Self-Disclosure%20on%20Online%20Dating %20versus%20Traditional%20Dating.pdf

17 Dominick, J. R. (1999, Winter). Who do you think you are? Personal home pages and self-presentation on the World Wide Web. *Journal & Mass Communication, 76(4),* 646–658.

18 More acronyms can be found at http://www.aim.com/acronyms.adp?aolp or at http://en.wikipedia.org/wiki/List_of_Internet_slang_phrases

19 Here are some common smilies:

    :-(or :-< represents sadness or unhappiness
:'(or :_(or even :*(indicates crying or shedding a tear
>:=(shows that you are angry or grumpy
;-) is a wink
:-D depicts a wide grin or very happy smile
:-P shows the tongue sticking out and is used to highlight a joke, sarcastic remark, or even a groan upon hearing a joke
:-o or :-O can be used to show surprise

:* is often used to show the delivery of a kiss

:-/ is a slight frown showing annoyance or skepticism

20 Prensky, M. (2001). Digital native, digital immigrants. *On the Horizon, 9(5)*, 1–6. Retrieved from http://www.marcprensky.com/writing/Prensky%20-%20 Digital%20Natives,%20Digital%20Immigrants%20-%20Part1.pdf

21 Huffaker, D. A., & Calvert, S. L. (2005). Gender, identity, and language use in teenage blogs. *Journal of Computer-Mediated Communication, 10(2), article 1.* Retrieved from http://jcmc.indiana.edu/vol10/issue2/huffaker.html

22 Constantin, C., Kalyanaraman, S., Stavrositu, C., & Wagoner, N. (2002, November). *Impression formation effects in moderated chatrooms: An experimental study of gender differences.* Paper presented at the eighty-eighth annual meeting of the National Communication Association, New Orleans, LA. Retrieved from http:// www.psu.edu/dept/medialab/research/NCA.htm

23 Huffaker, D. (2005). The educated blogger: Using weblogs to promote literacy in the classroom. *AACE Journal, 13(2)*, 91–98.

24 Fresco, A. (2005, October 31). Texting teenagers are proving "more literate than ever before." *Times Online.* Retrieved from http://www.timesonline.co.uk/tol/ life_and_style/education/article584810.ece

25 Plester, B, & Wood, C. (2006). *Cognitive factors in text messaging and literacy.* Poster Presentation at BPS Developmental Section Conference. London, September 2006. Plester, B., Bell, V, & Wood, C. (2006) *Exploring the relationship between text messaging and literacy attainment.* Poster presentation at Society for Scientific Study of Reading conference, Vancouver, BC, July 2006.

26 Baron, N. S. (2005, July). Instant messaging and the future of language. *Communications of the ACM, 48(7)*, 29–31. For additional information, see Crystal, D. (2006). *Language and the Internet.* Cambridge: Cambridge University Press.

27 http://abcnews.go.com/WNT/BrianRoss/story?id=2509586&page=1

28 http://sports.espn.go.com/nba/playoffs2006/news/story?id=2440355

29 http://www.wired.com/culture/lifestyle/news/2004/12/65912

30 http://www.usatoday.com/tech/news/internetprivacy/2006-03-08-facebook -myspace_x.htm?POE=TECISVA

31 Farnham, K., & Farnham, D. (2006). *MySpace safety: 51 tips for teens and parents.* Pomfret, CT: How-To-Primers.

32 The Pew Study found that bloggers provided the following information: first name (70%), full name (31%), age (67%), e-mail address (44%), IM screen name (44%), location- city and state (59%), birth date (39%). Lenhart, A., & Madden, M. (2007, April 18). *Teens, privacy & online social networks: How teens manage their online identities and personal information in the age of MySpace.* Washington, DC: Pew Internet & American Life Project. Retrieved from http://www.pewinternet.org/pdfs/PIP_Teens_Privacy_SNS_Report_Final.pdf. My recent research with MySpacers found similar results with 74% giving out the name of their school and 46% providing information about the date and location of social

events they planned to attend. More than one-third of the parents were not even sure if their teens had given out any information and those who thought they knew underestimated how much their teenagers were disclosing. For example, while 74% of the teens gave out their school name, only 43% of the parents were aware of that. The trend was similar for all disclosed material.

33 The National Center on Addiction and Substance Abuse (2005, September). *The importance of family dinners II*. New York: Columbia University Press. Retrieved from   http://www.casacolumbia.org/Absolutenm/articlefiles/380-2005_family _dinners_ii_final.pdf

34 Gibbs, N. (2006, June 4). The magic of the family meal. *Time*. Retrieved from http://www.time.com/time/magazine/article/0,9171,1200760,00.html

35 National Pork Producers Council (2000). *The kitchen report IIIA survey from the National Pork Producers Council*. Reported in Pohlman, D. *Background research on family needs*. Lincoln, NE: UNL for Families. Retrieved from http://unlforfamilies .unl.edu/FoodNutrition/BackgroundResearch.htm

Chapter 6: Sex and the Media

1 Third Way Culture Project (2005). *The porn standard: Children and pornography on the Internet*. Retrieved from http://www.third-way.com/data/product/file/14/ porn_standard.pdf

2 Thornburgh, D., & Lin, H. S. (2002). *Youth, pornography and the Internet*. Washington, DC: National Academies Press.

3 Pardun, C. J., L'Engle, K. L., & Brown, J. D. (2005). Linking exposure to outcomes: Early adolescents' consumption of sexual content in six media. *Mass Communication & Society, 8(2)*, 75–91.

4 Kunkel, D., Eyal, K., Finnerty, K., Biely, E., & Donnerstein, E. (2005, November). *Sex on TV: 2005*. Menlo Park, CA: Kaiser Family Foundation.

5 Quoted in *Teen sexual behaviors: Issues and concerns*. Retrieved from http://www .focusas.com/SexualBehavior.html

6 Pardun, C. J., L'Engle, K. L., & Brown, J. D. (2005). Linking exposure to outcomes: Early adolescents' consumption of sexual content in six media. *Mass Communication & Society, 8(2)*, 75–91.

7 Collins, R. L., Elliott, M. N., Berry, S. H., Kanouse, D. E., Kunkel, D., Hunter, S. B., et al. (2004, September). Watching sex on television predicts adolescent initiation of sexual behavior. *Pediatrics, 114(1)*. e280–e289.

8 Kunkel, D., Eyal, K., Finnerty, K., Biely, E., & Donnerstein, E. (2005, November). *Sex on TV: 2005*. Menlo Park, CA: Kaiser Family Foundation.

9 Escobar-Chaves, S. L., Tortolero, S. R., Markham, C. M., Low, B. J., Eitel, P., & Thickstun, P. (2005, July). Impact of the media on adolescent sexual attitudes and behaviors. *Pediatrics, 116(1)*, 303–326.

10 Escobar-Chaves, S. L., Tortolero, S. R., Markham, C. M., Low, B. J., Eitel, P., & Thickstun, P. (2005, July). Impact of the media on adolescent sexual attitudes and behaviors. *Pediatrics, 116(1)*, 303–326. Kunkel, D., Eyal, K., Finnerty,

K., Biely, E., & Donnerstein, E. (2005, November). *Sex on TV: 2005.* Menlo Park, CA: Kaiser Family Foundation. Results from Center for Disease Control's YRBSS study on sexual behaviors can be found at http://apps.nccd.cdc.gov/yrbss/CategoryQuestions.asp?Cat=4&desc=Sexual%20Behaviors

11 Halpern-Felscher, B. L., Cornell, J. L., Kropp, R. Y., & Tschann, J. M. (2005, April). Oral versus vaginal sex among adolescents: Perceptions, attitudes, and behavior. *Pediatrics, 115(4),* 845–851.

12 See http://www.oprah.com/relationships/relationships_content.jhtml?contentId =con_20031002_slang.xml&section=Family&subsection=Parenting; http://www .oprah.com/tows/pastshows/200310/tows_past_20031002.jhtml; and http:// www.nerve.com/screeningroom/books/rainbowparty/

13 See http://www.nytimes.com/2005/06/30/fashion/thursdaystyles/30rainbow.html ?pagewanted=1&ei=5070&en=63e9983fc6d55ac7&ex=1177905600

14 Statistics from a U.S. Department of Health and Human Services study, displayed in Table 6.1, separated sexual relations into those who had oral sex only or vaginal sex. Their data, although collected back in 2002, show the trends from ages fifteen to eighteen. This study also found that 22% of males fifteen–nineteen years of age had multiple partners compared to 17% of females.

Table 6.1 Sexual Relations in Teenagers: Oral Sex Only Compared with Vaginal Sex

Age	Oral Sex Only	Vaginal Sex
Males		
15 years old	15%	25%
16 years old	12%	37%
17 years old	14%	46%
18 years old	10%	62%
Females		
15 years old	8%	26%
16 years old	12%	37%
17 years old	15%	49%
18 years old	8%	70%

15 Denizet-Lewis, B. (2004, May 30). *New York Times Magazine.* Retrieved from http://www.nytimes.com/2004/05/30/magazine/30NONDATING.html?ei =5007&en=b8ab7c02ae2d206b&ex=1401249600

16 Kaplowitz, P. B., Slora, E. J., Wasserman, R. C., Pedlow, S. E., & Herman-Giddens, M. E. (2001). Earlier onset of puberty in girls: Relation to increased body mass index and race. *Pediatrics, 108,* 347–353.

17 As reported in http://blogs.modestlyyours.net/modestlyyours/2006/10/cbs _retracts_ap.html

18 Escobar-Chaves, S. L., Tortolero, S. R., Markham, C. M., Low, B. J., Eitel, P., & Thickstun, P. (2005, July). Impact of the media on adolescent sexual attitudes and behaviors. *Pediatrics, 116(1),* 303–326.

19 Escobar-Chaves, S. L., Tortolero, S. R., Markham, C. M., Low, B. J., Eitel, P., & Thickstun, P. (2005, July). Impact of the media on adolescent sexual attitudes and behaviors. *Pediatrics, 116(1),* 303–326.

20 These studies and more can be found in: Strasburger, V. C., & Wilson, B. J. (2002). *Children, adolescents, and the media.* Thousand Oaks, CA: Sage Publications.

21 Collins, R. L., Elliott, M. N., Berry, S. H., Kanouse, D. E., Kunkel, D., Hunter, S. B., et al. (2004, September). Watching sex on television predicts adolescent initiation of sexual behavior. *Pediatrics, 114(1).* e280–e289.

22 Collins, R. L., Elliott, M. N., Berry, S. H., Kanouse, D. E., & Hunter, S. B. (2003, November). Entertainment television as a healthy sex educator: The impact of condom-efficacy information in an episode of *Friends. Pediatrics, 112(5),* 1115–1121.

23 Collins, R. L., Elliott, M. N., Berry, S. H., Kanouse, D. E., Kunkel, D., Hunter, S. B., et al. (2004, September). Watching sex on television predicts adolescent initiation of sexual behavior. *Pediatrics, 114(1).* e280–e289.

24 Stock, P. (2004, November). *The harmful effects on children of exposure to pornography.* Canadian Institute for Education on the Family. Retrieved from http://www.cief.ca/pdf/harmpornography.pdf. Also as reported by Hughes, D. R. (1998). How pornography harms children. ProtectKids.com. Retrieved from http://www.protectkids.com/effects/harms.htm#ix

25 Haninger, K., & Thompson, K. M. (2004). Content and ratings of teen-rated video games. *JAMA, 291,* 856–865. More information on ESRB video game ratings can be found at www.esrb.org.

26 Strasburger, V. C., & Wilson, B. J. (2002). *Children, adolescents, and the media.* Thousand Oaks, CA: Sage Publications.

27 Escobar-Chaves, S. L., Tortolero, S. R., Markham, C. M., Low, B. J., Eitel, P., & Thickstun, P. (2005, July). Impact of the media on adolescent sexual attitudes and behaviors. *Pediatrics, 116(1),* 303–326.

28 Strasburger, V. C., & Wilson, B. J. (2002). *Children, adolescents, and the media.* Thousand Oaks, CA: Sage Publications.

29 Escobar-Chaves, S. L., Tortolero, S. R., Markham, C. M., Low, B. J., Eitel, P., & Thickstun, P. (2005, July). Impact of the media on adolescent sexual attitudes and behaviors. *Pediatrics, 116(1),* 303–326.

30 Escobar-Chaves, S. L., Tortolero, S. R., Markham, C. M., Low, B. J., Eitel, P., & Thickstun, P. (2005, July). Impact of the media on adolescent sexual attitudes and behaviors. *Pediatrics, 116(1),* 303–326. Strasburger, V. C., & Wilson, B. J. (2002). *Children, adolescents, and the media.* Thousand Oaks, CA: Sage Publications.

31 Escobar-Chaves, S. L., Tortolero, S. R., Markham, C. M., Low, B. J., Eitel, P., & Thickstun, P. (2005, July). Impact of the media on adolescent sexual attitudes and behaviors. *Pediatrics, 116(1),* 303–326.

32 Martino, S. C., Collins, R. L., Elliott, M. N., Strachman, A., Kanouse, D. E., & Berry, S. H. (2006). Exposure to degrading versus nondegrading music lyrics and sexual behavior among youth. *Pediatrics, 118*, 430–441.

33 Escobar-Chaves, S. L., Tortolero, S. R., Markham, C. M., Low, B. J., Eitel, P., & Thickstun, P. (2005, July). Impact of the media on adolescent sexual attitudes and behaviors. *Pediatrics, 116(1)*, 303–326. Strasburger, V. C., & Wilson, B. J. (2002). *Children, adolescents, and the media.* Thousand Oaks, CA: Sage Publications.

34 Eichenwald, K. (2006, August 10). With child sex sites on the run, nearly nude photos hit the web. *New York Times.* Retrieved from http://select.nytimes.com/gst/abstract.html?res=F70F14F63E5A0C738EDDA10894DE404482&n=Top%2fReference%2fTimes%20Topics%2fPeople%2fE%2fEichenwald%2c%20Kurt

35 Hauser, D. (2004). *Five years of abstinence-only-until-marriage education: Assessing the impact.* Washington, DC: Advocates for Youth. Retrieved from http://www.advocatesforyouth.org/publications/stateevaluations/index.htm

36 Bruckner, H., & Bearman, P. (2005). After the promise: the STD consequences of adolescent virginity pledges. *Journal of Adolescent Health, 36*, 271–278. Retrieved from http://www.yale.edu/ciqle/PUBLICATIONS/AfterThePromise.pdf. Quoted in Connolly, C. (2005, March 19). Teen pledges barely cut STD rate, study says. *Washington Post,* p. A03.

37 Collins, R. L., Elliott, M. N., Berry, S. H., Kanouse, D. E., Kunkel, D., Hunter, S. B., et al. (2004, September). Watching sex on television predicts adolescent initiation of sexual behavior. *Pediatrics, 114(1).* e280–e289.

38 Escobar-Chaves, S. L., Tortolero, S. R., Markham, C. M., Low, B. J., Eitel, P., & Thickstun, P. (2005, July). Impact of the media on adolescent sexual attitudes and behaviors. *Pediatrics, 116(1)*, 303–326. Strasburger, V. C., & Wilson, B. J. (2002). *Children, adolescents, and the media.* Thousand Oaks, CA: Sage Publications.

39 Jancin, B. (2005). Addiction to cybersex called pervasive. *Clinical Psychiatry News, 33(6)*, 32.

40 Cooper, A., & McLoughlin, I. P. (2001). What clinicians need to know about Internet sexuality. *Sexual and Relationship Therapy, 16(4)*, 321–327.

41 Ross, M. W. (2005). Typing, doing, and being: Sexuality and the Internet. *Journal of Sex Research, 42(4)*, 342–352.

42 Wolak, J., Mitchell, K., & Finkelhor, D. (2007). Unwanted and wanted exposure to online pornography in a national sample of youth Internet Users. *Pediatrics, 119*, 247–257.

43 Wolak, J., Mitchell, K., & Finkelhor, D. (2007). Unwanted and wanted exposure to online pornography in a national sample of youth Internet Users. *Pediatrics, 119*, 247–257. Pierce, T. A. (2007). X-Posed on MySpace: A content analysis of "MySpace" social networking sites. *Journal of Media Psychology, 12.* Retrieved from http://www.calstatela.edu/faculty/sfischo/X-posed_on_%20MySpace.htm

44 Mosher, W. D., Chandra, A., & Jones, J. (2005, September 15). *Sexual behavior and selected health measures: Men and women 15–44 years of age, United States,*

2002. number 362. U.S. Department of Health and Human Services, Centers for Disease Control. Retrieved from http://www.cdc.gov/nchs/data/ad/ad362.pdf

45 Kim, E. K. (2006, June 23). Many gay teens are coming out at earlier ages. *St. Louis Post-Dispatch*, p. A1.

46 Gallup Poll (2006, May). *Homosexual relations: Gallup's pulse of democracy.* Retrieved from http://www.galluppoll.com/content/?ci=1651&pg=1

47 Kunkel, D., Eyal, K., Finnerty, K., Biely, E., & Donnerstein, E. (2005, November). *Sex on TV: 2005.* Menlo Park, CA: Kaiser Family Foundation.

48 Blum, R. W. (2002). *Mothers' influence on teen sex: Connections that promote postponing sexual intercourse.* Minneapolis: Center for Adolescent Health and Development, University of Minnesota. Quoted in The Media Project. *Parent-child communication: Helping teens make healthy decisions about sex.* Retrieved from http://www.themediaproject.com/topics/pcc.htm

49 Escobar-Chaves, S. L., Tortolero, S. R., Markham, C. M., Low, B. J., Eitel, P., & Thickstun, P. (2005, July). Impact of the media on adolescent sexual attitudes and behaviors. *Pediatrics, 116(1),* 303–326. Strasburger, V. C., & Wilson, B. J. (2002). *Children, adolescents, and the media.* Thousand Oaks, CA: Sage Publications.

50 CommonSense Media (2006, June 7). *Parents Internet poll: What parents are saying about Internet Safety.* Retrieved from http://www.commonsensemedia.org/news/press-releases.php?id=24

51 http://home.aol.com/eklusmann/AOL/AOL-Safe.htm

Chapter 7: Just a Few More Minutes, Mom

1 Young, K.S. (1996). *Pathological Internet use: The emergence of a new clinical disorder.* Paper presented at the American Psychological Association Convention, Toronto, Canada.

2 Young, K. S. (2001). *Caught in the Net: How to recognize the signs of Internet addiction and a winning strategy for recovery.* New York: Wiley.

3 Center for Internet Addiction Recovery. http://www.netaddiction.com

4 Rosen, L. D., Cheever, N. A., & Carrier, L. M. (2007). *The impact of parental attachment style, limit setting and monitoring on teen MySpace behavior.* Paper submitted for publication. Retrieved from http://www.csudh.edu/psych/The%20Impact%20of%20Parental%20Attachment%20Style%20Rosen-Cheever-Ca.pdf

5 Kim, K., Ryu, E., Chon, M. Y., Yeun, E., Choi, S., Seo, J., et al. (2006). Internet addiction in Korean adolescents and its relation to depression and suicidal ideation: A questionnaire study. *International Journal of Nursing Studies, 43,* 185–192. Laino, C. (2005, May 23). Internet addiction may mask teen depression. Paper presented at American Psychiatric Association convention, Atlanta, GA. Kaltiala-Heino, R., Lintonen, T., & Rimpela, A. (2004). Internet addiction? Potentially problematic use of the Internet in a population of 12–18 year-old adolescents. *Addiction Research and Theory, 12(1),* 89–96. Niemz, K., Griffiths, M., & Banyard, P. (2005). Prevalence of pathological Internet use among university students

and correlations with self-esteem, the General Health Questionnaire (GHQ), and disinhibition. *CyberPsychology & Behavior, 8(6)*, 562–570. Widyanto, L., & Griffiths, M. (2006). "Internet addiction": A critical review. *International Journal of Mental Health and Addiction, 4(1)*, 31–51.

6 Yang, C., Choe, B., Baity, M., Lee, J., & Cho, J. (2005). SCL-90-R and 16PF profiles of senior high school students with excessive internet use. *Canadian Journal of Psychiatry, 50(7)*, 407–414.

7 Rosen, L. D., Cheever, N. A., & Carrier, L. M. (2007). *The impact of parental attachment style, limit setting and monitoring on teen MySpace behavior.* Paper submitted for publication. Retrieved from http://www.csudh.edu/psych/The%20 Impact%20of%20Parental%20Attachment%20Style%20Rosen-Cheever-Ca .pdf. More information on parenting styles can be found in chapter 8.

8 Young, K. S. (2001). *Caught in the Net: How to recognize the signs of Internet addiction and a winning strategy for recovery.* New York: Wiley. Wallis, D. (1997). Just click no. *New Yorker, 72(42)*, 28. Morahan-Martin, J. (2005). Internet abuse: Addiction? Disorder? Symptom? Alternative explanations? *Social Science Computer Review, 23(1)*, 39–48.

9 Young, K. S. (2001). *Caught in the Net: How to recognize the signs of Internet addiction and a winning strategy for recovery.* New York: Wiley.

10 Geirland, J. (1996, September). Go with the flow. *Wired, 4(9)*. Retrieved from http://www.wired.com/wired/archive/4.09/czik.html. Csikszentmihalyi, M (1990). *Flow: The psychology of optimal experience.* New York: Harper & Row. Csikszentmihalyi, M. (1998). *Finding flow: The psychology of engagement with everyday life.* New York: Basic Books.

11 Niemz, K., Griffiths, M., & Banyard, P. (2005). Prevalence of pathological Internet use among university students and correlations with self-esteem, the General Health Questionnaire (GHQ), and disinhibition. *CyberPsychology & Behavior, 8(6)*, 562–570. Widyanto, L., & Griffiths, M. (2006). "Internet addiction": A critical review. *International Journal of Mental Health and Addiction, 4(1)*, 31–51. Yang, C., Choe, B., Baity, M., Lee, J., & Cho, J. (2005). SCL-90-R and 16PF profiles of senior high school students with excessive internet use. *Canadian Journal of Psychiatry, 50(7)*, 407–414.

12 Song, I., LaRose, R., Eastin, M. S., & Lin, C. A. (2004). Internet gratifications and Internet addiction: On the uses and abuses of new media. *CyberPsychology & Behavior, 7(4)*, 384–394.

13 Adapted from Eastin, M. S. (2005). Teen Internet use: Relating social perceptions and cognitive models to behavior. *CyberPsychology & Behavior, 8(1)*, 62–75.

14 Young, K. S. (2001). *Caught in the Net: How to recognize the signs of internet addiction and a winning strategy for recovery.* New York: Wiley. Center for Internet Addiction Recovery. http://www.netaddiction.com.

Chapter 8: MySpace and Your Family

1 Kraut, R., Patterson, M., Lundmark, V. (1998). Internet paradox: A social technology that reduces social involvement and psychological well-being. *American Psychologist, 53(9),* 1017–1031.

2 Kraut, R., Kiesler, S., & Boneva, B. (2002). Internet paradox revisited. *Journal of Social Issues, 58(1),* 49–74.

3 Lenhart, A., Madden, M., & Hitlin, P. (2005, July 27). *Youth are leading the transition to a fully wired and mobile nation.* Washington, DC: Pew Internet & American Life Project. Boase, J., Horrigan, J. B., Wellman, B., & Rainie, L. (2006, January 25). *The strength of Internet ties.* Washington, DC: Pew Internet & American Life Project.

4 Rosen, L. D., Cheever, N. A., & Carrier, L. M. (2007). *The impact of parental attachment style, limit setting and monitoring on teen MySpace behavior.* Paper submitted for publication. Retrieved from http://www.csudh.edu/psych/The%20 Impact%20of%20Parental%20Attachment%20Style%20Rosen-Cheever-Ca .pdf. In my research nearly one in three parents felt that time on MySpace interfered with the family. Further, half the parents of teens who spent more than two hours per day on MySpace were convinced it was interfering with family time, schoolwork, outdoor activities, and chores. Teens spending more time on MySpace felt they were getting less support from their parents and other studies have shown that more time spent apart from parents is related to less family cohesiveness.

5 Mesch, G. S. (2006). Family relations and the Internet: Exploring a family boundaries approach. *Journal of Family Communication, 6(2),* 119–138.

6 Mesch, G. S. (2006). Family relations and the Internet: Exploring a family boundaries approach. *Journal of Family Communication, 6(2),* 119–138.

7 Dombeck, M. (2006). Boundaries and dysfunctional family systems. *Mental-Help.net.* Retrieved from http://mentalhelp.net/poc/view_doc.php?type=doc&id =10179

8 Macoby, E. E., & Martin, J. A. (1983). Socialization in the context of the family: Parent–child interaction. In P. H. Mussen & E. M. Hetherington (Eds.), *Handbook of child psychology: Vol. 4. Socialization, personality, and social development* (4th ed., pp. 1-101). New York: Wiley.

9 Baumrind, D. (1991). The influence of parenting style on adolescent competence and substance use. *Journal of Early Adolescence, 11,* 56–95.

10 Slicker, E. K., & Thornberry, I. (2002). Older adolescent well-being and authoritative parenting. *Adolescent & Family Health, 3,* 9–19. Amato, P. R., & Flower, F. (2002). Parenting practices, child adjustment, and family diversity. *Journal of Marriage and the Family, 64,* 703–716. Lamborn, S. D., Mounts, N. S., Steinberg, L. and Dornbusch, S. M. (1991). Patterns of competence and adjustment among adolescents from authoritative, authoritarian, indulgent, and neglected families. *Child Development, 62,* 1049–1065. Kaufmann, D., Gesten, E, & Santa-Lucia, R. C. (2000). The relationship between parenting style and children's adjustment:

The parents' perspective. *Journal of Child and Family Studies, 9,* 231–245. Lee, S. M., Daniels, M. H., & Kissinger, D. B. (2006). Parental influences on adolescent adjustment: Parenting styles versus parenting practices. *Family Journal: Counseling and Therapy for Couples and Families, 14,* 253–259. Adamczyk-Robinette, S. L., Fletcher, A. C., & Wright, K. (2002). Understanding the authoritative parenting early adolescent tobacco use link: The mediating role of peer tobacco use. *Journal of Youth and Adolescence, 31,* 311–318. Aunola, K., Stattin, H, & Nurmi, J. E. (2000). Parenting styles and adolescents' achievement strategies. *Journal of Adolescence, 23,* 205–222. Chasin, L., Presson, C. C., Rose, J., Sherman, S. J., Davis, M. J., & Gonzalez, J. L. (2005). Parenting style and smoking-specific parenting practices: Predictors of adolescent smoking onset. *Journal of Pediatric Psychology, 30,* 333–344. Steinberg, L., Blatt-Eisengart, I., & Cauffman, E. (2006). Patterns of competence and adjustment among adolescents from authoritative, authoritarian, indulgent, and neglectful homes: A replication in a sample of serious juvenile offenders. *Journal of Research on Adolescence, 16,* 47–58. Stone, A. L. (2006). Parental functioning and adolescent marijuana involvement (Doctoral dissertation, Johns Hopkins University). *Dissertation Abstracts International: Section B: The Sciences and Engineering, 66(12-B),* 6562.

11 Lamborn, S. D., Mounts, N. S., Steinberg, L, & Dornbusch, S. M. (1991). Patterns of competence and adjustment among adolescents from authoritative, authoritarian, indulgent, and neglected families. *Child Development, 62,* 1049–1065.

12 Rosen, L. D., Cheever, N. A., & Carrier, L. M. (2007). *The impact of parental attachment style, limit setting and monitoring on teen MySpace behavior.* Paper submitted for publication. Retrieved from http://www.csudh.edu/psych/The%20 Impact%20of%20Parental%20Attachment%20Style%20Rosen-Cheever-Ca.pdf

13 Schmitt, K. L. (2000). *Public policy, family rules and children's media use in the home.* Philadelphia: Annenberg Public Policy Center of the University of Pennsylvania.

14 Rosen, L. D., Cheever, N. A., & Carrier, L. M. (2007). *The impact of parental attachment style, limit setting and monitoring on teen MySpace behavior.* Paper submitted for publication. Retrieved from http://www.csudh.edu/psych/The%20 Impact%20of%20Parental%20Attachment%20Style%20Rosen-Cheever-Ca.pdf

Chapter 9: Hate Mail

1 Belsey, B. http://www.cyberbullying.ca

2 Anne Collier's work and writings can be found at http://www.netfamilynews. org, http://blogsafety.com, and http://stopcyberbullying.ning.com. She is the author of *MySpace unraveled: What it is and how to use it safely.* Berkeley, CA: Peachpit Press (2006). Nancy Willard's work and thoughts can be found at http:// www.cyber-safe-kids.com and the Center for Safe and Responsible Internet Use at http://www.csriu.org. She is the author of *Cyber-Safe Kids, Cyber-Savvy Teens* (2007). San Francisco: Jossey-Bass.

3 Kowalski, R. M., & Limber, S. (2007). *Cyber bullying among middle school children*. Unpublished manuscript.
4 Mitchell, K. J., Wolak, J., & Finkelhor, D. (2007). Trends in youth reports of sexual solicitations, harassment and unwanted exposure to pornography on the Internet. *Journal of Adolescent Health, 40(2)*, 116–126. The complete report of the YISS project, entitled *Online victimization of youth: Five years later*, can be found at http://www.unh.edu/ccrc/pdf/CV138.pdf
5 Rosen, L. D., Cheever, N. A., & Carrier, L. M. (2007). *The impact of parental attachment style, limit setting and monitoring on teen MySpace behavior*. Paper submitted for publication. Retrieved from http://www.csudh.edu/psych/The%20 Impact%20of%20Parental%20Attachment%20Style%20Rosen-Cheever-Ca.pdf
6 Rosen, L. D. (2006, August). *Blocking sexual predators and Cyberbullies on MySpace: The kids are alright*. California State University, Dominguez Hills, Short Report 2006-03 retrieved from http://www.csudh.edu/psych/BLOCKING%20SEXUAL %20PREDATORS%20&%20CYBERBULLIES%20ON%20MYSPACE%20 Short%20Report%202006-03.pdf
7 Rosen, L. D., Cheever, N. A., & Carrier, L. M. (2007). *The impact of parental attachment style, limit setting and monitoring on teen MySpace behavior*. Paper submitted for publication. Retrieved from http://www.csudh.edu/psych/The%20 Impact%20of%20Parental%20Attachment%20Style%20Rosen-Cheever-Ca.pdf
8 Kowalski, R., Limber, S., Scheck, A., Redfearn, M., Allen, J., Calloway, A., et al. (2005, August). *Electronic bullying among school-aged children and youth*. Poster presented at the annual meeting of the American Psychological Association, Washington, DC.
9 In the 2005 YISS study of adolescents on the Internet 31% of the teens told their parents and 45% told friends. Overall, 67% told someone (some told both parents and friends), 49% blocked the person or left the situation, 8% ignored it, and 17% told the person to stop. The complete report of the YISS project, entitled *Online victimization of youth: Five years later*, can be found at http://www .unh.edu/ccrc/pdf/CV138.pdf. In my study, 9% told someone, 40% blocked the person or left the situation, 21% ignored it, and 19% told the person to stop. Note: the YISS study allowed for multiple responses while my study only asked for a single response of what the person did in the most recent instance of cyberbullying.
10 Kim, J. (2006). The effect of a bullying prevention program on responsibility and victimization of bullied children in Korea. *International Journal of Reality Therapy, 26(1)*, 4–8. Greif, J. L., & Furlong, M. J. (2006). The assessment of school bullying: Using theory to inform practice. *Journal of School Violence, 5(3)*, 33–50. Scheithauer, H., Hayer, T., & Petermann, F. (2006). Physical, verbal, and relational forms of bullying among German students: Age trends, gender differences, and correlates. *Aggressive Behavior, 32(3)*, 261–275. Olweus, D. (2005). A useful evaluation design, and effects of the Olweus Bullying Prevention Program. *Psychology, Crime & Law, 11(4)*, 389–402.

11 Olweus, D., & Huesmann, L. R. (1994). Bullying at school: Long-term outcomes for the victims and an effective school-based intervention program. In L.
R. Heusmann & L. Miller (Eds.), *Aggressive Behavior: Current Perspectives* (pp.
97–130). New York: Plenum Press.

12 Olweus, D. (1993). *Bullying at school: What we know and what we can do.* Oxford:
Blackwell.

13 Marano, H. E. (1995, September/October). Big bad bully. *Psychology Today,
28(5),* 50–57.

Chapter 10: Proactive Parenting

1 Hinduja, S., & Patchin, J. W. (in press). Personal information of adolescents on
the Internet: A quantitative content analysis of MySpace. *Journal of Adolescence.*

2 Quoted in Belden, A. C. *Virtual lives: Your child's secret high-tech world.* Retrieved
from http://www.parenthood.com/articles.html?article_id=9514

3 Quoted in Belden, A. C. *Virtual lives: Your child's secret high-tech world.* Retrieved
from http://www.parenthood.com/articles.html?article_id=9514

4 This does not include additional hours spent online, but not on MySpace. Rosen,
L. D., Cheever, N. A., & Carrier, L. M. (2007). *The impact of parental attachment
style, limit setting and monitoring on teen MySpace behavior.* Paper submitted for
publication. Retrieved from http://www.csudh.edu/psych/The%20Impact%20of
%20Parental%20Attachment%20Style%20Rosen-Cheever-Ca.pdf

5 Bausch, S., & Han, L. (2006, October 11). *U.S. teens graduate from choosing
IM buddy icons to creating elaborate social networking profiles, according to Nielsen/
NetRatings: Kids and teens spending more time online than ever before.* Nielsen/
NetRatings. Retrieved from http://www.nielsen-netratings.com/pr/pr_061011.pdf

6 According to a Kaiser Family Foundation national study, tweens and teens are
spending six hours and 21 minutes per day using media for a total of 45 hours
per week. Roberts, D. F., Foehr, U. G., & Rideout, V. (2005). *Generation M:
Media in the lives of 8–18 year-olds.* Menlo Park, CA: Kaiser Family Foundation.
Retrieved from http://www.kff.org/entmedia/upload/Generation-M-Media-in
-the-Lives-of-8-18-Year-olds-Report.pdf

7 Zandl Group (2006, November 6). *The 11 key teen consumer trends for 2007.*
Retrieved from http://www.zandlgroup.com/wisemarketer061108.html

8 Newman, B. M., & Newman, P. R. (2001). Group identity and alienation: Giving the we its due. *Journal of Youth and Adolescence, 30(5),* 515–538.

9 boyd, d. (2006, February 19). *Identity production in a networked culture: Why youth
heart MySpace.* Paper presented at the American Association for the Advancement
of Science Convention. St. Louis, MO.

10 This is from a study by Virgin Mobile and was quoted by Anastasia Goodstein in
Ypulse at http://ypulse.com/archives/2006/07/the_ten_biggest.php

11 Zandl Group (2006, November 6). *The 11 key teen consumer trends for 2007.*
Retrieved from http://www.zandlgroup.com/wisemarketer061108.html

12 According to collegeadmissioninfo.com over 53% of U.S. colleges received more applications in 2005 than 2004 and had sharply lower acceptance rates. An enlightening article about college admissions: Dillon, S. (2007, April 4). A great year of ivy leagues schools, but not so good for applicants to them. *New York Times.* Retrieved from http://www.nytimes.com/2007/04/04/education/04colleges.html?ex=13333 39200&en=3b78ac1fa18e4512&ei=5089&partner=rssyahoo&emc=rss.

13 These ratings can be found at http://internet-filter-review.toptenreviews.com. Other interesting information about Internet filters—including information about how teens can bypass these filters—can be found at the following Web sites: http://www.netalert.net.au/02325-Filters.pdf, http://www.sanonofre.com/censorship.html, and http://nautopia.coolfreepages.com/libertades_civiles/howto_bypass_internet_censorship.htm.

14 Lenhart, A., & Madden, M. (2007, April 18). *Teens, privacy & online social networks: How teens manage their online identities and personal information in the age of MySpace.* Washington, DC: Pew Internet & American Life Project. Retrieved from http://www.pewinternet.org/pdfs/PIP_Teens_Privacy_SNS_Report_Final.pdf

15 Eastin, M. S., Greenberg, B. S., & Hofschire, L. (2006). Parenting the Internet. *Journal of Communication, 56,* 486–504.

16 In my research, 70% of teens said that they felt comfortable showing their parents their MySpace page.

17 In my research studies, parents underestimated how much information their teens actually disclosed, including full name (teen 42%; parent 28%), home address (teen 8%; parent 3%), school name (teen 64%; parent 44%), phone number (teen 21%; parent 8%), e-mail address (teen 54%; parent 34%), IM name (teen 55%; parent 32%) and social activities (teen 37%; parent 17%).

18 *Researchers find most teens limit personal information on MySpace, but some youth still at risk.* Press Release for University of Wisconsin, Eau Claire, December 4, 2006. Retrieved from http://www.uwec.edu/newsreleases/06/dec/1204MySpaceresearch.htm

19 Installing AIM is straightforward and you can download the latest version at http://www.aim.com

20 *The importance of family dinners III.* The National Center on Addiction and Substance Abuse at Columbia University, September 2006. Retrieved from http://www.casacolumbia.org/absolutenm/articlefiles/380-Family%20Dinners%20III%20Final%20report.pdf. Gibbs, N. (2006, June 4). The magic of the family meal. *Time.* Retrieved from http://www.time.com/time/magazine/article/0,9171,1200760,00.html

21 Bronson, P. (2007, February 19). *How not to talk to your kids: The inverse power of praise. New York Magazine.* Retrieved from http://nymag.com/news/features/27840/index4.html

22 Usually the tip-off to situations such as these is a change in behavior such as late nights spent online, a sudden drop in grades, or moodiness.

23 Parents and teens were asked about where the teen used computers other than in the home. While 64% of teens use a computer at a friend's house, only 47% of the parents were aware of this. Similar results were found for computers used at a library (teen: 32%; parent: 24%) and school (teen: 53%; parent: 46%).

24 Rosen, L. D., Cheever, N. A., & Carrier, L. M. (2007). *The impact of parental attachment style, limit setting and monitoring on teen MySpace behavior*. Paper submitted for publication. Retrieved from http://www.csudh.edu/psych/The%20 Impact%20of%20Parental%20Attachment%20Style%20Rosen-Cheever-Ca .pdf. Eastin, M. S., Greenberg, B. S., & Hofschire, L. (2006). Parenting the Internet. *Journal of Communication, 56*, 486–504.

25 Sharif, I., & Sargent, J. D. (2006). Association between television, movie, and video game exposure and school performance. *Pediatrics, 118(4)*, 1061–1070.

26 Rosen, L. D., Cheever, N. A., & Carrier, L. M. (2007). *The impact of parental attachment style, limit setting and monitoring on teen MySpace behavior*. Paper submitted for publication. Retrieved from http://www.csudh.edu/psych/The%20 Impact%20of%20Parental%20Attachment%20Style%20Rosen-Cheever-Ca.pdf

27 http://www.clubpenguin.com or Disney.go.com

28 Video game ratings can be found at www.esrb.org

29 Rosen, L. D., Cheever, N. A., & Carrier, L. M. (2007). *The impact of parental attachment style, limit setting and monitoring on teen MySpace behavior*. Paper submitted for publication. Retrieved from http://www.csudh.edu/psych/The%20 Impact%20of%20Parental%20Attachment%20Style%20Rosen-Cheever-Ca .pdf. Eastin, M. S., Greenberg, B. S., & Hofschire, L. (2006). Parenting the Internet. *Journal of Communication, 56*, 486–504.

Index

Acceptable Use Policy, 201–203
ADD, *see* Attention Deficit Disorder
Addiction, *see* Internet addiction
ADHD, *see* Attention Deficit Hyperactivity
  Disorder
ADHD Generation, 1, 28. *See also* Attention
  Deficit Hyperactivity Disorder
Adolescent moratorium, 68–69, 74–75, 76, 79
AIDS, 121, 192
AIM, *see* America Online Instant Messenger
Ainsworth, Mary, 26. *See also* Attachment
  theory
Alter ego, 78
Alvy, Kerby, 188–192
America Online, 6, 93, 144. *See also* America
  Online Instant Messenger
America Online Instant Messenger, 42, 212
American Academy of Pediatrics, 138
American Medical Association, 139
American Psychiatric Association, 27
Anderson, Tom, 3, 36, 81, 106, 193, 200
Annenberg Public Policy Center, 184
Anonymity, 40, 69, 87–88, 116, 157,
  196–198, 201, 205
Antecedent, 161, 163
AOL, *see* America Online
Arbitron, 67
Archive.org, 107
Attachment theory, 26–27
Attention Deficit Disorder, 7
Attention Deficit Hyperactivity Disorder,
  27–28, 159, 163

AUP, *see* Acceptable Use Policy
Authoritarian parenting, *see* Parenting styles
Authoritative parenting, *see* Parenting styles
Automatic tasks, 12

Baby Boomers, 2, 19–36, 67, 208
Back-stage, 71
Bandura, Albert, 47, 131–133, 161. *See also*
  Social cognitive theory
Baumrind, Diana, 181
Behavioral consequences, 165
Behavioral contract, 166–168
Behavioral limits, 184
Behind the screen, 5, 69–70, 87, 95, 106,
  157, 196
Behl, Taylor, 4
Big Talk, The, 139–140
Bisexuality, 122, 136, 150
Blog, 3, 6, 14, 35, 39, 40, 58, 64, 76, 77, 78,
  91–116, 149, 209, 211, 223
Blog Beware Quiz, 109–110
Blogosphere, 91
BlogSafety.com, 194, 204, 222
Bobo doll, 131–132
Bowlby, John, 26. *See also* Attachment theory
boyd, danah, 57–61, 77, 78, 86–89, 98
Boys & Girls Clubs of America, 108
Brand, Stewart, 3
Brilliant, Larry, 3
Browser history, search History, 85, 143, 165
Buddy list, 42, 56, 65–66, 97, 145
Bulletins, 14, 49, 68, 78, 92, 114, 193, 209

Cable TV, 3, 25
Caffeinated drinks, *see* Caffeine
Caffeine, 32–34, 219–220
Calvert, Sandra, 95
Campaign for a Commercial-Free Childhood, 118
Carnegie-Mellon University, 20, 98, 174
Catch them being good, 113–114
CBS NewsWatch, 6
Center for Safe and Responsible Internet Use, 94, 194, 204
Center for the Improvement of Child Caring, 188
Child Online Protection Act, 129
Children's Digital Media Center at Georgetown University, 1, 63, 95
Children's Digital Media Project, 6
Children's Internet Protection Act, 129
Chris Hansen, *see Dateline: To Catch a Predator*
Clique, 38, 48, 53, 66–67, 77
Club Penguin, 218
Cognitive distraction, 13–14
Cole, Jeffrey, 207
Collier, Anne, 194, 200, 204–206
Collins, Rebecca, 119, 131
Coming out, 137
Commitments, 74
Common Sense Media, 16, 141
Communications Decency Act, 128
Cooper, Al, 136
Couric, Katie, 120
Co-viewing, 211
Cox Communications, 54
Crimes Against Children Research Center, 147, 195
Crowd, 38, 48, 53, 66
    Merged, 38
    Reputation-based, 38
Csikszentmihalyi, Mihaly, 157–158
Cuban, Mark, 106
Cultivation theory, 134
Cyberbullying, 15–16, 30, 116, 191, 193–206
Cybercocoon, *see* TechnoCocoon
CyberPatrol, 210. *See also* Internet filters
Cybersex, 135–136, 138
CyberSitter, 210. *See also* Internet filters

Daily media consumption, 6. *See also* Media Diet
Dateline: To Catch a Predator, 4 to 5
Deleting Online Predators Act, 129
Depression, 13, 15, 47, 158, 163, 167, 169, 182, 198
DeRosier, Melissa, 199
DeWolfe, Chris, 3
Diagnostic and Statistical Manual of Mental Disorders, 156, 159
Digital immigrants, 104
Digital natives, 104
Discriminative Stimulus, 161, 163
Disinhibition, 44, 53, 69–70, 157, 197
    Benign, 69
    Toxic, 69–70
Disney Extreme Digital, 218
Displacement effect, 190
Dombeck, Mark, 177
Dominick, Joseph, 101–102. *See also* Strategies of self-presentation
Dramatic realization, 71
Driver distraction, 12
DSM-V, *see* Diagnostic and Statistical Manual of Mental Disorders
Dungeons and Dragons, 3
Dweck, Carol, 213
Dysfunctional family, 178. *See also* Family systems theory

Eastin, Matthew, 159, 188–192
eHarmony, 53
Eichenwald, Kurt, 129
Electronic monitoring, 192
Electronic tracking, *see* Electronic monitoring
Emoticons, *see* Netspeak
Erikson, Erik, 63–64, 68, 74, 76, 122, 136
Escobar-Chaves, Liliana, 124

Face time, 214
Facebook, 17, 40, 51, 79, 96, 115, 137, 169
Family cohesion, 175, 177, 187
Family meals, 25, 112–113, 214
Family systems theory, 175–181
    Boundaries, 176–178, 180
    Boundary violation, 180
    Communications, 176, 178, 179, 181

Differentiation, 176, 178, 179, 180
Dyadic identity, 178
Dyads, 176–180
Family identity, 177, 180
Hierarchies, 176, 179, 202
Homeostasis, 176, 178, 179, 181, 188
Identity boundaries, 177, 180
Separateness, 178, 180, 188
Triangles, 176–177, 179, 180
Farnham, Kevin, 107
FBI, 91, 141
Filling in the blanks, 45
Flaming, 194, 197
Flow theory, 157
Foley, Mark, 106
Freud, Sigmund, 45, 53. *See also* Projection
Friend time, 174
Friending, 6
Friends (TV show), 126, 138, 192
Friends with benefits, 120
Friendship,
    Characteristics, 40, 44
    Core ties, 47
    Group, 48–52
    Self-disclosure, 40, 43–44, 53–54
    Significant ties, 47
Friendster, 57, 79, 86
Front stage, 71

Gallup, 137
Game Boy, 25, 214
Gating characteristics, 44
Gay-Straight Alliance, 136–137
Gender identity, 122, 136
Gender-bending, 70
Generation M, 1, 8
Generation X, 20, 25, 28, 35
Generation Y, 1, 35
Gerbner, George, 134
Goffman, Erving, 71–72, 76, 87, 96
Goodstein, Anastasia, 35–36, 80
Google, 4, 6, 19, 107, 203, 208
Googling, 6, 107
Gore, Al, 6
Grand Theft Auto, 31
Greenfield, Patricia, 1
GSA, *see* Gay-Straight Alliance

Habit strength, 161–162
Hallowell, Edward, 6
Harassment, 116, 195, 205. *See also* Cyberbullying
Harrison Group, 9. *See also* Teen Trends Study
Helicopter parenting, 35
Herring, Susan, 91
Hinduja, Sameer, 207
HIV, 192
Holding power, 156
Homophily, 51
Homosexuality, 70, 96, 122, 136–137
Hooking up, 120–121
Huffaker, David, 95, 104–105, 114–116
Humanistic personality theory, 71
Hyperpersonal, 44, 45, 46, 53

IAD, *see* Internet Addiction Disorder
IAT, *see* Internet Addiction Test
Identity status model, 73–74. *See also* Stages of identity formation
Identity theft, 191
Impression management, 87
Individual's digital representation, 64
Indulgent parenting, *see* Parenting styles
Information Superhighway, 6
Internet addiction, 151–171, 191
    Operant conditioning, 31, 159, 160–163
    Psychological gratification, 159, 162–163
    Social cognition, 161–163, 169
Internet Addiction Disorder, 156, 159
Internet Addiction Test, 152, 154
Internet bullying, 193. *See also* Cyberbullying
Internet Explorer, 144
Internet filters, 103, 210
iSafe, 222

Jenkins, Henry, 65, 207
Joinson, Adam, 44. *See also* Disinhibition
Jones, Edward Ellsworth, 101. *See also* Strategies of self-presentation

Kaiser Family Foundation, 6, 8, 20, 32, 33, 85, 119, 126, 138, 208
Kay, Alan, 87
Kowalski, Robin, 194

Lamborn, Susie, 183
LaRose, Robert, 159
Least restrictive alternative, 215
Lenhart, Amanda, 11
Lewinsky, Monica, 121
Lin, Carolyn, 159
Listserv, 49
LiveJournal, 79, 91, 116

Magid, Larry, 200
Mapquest, 6
Marcia, James, 73–76, 97. *See also* Identity status model
Massachusetts Institute of Technology, 20, 65, 68, 207
Massey, Alf, 105
match.com, 53
McKenna, Katelyn, 73
Me Generation, 24
Media Diet, 8–9, 118, 138
Mild social disapproval, 215
Millennials, 1, 35
MindShare, 67
Mitchell, Kimberly, 147–150
MIT's Media Laboratory, 20
Molesters, 5, 149. *See also* Sexual predation
Moratorium, *see* Adolescent moratorium
MTV, 25, 121, 128
Multitasking, 5, 6, 11, 12, 13, 16, 19–20, 22, 27, 29, 32–34, 35, 67, 98, 118, 173, 190, 208, 221
Murdock, Rupert, 4
MySpace Generation, 16, 19–36, 43, 67, 98, 102, 106, 112, 118, 138, 160, 209
MySpace whores, 59

National Center for Missing & Exploited Children, 6, 54, 108
National Highway Traffic Safety Administration, 12
National Longitudinal Study of Adolescent Health, 124
National Sleep Foundation, 13, 32
Neglectful parenting, *see* Parenting styles
NetNanny, 210. *See also* Internet filters
NetSmartz Workshop, 108–109
Netspeak, 102, 104–105

Emoticons, 102–104, 115
leetspeak, 102–104
Nickelodeon's U.S. Multicultural Kids Study, 8
Nielsen Media Service, 6, 124, 126

Obesity epidemic, 122, 189
Online acronyms,
ASL, 102–103
BF/GF, 102–103
BRB, 102–103
CYA, 102–103
GTG, 102–103
IDK, 102–103
IMHO, 102–103
JK, 102–103
LMAO, 102–103
LOL, 102–103
P911, 102–103
POS, 102–103
ROTFLOL, 102–103
TTYL, 102–103
W/E, 102–103
WTF, 102–103
Online addiction, *see* Internet addiction
Online bullying, *see* Cyberbullying
Online dating, 53, 69
Online romance, *see* Online dating
Open door policy, 85–86, 164, 219
Operant conditioning theory of learning, 31–32. *See also* Internet addiction
Oral sex, 120–121, 128
Oxford English Dictionary, 6

Paralanguage, 102
Parental controls, 144
Parenting,
Proactive, 55–57, 79–80, 84, 86, 138, 164–165, 200, 204, 207–225
Reactive, 55, 165–166, 200, 202, 204, 208, 210, 212, 214–215, 221
Parenting styles,
Authoritarian, 181–183, 217
Authoritative, 181–184, 217
Indulgent, 181–184, 217
Neglectful, 181–183, 217
Parent's Guide to Internet Safety, A, 141
Partnership for Safe Driving, 12

Patchin, Justin, 207, 212
PDA, 35
Pedophiles, 129, 225
Penetration Rate,
    Blog, 3
    Cell Phones, 3
    Instant Messaging, 3
    Internet, 3
    iPod, 3
    MySpace, 3
    Radio, 2
    Telephone, 2
    Television, 2 to 3
    YouTube, 3
Penthouse Magazine, 128
Personal Responsibility & Work
    Opportunities Reconciliation Act, 130
Peter, Jochen, 40
Pew Internet & American Life Project, 6, 11,
    14, 20, 42, 47, 70, 78, 81, 97, 109, 174
Phishing, 6
Physiological gender, 122
Piaget, Jean, 133
Pierce, Tamyra, 27
Playboy Magazine, 117, 128, 147–148
Podcasting, 6
Point system, 185–188
Pornography, 15, 16, 30, 70, 127, 136, 138,
    148, 149, 169, 214, 218
Positive reinforcement, 32, 113–114, 157,
    161, 163, 182, 185, 213, 221
Prefrontal cortex, 13. *See also* Multitasking
Premarital sex, 128
Prensky, Mark, 104
Proactive parenting, *see* Parenting
Projection, 45, 53
Psychosocial moratorium, 68
Public display of identity, 78
Punishment, 114, 131–132, 161, 166, 170,
    181–183, 186, 201, 214–217, 221

Queer, 57, 88, 137. *See also* Homosexuality

Rainbow party, 120
RAND Corporation, 118–119, 126, 131
Reactive parenting, *see* Parenting
Real life, 47, 68, 73, 137, 158, 162, 223–225
Reinforcement, *see* Positive reinforcement

Rich-get-richer theory, 40
Ritalin, 27–28
RL, *see* Real life
Rogers, Carl, 71, 76. *See also* Humanistic
    personality theory
Role-playing game, 95
Rorschach test, 68, 77
Ross, Michael, 136
RPG, *see* Role-playing game
Russell, Stephen, 147–150

Schemas, 133
Schouten, Alexander, 40
Schroeder, Teri, 222–225
Screen sucking, 7
Screen time, 217–220
Scripts, 133–135. *See also* Schemas
SD, *see* Discriminative Stimulus
Self, aspects of,
    Ideal self, 71–72
    Ought self, 71–73
    True self, 71–73
Self-efficacy, *see* Social cognitive theory
Self-esteem, 15, 40, 46, 63, 65–66, 73, 85,
    93, 153, 158, 182, 197–198, 217
Self-reactive outcome expectations, *see* Social
    cognitive theory
Self-regulation, *see* Social cognitive theory
Sex and the City (TV show), 121
Sex offender, 5, 141
Sexual abstinence programs, 130
Sexual media diet, 118, 138, 150
Sexual orientation, 122–124, 135–137
Sexual predation, 4, 5, 14–15, 31, 46, 84, 107,
    109, 111, 116, 129, 141–142, 144, 191
Sexual solicitation, 15, 129, 148–149
Shadow page, 79
Silent Generation, 24–25
Skinner, B. F., 31–32, 161. *See also* Operant
    conditioning theory of learning
Sleep debt, 13, 32, 33
SMD, *see* Sexual media diet
Smilies, *see* Emoticons
Social cognitive theory, 47–48
    Self-efficacy, 47–48, 161
    Self-reactive outcome expectations, 161
    Self-regulation, 161
Social compensation theory, 40

Social learning theory, 131, 133
Song, Indeok, 159
Spears, Britney, 121
Stages of identity formation,
    Foreclosure, 74, 75, 79
    Identity achievement, 74–76, 85, 97
    Identity diffusion, 74, 75, 79
    Moratorium, 68–69, 74–76, 79
Starbucks, 33
STD epidemic, 120, 128, 130, 141, 192
Stranger danger, 116, 224
Stranger-on-a-train phenomenon, 69
Strategies of web self-presentation,
    Competence, 101
    Exemplification, 101
    Ingratiation, 101–102
    Intimidation, 101
    Supplication, 102
Suler, John, 69. *See also* Disinhibition
Support types,
    Informational support, 39
    Instrumental support, 40
    Self-esteem support, 40
    Social companionship, 39
Surreptitious texting, 10

TALK, 210
Taylor, Jim, 9. *See also* Teen Trends Study
TechnoCocoon, 9, 85, 189, 191, 209, 214
Technorati, 91
Teen Trends Study, 9
Tell Me About Yourself Quiz, 99
Terminal Time Warp, 157, 168
Text messaging, 9–11, 43, 48, 190, 202, 209
Thorndike, Edmund, 160
TiVo, 6, 8, 11, 19, 30, 119, 127, 138, 139, 220
Toffler, Alvin, 3
Top 8, 14, 36, 38, 41–42, 55, 76, 82, 99,
    193, 211
Traditionalist Generation, 24
Tunnel vision, 12
Turkle, Sherry, 68–69, 72, 77, 79, 156, 167
Twenty-four-hour cooling-off period, 200

Unitask, 29
U.S. Department of Health and Human
    Services, 120, 136

USA Today, 107
USC Annenberg Digital Future Project, 16
Usenet, 49–50
Vaginal sex, 120
Valkenburg, Patti, 40, 52
Van Zandt, Cliff, 91, 106
V-Chip, 138
VCR, 8, 9, 25, 89
Vicarious reinforcement, 28
Video Game Consoles, 6, 9, 25
    Wii, 6, 8
    X-Box, 6, 8, 179
Virginia Tech, 51
Virginity pledge, 130
Virtual community, 3, 159–160
Vogensen, April, 76

Walther, Joe, 44. *See also* Hyperpersonal
Wasson, Christine, 10
Wayback Machine, *see* Archive.org
Web self-presentation strategies, *see* Strategies
    of self-presentation
WebMD, 188
What Parents Can Do guide, 169
What-I-Want When-I-Want-It Generation, 2
Whois, 203
Whole Earth 'Lectronic Link (WELL), 3
Wiki, 6, 8, 80
Wikipedia, *see* Wiki
Willard, Nancy, 94, 194, 200, 204–206
Winfrey, Oprah, 120
Wired Generation, 1–2
Wired Magazine, 106
World of Warcraft, 57
WoW, see World of Warcraft

Yahoo! Groups, 50
Yan, Zheng, 1, 63
YISS, *see* Youth Internet Safety Surveys
Young, Kimberly, 151–152, 157, 168–171
Youth Internet Safety Surveys, 195
YouTube, 3, 6, 17, 31, 71, 80, 116, 208,
    209, 221
Ypulse, online blog, 35, 80

Zandl Group, 208